Hannah Arendt

Totalitarianism

Part Three of *The Origins of Totalitarianism*

A Harvest Book • Harcourt, Inc.
San Diego New York London

Library of Congress Cataloging-in-Publication Data
Arendt, Hannah.
The origins of totalitarianism.
"A Harvest book."
Includes bibliographies and indexes.
Contents: pt. 1. Antisemitism — pt. 2. Imperialism—
pt. 3. Totalitarianism.
1. Totalitarianism. 2. Imperialism. 3. Antisemitism.
I. Title
JC481.A62 1985 321.9 84-22579
ISBN 978-0-15-690650-0

Printed in the United States of America
Z Y X W

Introduction

I

THE ORIGINAL manuscript of *The Origins of Totalitarianism* was finished in autumn 1949, more than four years after the defeat of Hitler Germany, less than four years before Stalin's death. The first edition of the book appeared in 1951. In retrospect, the years I spent writing it, from 1945 onwards, appear like the first period of relative calm after decades of turmoil, confusion, and plain horror—the revolutions after the First World War, the rise of totalitarian movements and the undermining of parliamentary government, followed by all sorts of new tyrannies, Fascist and semi-Fascist, one-party and military dictatorships, finally the seemingly firm establishment of totalitarian governments resting on mass support:[1] in Russia in 1929, the year of what now is often called the "second revolution," and in Germany in 1933.

With the defeat of Nazi Germany, part of the story had come to an end. This seemed the first appropriate moment to look upon contemporary events with the backward-directed glance of the historian and the analytical zeal of the political scientist, the first chance to try to tell and to understand what had happened, not yet *sine ira et studio,* still in grief and sorrow and, hence, with a tendency to lament, but no longer in speechless outrage and impotent horror. It was, at any rate, the first possible

[1] No doubt, the fact that totalitarian government, its open criminality notwithstanding, rests on mass support is very disquieting. It is therefore hardly surprising that scholars as well as statesmen often refuse to recognize it, the former by believing in the magic of propaganda and brainwashing, the latter by simply denying it, as for instance Adenauer did repeatedly. A recent publication of secret reports on German public opinion during the war (from 1939 to 1944), issued by the Security Service of the SS (*Meldungen aus dem Reich. Auswahl aus den Geheimen Lageberichten des Sicherheitsdienstes der SS 1939–1944,* edited by Heinz Boberach, Neuwied & Berlin, 1965), is very revealing in this respect. It shows, first, that the population was remarkably well informed about all so-called secrets—massacres of Jews in Poland, preparation of the attack on Russia, etc.—and, second, the "extent to which the victims of propaganda had remained able to form independent opinions" (pp. XVIII–XIX). However, the point of the matter is that this did not in the least weaken the general support of the Hitler regime. It is quite obvious that mass support for totalitarianism comes neither from ignorance nor from brainwashing.

moment to articulate and to elaborate the questions with which my generation had been forced to live for the better part of its adult life: *What happened? Why did it happen? How could it have happened?* For out of the German defeat, which left behind a country in ruins and a nation that felt it had arrived at "point zero" of its history, mountains of paper had emerged virtually intact, a super-abundance of documentary material on every aspect of the twelve years that Hitler's *Tausendjähriges Reich* had managed to last. The first generous selections from this *embarras de richesses,* which even today are by no means adequately published and investigated, began to appear in connection with the Nuremberg Trial of the Major War Criminals in 1946, in the twelve volumes of *Nazi Conspiracy and Aggression.*[2]

Much more documentary and other material, however, bearing on the Nazi regime, had become available in libraries and archives when the second (paperback) edition appeared in 1958. What I then learned was interesting enough, but it hardly required substantial changes in either the analysis or the argument of my original presentation. Numerous additions and replacements of quotations in the footnotes seemed advisable, and the text was considerably enlarged. But these changes were all of a technical nature. In 1949, the Nuremberg documents were known only in part and in English translations, and a great number of books, pamphlets, and magazines published in Germany between 1933 and 1945 had not been available. Also, in a number of additions I took into account some of the more important events after Stalin's death—the successor crisis and Khrushchev's speech at the Twentieth Party Congress—as well as new information on the Stalin regime from recent publications. Moreover, there were certain insights of a strictly theoretical nature, closely connected with my analysis of the elements of total domination, which I did not possess when I finished the original manuscript that ended with rather inconclusive "Concluding Remarks." The last chapter of this edition, "Ideology and Terror," replaced these "Remarks," which, to the extent that they still seemed valid, were shifted to other chapters. To the second edition, I had added an Epilogue where I discussed briefly the introduction of the Russian system into the satellite countries and the Hungarian Revolution. This discussion, written much later, was different in tone since it dealt with contemporary events and has become obsolete in many details. I have now eliminated it, and this is the only substantial change of this edition as compared with the second (paperback) edition.

Obviously, the end of the war did not spell the end of totalitarian government in Russia. On the contrary, it was followed by the Bolshevization of Eastern Europe, that is, the spread of totalitarian government, and

[2] From the beginning, investigation and publication of documentary material have been guided by concern for criminal activities, and the selection has usually been made for the purpose of prosecution of war criminals. The result is that a great amount of highly interesting material has been neglected. The book mentioned in note 1 is a very welcome exception from the rule.

peace offered no more than a significant turning point from which to analyze the similarities and differences in methods and institutions of the two totalitarian regimes. Not the end of the war but Stalin's death eight years later was decisive. In retrospect, it seems that this death was not merely followed by a successor crisis and a temporary "thaw" until a new leader had asserted himself, but by an authentic, though never unequivocal, process of detotalitarization. Hence, from the viewpoint of events, there was no reason to bring this part of my story up to date now; and as far as our knowledge of the period in question is concerned, it has not changed drastically enough to require extensive revisions and additions. In contrast to Germany, where Hitler used his war consciously to develop and, as it were, perfect totalitarian government, the war period in Russia was a time of temporary suspense of total domination. For my purposes, the years from 1929 to 1941 and then again from 1945 down to 1953 are of central interest, and for these periods our sources are as scarce and of the same nature as they were in 1958 or even in 1949. Nothing has happened, or is likely to happen in the future, to present us with the same unequivocal end of the story or the same horribly neat and irrefutable evidence to document it as was the case for Nazi Germany.

The only important addition to our knowledge, the contents of the Smolensk Archive (published in 1958 by Merle Fainsod) have demonstrated to what an extent dearth of the most elementary documentary and statistical material will remain the decisive handicap for all inquiries into this period of Russian history. For although the archives (discovered at party headquarters in Smolensk by German intelligence and then captured by the American occupation force in Germany) contain some 200,000 pages of documents and are virtually intact for the period from 1917 to 1938, the amount of information they fail to give us is truly amazing. Even with "an almost unmanageable abundance of material on the purges" from 1929 to 1937, they contain no indication of the number of victims or any other vital statistical data. Wherever figures are given, they are hopelessly contradictory, the various organizations all giving different sets, and all we learn beyond doubt is that many of them, if they ever existed, were withheld at the source by order of the government.[3] Also, the Archive contains no information on the relations between the various branches of authority, "between Party, the military and NKVD," or between party and government, and it is silent about the channels of communication and command. In short, we learn nothing about the organizational structure of the regime, of which we are so well informed with respect to Nazi Germany.[4] In other words, while it has always been known that official Soviet publications served propaganda

[3] See Merle Fainsod, *Smolensk under Soviet Rule*, Cambridge, 1958, pp. 210, 306, 365, etc.

[4] *Ibid.*, pp. 73, 93.

purposes and were utterly unreliable, it now appears that reliable source and statistical material probably never existed anywhere.

A much more serious question is whether a study of totalitarianism can afford to ignore what has happened, and is still happening, in China. Here our knowledge is even less secure than it was for Russia in the thirties, partly because the country has succeeded in isolating itself against foreigners after the successful revolution much more radically, and partly because defectors from the higher ranks of the Chinese Communist Party have not yet come to our aid—which, of course, in itself is significant enough. For seventeen years, the little we knew beyond doubt pointed to very relevant differences: after an initial period of considerable bloodshed—the number of victims during the first years of dictatorship is plausibly estimated at fifteen million, about three percent of the population in 1949 and, in terms of percentage, considerably less than the population losses due to Stalin's "second revolution"—and after the disappearance of organized opposition, there was no increase in terror, no massacres of innocent people, no category of "objective enemies," no show trials, though a great deal of public confession and "self-criticism," and no outright crimes. Mao's famous speech in 1957, "On the Correct Handling of Contradictions among the People," usually known under the misleading title "Let a Hundred Flowers Bloom," was certainly no plea for freedom, but it did recognize non-antagonistic contradictions between classes and, more importantly, between the people and the government even under a Communist dictatorship. The way to deal with opponents was "rectification of thought," an elaborate procedure of constant molding and remolding of the minds, to which more or less the whole population seemed subject. We never knew very well how this worked in everyday life, who was exempt from it—that is, who did the "remolding"—and we had no inkling of the results of the "brainwashing," whether it was lasting and actually produced personality changes. If one were to trust the present announcements of the Chinese leadership, all it produced was hypocrisy on a gigantic scale, the "breeding grounds for counter-revolution." If this was terror, as it most certainly was, it was terror of a different kind, and whatever its results, it did not decimate the population. It clearly recognized national interest, it permitted the country to develop peacefully, to use the competence of the descendants of the formerly ruling classes, and to uphold academic and professional standards. In brief, it was obvious that Mao Tse-tung's "thought" did not run along the lines laid down by Stalin (or Hitler, for that matter), that he was not a killer by instinct, and that nationalist sentiment, so prominent in all revolutionary upheavals in formerly colonial countries, was strong enough to impose limits upon total domination. All this seemed to contradict certain fears expressed in this book (p. 9).

On the other hand, the Chinese Communist Party after its victory had at once aimed at being "international in organization, all-comprehensive in its ideological scope, and global in its political aspiration" (p. 87), that is, its totalitarian traits have been manifest from the beginning. These traits became more prominent with the development of the Sino-Soviet conflict, although the conflict itself might well have been touched off by national rather than ideological issues. The insistence of the Chinese on rehabilitating Stalin and denouncing the Russian attempts at detotalitarization as "revisionist" deviation was ominous enough, and, to make matters worse, it was accompanied by an utterly ruthless, though thus far unsuccessful, international policy which aimed at infiltrating all revolutionary movements with Chinese agents and at reviving the Comintern under Peking's leadership. All these developments are difficult to judge at the present moment, partly because we don't know enough and partly because everything is still in a state of flux. To these uncertainties, which are in the nature of the situation, we unhappily have added our own self-created handicaps. For it does not facilitate matters in either theory or practice that we have inherited from the cold-war period an official "counter-ideology," anti-Communism, which also tends to become global in aspiration and tempts us into constructing a fiction of our own, so that we refuse on principle to distinguish the various Communist one-party dictatorships, with which we are confronted in reality, from authentic totalitarian government as it may develop, albeit in different forms, in China. The point, of course, is not that Communist China is different from Communist Russia, or that Stalin's Russia was different from Hitler's Germany. Drunkenness and incompetence, which loom so large in any description of Russia in the twenties and thirties and are still widespread today, played no role whatsoever in the story of Nazi Germany, while the unspeakable gratuitous cruelty in the German concentration and extermination camps seems to have been largely absent from the Russian camps, where the prisoners died of neglect rather than of torture. Corruption, the curse of the Russian administration from the beginning, was also present during the last years of the Nazi regime but apparently has been entirely absent from China after the revolution. Differences of this sort could be multiplied; they are of great significance and part and parcel of the national history of the respective countries, but they have no direct bearing on the form of government. Absolute monarchy, no doubt, was a very different affair in Spain, in France, in England, in Prussia; still it was everywhere the same form of government. Decisive in our context is that totalitarian government is different from dictatorships and tyrannies; the ability to distinguish between them is by no means an academic issue which could be safely left to the "theoreticians," for total domination is the only form of government with which coexistence is not possible.

Hence, we have every reason to use the word "totalitarian" sparingly and prudently. On the other hand, we have every reason to be greatly worried. We witness now the first nationwide party purge in China with open threats of massacres. Should these threats be carried out, they might well create the same conditions we know so well from Russia under Stalin's rule. We don't know what caused this sudden development, "which is said to have caught even experienced Chinese officials off guard" (Max Frankel in the *New York Times*, June 26, 1966), whether it is the outcome of a carefully concealed succession struggle or the result of the recent disasters in Chinese foreign relations. But the hysterical claims of an obviously non-existent "bourgeois counter-revolution," aided and abetted by "revisionists," "anti-party" elements within the party, "rattlesnakes" and "poisonous weeds" among the intellectuals, could easily introduce the same change of regime which like a "second revolution" abolished Lenin's dictatorship and established Stalin's totalitarian rule. However, such observations are still mere speculations, and the fact remains that China is still less known than Russia was during her worst period. It would be presumptuous to even attempt an analysis of her present form of government if only because it has not yet been established.

In stark contrast to the scarcity and uncertainty of new sources for factual knowledge with respect to totalitarian government, we find an enormous increase in studies of all the varieties of new dictatorships, be they totalitarian or not, during the last fifteen years. This is of course particularly true for Nazi Germany and Soviet Russia. There exist now many works which are indeed indispensable for further inquiry and study of the subject, and I have tried my best to supplement my old bibliography accordingly. (The second [paperback] edition carried no bibliography.) The only kind of literature which, with few exceptions, I left out on purpose are the numerous memoirs published by former Nazi generals and high functionaries after the end of the war. That this sort of apologetics does not shine with honesty is understandable enough and should not rule it out of our consideration. But the lack of comprehension these reminiscences display of what actually happened and of the roles the authors themselves played in the course of events is truly astonishing and deprives them of all but a certain psychological interest.)

II

AS FAR AS evidence is concerned, the early date this book was conceived and written has proved to be less of a handicap than might reasonably be assumed, and this is true of the material on both the Nazi and the Bolshevik variety of totalitarianism. It is one of the oddities of the literature on totalitarianism that very early attempts by contemporaries at writing its "history," which according to all academic rules were bound to founder on the lack of impeccable source material and emotional overcommitment, have stood the test of time remarkably well. Konrad Heiden's biography of Hitler and Boris Souvarine's biography of Stalin, both written and published in the thirties, are in some respects more accurate and in almost all respects more relevant than the standard biographies by Alan Bullock and Isaac Deutscher respectively. This may have many reasons, but one of them certainly is the simple fact that documentary material in both cases has tended to confirm and to add to what had been known all along from prominent defectors and other eye-witness accounts.

To put it somewhat drastically: We did not need Khrushchev's Secret Speech to know that Stalin had committed crimes, or that this allegedly "insanely suspicious" man had decided to put his trust in Hitler. As to the latter, nothing indeed proves better than this trust that Stalin was not insane; he was justifiably suspicious with respect to all people he wished or prepared to eliminate, and these included practically everybody in the higher echelons of party and government; he naturally trusted Hitler because he did not wish him ill. As to the former, Khrushchev's startling admissions, which—for the obvious reason that his audience and he himself were totally involved in the true story—concealed considerably more than they revealed, had the unfortunate result that in the eyes of many (and also, of course, of scholars with their professional love of official sources) they minimized the gigantic criminality of the Stalin regime which, after all, did not consist merely in the slander and murder of a few hundred or thousand prominent political and literary figures, whom one may "rehabilitate" posthumously, but in the extermination of literally untold millions of people whom no one, not even Stalin, could have suspected of "counter-revolutionary" activities. It was precisely by conceding some crimes that Khrushchev concealed the criminality of the regime as a whole, and it is precisely against this camouflage and the hypocrisy of the present Russian rulers—all of them trained and promoted under Stalin—that the younger generation of Russian intellectuals is now in an almost open rebellion. For they know everything there is to know about "mass purges, and the deportation and annihilation of entire peoples." [5] Moreover, Khrushchev's explanation of the crimes he conceded—Stalin's insane suspiciousness—concealed the most characteristic aspect of totalitarian terror, that it is let loose when all organized opposition has died down and the totalitarian ruler knows that he no longer need to be afraid. This is particularly true for the Russian development. Stalin started his gigantic purges not in 1928 when he conceded, "We have internal enemies," and actually had still reason to be afraid—he knew that Bukharin compared him to Genghis Khan and was convinced that Stalin's policy "was leading the country to famine, ruin, and a police regime," [6] as indeed it did—but in 1934, when all former opponents had "confessed their errors," and Stalin himself, at the Seventeenth Party Congress, also called by him the "Congress of the Victors," had declared: "At this Congress . . . there is nothing more to prove and, it seems, no one to fight." [7] Neither the sensational character nor the decisive political importance of the Twentieth Party Congress for Soviet Russia and the Communist movement at large are in doubt. But the importance is political; the light official sources of the post-Stalin

[5] To an estimated nine to twelve million victims of the First Five Year Plan (1928–1933) must be added the victims of the Great Purge—an estimated three million executed while five to nine million were arrested and deported. (See Robert C. Tucker's important introduction, "Stalin, Bukharin, and History as Conspiracy," to the new edition of the verbatim report of the 1938 Moscow Trial, *The Great Purge Trial*, New York, 1965.) But all these estimates seem to fall short of the actual number. They do not take into account mass executions of which nothing was known until "German occupation forces discovered a mass grave in the city of Vinnitsa containing thousands of bodies of persons executed in 1937 and 1938." (See John A. Armstrong, *The Politics of Totalitarianism. The Communist Party of the Soviet Union from 1934 to the Present*, New York, 1961, pp. 65 f.) Needless to say, this recent discovery makes the Nazi and the Bolshevik systems look even more than before like variations of the same model.—To what extent the mass killings of the Stalin era are in the center of the present opposition can best be seen in the trial of Sinyavsky and Daniel, of which the *New York Times Magazine* published key sections on April 17, 1966, and from which I quoted.

[6] Tucker, *op. cit.*, pp. XVII–XVIII.

[7] Quoted from Merle Fainsod, *How Russia Is Ruled*, Cambridge, 1959, p. 516.—Abdurakhman Avtorkhanov (in *The Reign of Stalin*, published under the pseudonym Uralov in London, 1953) tells of a secret meeting of the Central Committee of the Party in 1936 after the first show trials, in which Bukharin reportedly accused Stalin of changing Lenin's party into a police state and was supported by more than two-thirds of the members. The story, especially the allegedly strong support of Bukharin in the Central Committee, does not sound very plausible; but even if true, in view of the fact that this meeting occurred while the Great Purge was already in full swing, the story does not indicate an organized opposition but rather its opposite. The truth of the matter, as Fainsod rightly points out, seems to be that "wide-spread mass discontent" was quite common, especially among the peasants, and that up to 1928, "at the beginning of the First Five Year Plan strikes . . . were not uncommon," but that such "oppositional moods never come to a focus in any form of organized challenge to the regime," and that by 1929 or 1930 "every organizational alternative had faded from the scene" if it ever had existed before. (See *Smolensk under Soviet Rule*, pp. 449 ff.)

period shed on what had happened before should not be mistaken for the light of truth.

As far as our knowledge of the Stalin era is concerned, Fainsod's publication of the Smolensk Archive, which I mentioned before, has remained by far the most important publication, and it is deplorable that this first random selection has not yet been followed up by a more extensive publication of the material. To judge from Fainsod's book, there is much to learn for the period of Stalin's struggle for power in the mid-twenties: We now know how precarious the position of the party was,[8] not only because a mood of outright opposition prevailed in the country but because it was riddled with corruption and drunkenness; that outspoken antisemitism accompanied nearly all demands for liberalization;[9] that the drive for collectivization and dekulakization from 1928 onward actually interrupted the NEP, Lenin's new economic policy, and with it a beginning reconciliation between the people and its government;[10] how fiercely these measures were resisted by the solidarity of the whole peasant class, which decided that "it's better not to be born than to join the kolkhoz"[11] and refused to be split up into rich, middle, and poor peasants in order to rise against the kulaks[12]—"there sits somebody who is worse than these kulaks and who is only planning how to hunt people down";[13] and that the situation was not much better in the cities, where the workers refused to co-operate with the party-controlled trade unions and addressed the management as "well-fed devils," "hypocritical walleyes," and the like.[14]

Fainsod rightly points out that these documents clearly show not only "wide-spread mass discontent" but also the lack of any "sufficiently organized opposition" against the regime as a whole. What he fails to see, and what in my opinion is equally supported by the evidence, is that there existed an obvious alternative to Stalin's seizure of power and transformation of the one-party dictatorship into total domination, and this

[8] "The wonder," as Fainsod, *op. cit.*, p. 38, points out, "is not merely that the Party was victorious, but that it managed to survive at all."

[9] *Ibid.*, pp. 49 ff.—A report from 1929 recounts violent antisemitic outbursts during a meeting; the Komsomol people "in the audience kept silent. . . . The impression was obtained that they were all in agreement with the anti-Jewish statements" (p. 445).

[10] All reports from 1926 show a significant "decline in so-called counter-revolutionary outbreaks, a measure of the temporary truce which the regime had worked out with the peasantry." Compared with 1926, the reports from 1929–1930 "read like communiqués from a flaming battle front" (p. 177).

[11] *Ibid.*, pp. 252 ff.

[12] *Ibid.*, especially pp. 240 ff. and 446 ff.

[13] *Ibid.* All such statements are taken from GPU reports; see especially pp. 248 f. But it is quite characteristic that such remarks became much less frequent after 1934, the beginning of the Great Purge.

[14] *Ibid.*, p. 310.

was the pursuance of the NEP policy as it had been initiated by Lenin.[15] Moreover, the measures taken by Stalin with the introduction of the First Five Year Plan in 1928, when his control of the party was almost complete, prove that transformation of classes into masses and the concomitant elimination of all group solidarity are the condition *sine qua non* of total domination.

With respect to the period of Stalin's undisputed rule from 1929 onward, the Smolensk Archive tends to confirm what we knew before from less irrefutable sources. This is even true for some of its odd lacunae, especially those concerning statistical data. For this lack proves merely that, in this as in other respects, the Stalin regime was ruthlessly consistent: all facts that did not agree, or were likely to disagree, with the official fiction—data on crop-yields, criminality, true incidences of "counter-revolutionary" activities as distinguished from the later conspiracy fictions—were treated as non-facts. It was indeed quite in line with the totalitarian contempt for facts and reality that all such data, instead of being collected in Moscow from the four corners of the immense territory, were first made known to the respective localities through publication in *Pravda, Izvestia,* or some other official organ in Moscow, so that every region and every district of the Soviet Union received its official, fictitious statistical data in much the same way it received the no less fictitious norms allotted to them by the Five Year Plans.[16]

I shall briefly enumerate a few of the more striking points, which could only be guessed at before and which are now supported by documentary evidence. We always suspected, but we now know that the regime was never "monolithic" but "consciously constructed around overlapping, duplicating, and parallel functions," and that this grotesquely amorphous structure was kept together by the same Führer-principle—the so-called "personality cult"—we find in Nazi Germany;[17] that the executive branch

[15] This alternative is usually overlooked in the literature because of the understandable, but historically untenable, conviction of a more or less smooth development from Lenin to Stalin. It is true that Stalin almost always talked in Leninist terms, so that it sometimes looks as though the only difference between the two men lay in the brutality or "insanity" of Stalin's character. Whether or not this was a conscious ruse on the side of Stalin, the truth of the matter is—as Tucker, *op. cit.*, p. XVI, rightly observes—that "Stalin filled these old Leninist concepts with a new, distinctively Stalinist content . . . The chief distinctive feature was the quite un-Leninist emphasis upon *conspiracy* as the hallmark of the present epoch."

[16] See Fainsod, *op. cit.*, especially pp. 365 f.

[17] *Ibid.*, p. 93 and p. 71: It is quite characteristic that messages on all levels habitually stressed the "obligations undertaken to Comrade Stalin," and not to the regime or the party or the country. Nothing perhaps underlines more convincingly the similarities of the two systems than what Ilya Ehrenburg and other Stalinist intellectuals have to say today in their efforts to justify their past or simply to report what they actually thought during the Great Purge. "Stalin knew nothing about the senseless violence committed against the Communists, against the Soviet intelligentsia," "they conceal it from Stalin" and "if only someone would tell Stalin about it," or, finally, the culprit was not Stalin at all but the respective chief of police.

of this particular government was not the party but the police, whose "operational activities were not regulated through party channels";[18] that the entirely innocent people whom the regime liquidated by the millions, the "objective enemies" in Bolshevik language, knew that they were "criminals without a crime";[19] that it was precisely this new category, as distinguished from the earlier true foes of the regime—assassins of government officials, arsonists, or bandits—that reacted with the same "complete passivity" [20] we know so well from the behavior patterns of the victims of Nazi terror. There was never any doubt that the "flood of mutual denunciations" during the Great Purge was as disastrous for the economic and social well-being of the country as it was effective in strengthening the totalitarian ruler, but we know only now how deliberately Stalin set this "ominous chain of denunciations in motion," [21] when he proclaimed officially on July 29, 1936: *"The inalienable quality of every Bolshevik under present conditions should be the ability to recognize an enemy of the Party no matter how well he may be masked."* [22] (Italics added.) For just as Hitler's "Final Solution" actually meant to make the command "Thou shalt kill" binding for the elite of the Nazi party, Stalin's pronouncement prescribed: "Thou shalt bear false testimony," as a guiding rule for the conduct of all members of the Bolshevik party. Finally, all doubts one still might have nourished about the amount of truth in the current theory, according to which the terror of the late twenties and thirties was "the high price in suffering" exacted by industrialization and economic progress, are laid at rest by this first glimpse into the actual state of affairs and the course of events in one particular region.[23] Terror produced nothing of the sort. The best documented re-

(Quoted from Tucker, *op. cit.*, p. XIII.) Needless to add, this was precisely what the Nazis had to say after the defeat of Germany.

[18] *Ibid.*, pp. 166 ff.

[19] The words are lifted from the appeal of a "class-alien element" in 1936: "I do not want to be a criminal without a crime" (p. 229).

[20] An interesting OGPU report from 1931 stresses this new "complete passivity," this horrible apathy which the random terror against innocent people produced. The report mentions the great difference between the former arrests of enemies of the regime when "an arrested man was led by two militiamen" and the mass arrests when "one militiaman may lead groups of people and the latter calmly walk and no one flees" (p. 248).

[21] *Ibid.*, p. 135.

[22] *Ibid.*, pp. 57–58. For the mounting mood of plain hysteria in these mass denunciations, see especially pp. 222, 229 ff., and the lovely story on p. 235, where we hear how one of the comrades has come to think "that Comrade Stalin has taken a conciliatory attitude toward the Trotskyite-Zinovievite group," a reproach which at the time meant immediate expulsion from the Party at least. But no such luck. The next speaker accused the man who had tried to outdo Stalin of being "politically disloyal," whereupon the former promptly "confessed" his error.

[23] Strangely enough, Fainsod himself still draws such conclusions from a mass of evidence that points into the opposite direction. See his last chapter, especially pp. 453 ff.—It is even stranger that this misreading of the factual evidence should be shared by so many authors in the field. To be sure, hardly any of them would go

sult of dekulakization, collectivization, and the Great Purge was neither progress nor rapid industrialization but famine, chaotic conditions in the production of food, and depopulation. The consequences have been a perpetual crisis in agriculture, an interruption of population growth, and the failure to develop and colonize the Siberian hinterland. Moreover, as the Smolensk Archive spells out in detail, Stalin's methods of rule succeeded in destroying whatever measure of competence and technical know-how the country had acquired after the October Revolution. And all this together was indeed an incredibly "high price," not just in suffering, exacted for the opening of careers in the party and government bureaucracies to sections of the population which often were not merely "*politically* illiterate." [24] The truth is that the price of totalitarian rule was so high that in neither Germany nor Russia has it yet been paid in full.

III

I MENTIONED before the detotalitarization process which followed upon Stalin's death. In 1958, I was not yet sure that the "thaw" was more than

so far in this subtle justification of Stalin as Isaac Deutscher in his biography, but many still insist that "Stalin's ruthless actions were . . . a way to the creation of a new equilibrium of forces" (Armstrong, *op cit.*, p. 64) and designed to offer "a brutal but consistent solution of some of the basic contradictions inherent in the Leninist myth" (Richard Lowenthal in his very valuable *World Communism. The Disintegration of a Secular Faith*, New York, 1964, p. 42). There are but few exceptions from this Marxist hangover, such as Richard C. Tucker (*op. cit.*, p. XXVII), who says unequivocally that the Soviet "system would have been better off and far more equipped to meet the coming test of total war had there been no Great Purge, which was, in effect, a great wrecking operation in Soviet society." Mr. Tucker believes that this refutes my "image" of totalitarianism, which, I think, is a misunderstanding. Instability is indeed a functional requisite of total domination, which is based on an ideological fiction and presupposes that a movement, as distinguished from a party, has seized power. The hallmark of this system is that substantial power, the material strength and well-being of the country, is constantly sacrificed to the power of organization, just as all factual truths are sacrificed to the demands of ideological consistency. It is obvious that in a contest between material strength and organizational power, or between fact and fiction, the latter may come to grief, and this happened in Russia as well as Germany during the Second World War. But this is no reason to underestimate the power of totalitarian movements. It was the terror of permanent instability that helped to organize the satellite system, and it is the present stability of Soviet Russia, its detotalitarization, which, on one side, has greatly contributed to her present material strength, but which, on the other, has caused her to lose control of her satellites.

[24] See the interesting details (Fainsod, *op. cit.*, pp. 345–355) about the 1929 campaign to eliminate "reactionary professors" against the protests of party and Komsomol members as well as the student body, who saw "no reason to replace the excellent non-Party" professors; whereupon of course a new commission promptly reported "the large number of class-alien elements among the student body." That it was one of the main purposes of the Great Purge to open the careers to the younger generation has always been known.

a temporary relaxation, a kind of emergency measure due to the successor crisis and not unlike the considerable loosening of totalitarian controls during the Second World War. Even today we cannot know if this process is final and irreversible, but it surely can no longer be called temporary or provisional. For however one may read the often bewildering zigzag line of Soviet policies since 1953, it is undeniable that the huge police empire was liquidated, that most of the concentration camps were dissolved, that no new purges against "objective enemies" have been introduced, and that conflicts between members of the new "collective leadership" are now being resolved by demotion and exile from Moscow rather than by show trials, confessions, and assassinations. No doubt, the methods used by the new rulers in the years after Stalin's death still followed closely the pattern set by Stalin after Lenin's death: there emerged again a triumvirate called "collective leadership," a term coined by Stalin in 1925, and after four years of intrigues and contest for power, there was a repetition of Stalin's *coup d'état* in 1929, namely, Khrushchev's seizure of power in 1957. Technically speaking, Khrushchev's coup followed the methods of his dead and denounced master very closely. He too needed an outside force in order to win power in the party hierarchy, and he used the support of Marshal Zhukov and the army exactly the same way Stalin had used his relationships to the secret police in the succession struggle of thirty years ago.[25] Just as in the case of Stalin, in which the supreme power after the coup continued to reside in the party, not in the police, so in Khrushchev's case "by the end of 1957 the Communist Party of the Soviet Union had attained a place of undisputed supremacy in all aspects of Soviet life";[26] for just as Stalin had never hesitated to purge his police cadres and liquidate their chief, so Khrushchev had followed up his inner-party maneuvers by removing Zhukov from the Presidium and Central Committee of the party, to which he had been elected after the coup, as well as from his post as highest commander of the army.

To be sure, when Khrushchev appealed to Zhukov for support, the army's ascendancy over the police was an accomplished fact in the Soviet Union. This had been one of the automatic consequences of the breaking up of the police empire whose rule over a huge part of Soviet industries, mines, and real estate had been inherited by the managerial group, who suddenly found themselves rid of their most serious economic

[25] Armstrong, *op. cit.*, p. 319, argues that the importance of Marshal Zhukov's intervention in the inner-party struggle has been "highly exaggerated" and maintains that Khrushchev "triumphed without any need for military intervention," because he was "supported by the Party apparatus." This seems not to be true. But it is true that "many foreign observers," because of the role of the army in support of Khrushchev against the party apparatus, arrived at the mistaken conclusion of a lasting power increase of the military at the expense of the party, as though the Soviet Union was about to change from a party dictatorship into a military dictatorship.

[26] *Ibid.*, p. 320.

competitor. The automatic ascendancy of the army was even more decisive; it now held a clear monopoly of the instruments of violence with which to decide inner-party conflicts. It speaks for Khrushchev's shrewdness that he grasped these consequences of what they presumably had done together more rapidly than his colleagues. But whatever his motives, the consequences of this shift of emphasis from the police to the military in the power game were of great consequence. It is true, ascendancy of the secret police over the military apparatus is the hallmark of many tyrannies, and not only the totalitarian; however, in the case of totalitarian government the preponderance of the police not merely answers the need for suppressing the population at home but fits the ideological claim to global rule. For it is evident that those who regard the whole earth as their future territory will stress the organ of domestic violence and will rule conquered territory with police methods and personnel rather than with the army. Thus, the Nazis used their SS troops, essentially a police force, for the rule and even the conquest of foreign territories, with the ultimate aim of an amalgamation of the army and the police under the leadership of the SS.

Moreover, the significance of this change in the balance of power had been manifest before, at the occasion of the suppression by force of the Hungarian Revolution. The bloody crushing of the revolution, terrible and effective as it was, had been accomplished by regular army units and not by police troops, and the consequence was that it did by no means represent a typically Stalinist solution. Although the military operation was followed by the execution of the leaders and the imprisonment of thousands, there was no wholesale deportation of the people; in fact, no attempt at depopulating the country was made. And since this was a military operation and not a police action, the Soviets could afford sending enough aid to the defeated country to prevent mass starvation and to stave off a complete collapse of the economy in the year following the revolution. Nothing, surely, would have been farther from Stalin's mind under similar circumstances.

The clearest sign that the Soviet Union can no longer be called totalitarian in the strict sense of the term is, of course, the amazingly swift and rich recovery of the arts during the last decade. To be sure, efforts to rehabilitate Stalin and to curtail the increasingly vocal demands for freedom of speech and thought among students, writers, and artists recur again and again, but none of them has been very successful or is likely to be successful without a full-fledged re-establishment of terror and police rule. No doubt, the people of the Soviet Union are denied all forms of political freedom, not only freedom of association but also freedom of thought, opinion and public expression. It looks as though nothing has changed, while in fact everything has changed. When Stalin died the drawers of writers and artists were empty; today there exists a whole literature that circulates in manuscript and all kinds of modern painting are tried out in the painters' studios and become known even though they are not exhibited. This is not to minimize the difference between tyrannical censorship and freedom of the arts, it is only to stress the fact that the difference between a clandestine literature and no literature equals the difference between one and zero.

Furthermore, the very fact that members of the intellectual opposition can have a trial (though not an open one), can make themselves heard in the courtroom and count upon support outside it, do not confess to anything but plead not guilty, demonstrates that we deal here no longer with total domination. What happened to Sinyavsky and Daniel, the two writers who in February 1966 were tried for having published works abroad which could not have been published in the Soviet Union and who were sentenced to seven and five years of hard labor respectively, was certainly outrageous by all standards of justice in constitutional government; but what they had to say was heard around the world and is not likely to be forgotten. They did not disappear in the hole of oblivion which totalitarian rulers prepare for their opponents. Less well known but perhaps even more convincing is that Khrushchev's own and most ambitious attempt at reversing the process of detotalitarization turned into a complete failure. In 1957, he introduced a new "law against social parasites," which would have enabled the regime to reintroduce mass deportations, re-establish slave labor on a large scale, and—most importantly for total domination—to let loose another flood of mass denunciations; for "parasites" were supposed to be selected by the people themselves in mass meetings. The "law," however, met with the opposition of Soviet jurists and was dropped before it could even be tried out.[27] In other words, the people of the Soviet Union have emerged from the nightmare of totalitarian rule to the manifold hardships, dangers, and injustices of one-party dictatorship; and while it is entirely true that this modern form of tyranny offers none of the guarantees of constitutional government, that "even accepting the presuppositions of Communist ideology, all power in the USSR is ultimately illegitimate," [28] and that the country therefore can relapse into totalitarianism between one day and another without major upheavals, it is also true that the most horrible of all new forms of government, whose elements and historical origins I set out to analyze, came no less to an end in Russia with the death of Stalin than totalitarianism came to an end in Germany with the death of Hitler.

This book deals with totalitarianism, its origins and its elements, whereas its aftermath in either Germany or Russia is pertinent to its considerations only insofar as it is likely to throw light on what happened before. Hence, not the period after Stalin's death but rather the postwar era of his rule is of relevance in our context. And these eight years. from 1945 to 1953, confirm and spin out, they don't either contradict or

[27] See *ibid.*, p. 325.
[28] *Ibid.*, pp. 339 ff.

add new elements to what had been manifest since the middle thirties. The events that followed upon victory, the measures taken to reaffirm total domination after the temporary relaxation of the war period in the Soviet Union as well as those by which totalitarian rule was introduced in the satellite countries, were all in accord with the rules of the game as we had come to know it. The Bolshevization of the satellites started with popular-front tactics and a sham parliamentary system, proceeded quickly to the open establishment of one-party dictatorships in which the leaders and members of the formerly tolerated parties were liquidated, and then reached the last stage when the native Communist leaders, whom Moscow rightly or wrongly mistrusted, were brutally framed, humiliated in show trials, tortured, and killed under the rulership of the most corrupt and most despicable elements in the party, namely those who were primarily not Communists but agents of Moscow. It was as though Moscow repeated in great haste all the stages of the October Revolution up to the emergence of totalitarian dictatorship. The story therefore, while unspeakably horrible, is without much interest of its own and varies little: what happened in one satellite country happened at almost the same moment in all others from the Baltic Sea down to the Adriatic. Events differed in regions which were not included into the satellite system. The Baltic states were directly incorporated into the Soviet Union and fared considerably worse than the satellites: more than half a million people were deported from the three small countries and an "enormous influx of Russian settlers" began to threaten the native populations with minority status in their own countries.[29] East Germany, on the other hand, is only now, after the erection of the Berlin Wall, slowly being incorporated into the satellite system, having been treated before rather as occupied territory with a Quisling government.

In our context, developments in the Soviet Union, especially after 1948 —the year of Zhdanov's mysterious death and the "Leningrad affair"— are of greater importance. For the first time after the Great Purge, Stalin had a great number of high and highest officials executed, and we know for certain that this was planned as the beginning of another nationwide purge. This would have been touched off by the "Doctors' plot" had Stalin's death not intervened. A group of mostly Jewish physicians were accused of having plotted "to wipe out the leading cadres of the USSR." [30] Everything that went on in Russia between 1948 and January 1953, when the "Doctors' plot" was being "discovered," bore a striking and ominous similarity to the preparations of the Great Purge during the thirties: the death of Zhdanov and the Leningrad purge corresponded to Kirov's no less mysterious death in 1934 which was immediately followed by a kind of preparatory purge "of all former oppositionists who re-

[29] See V. Stanley Vardys, "How the Baltic Republics fare in the Soviet Union," in *Foreign Affairs*, April, 1966.

[30] Armstrong, *op. cit.*, pp. 235 ff.

mained in the Party."[31] Moreover, the very content of the absurd accusation against the physicians, that they would kill off people in leading positions all over the country, must have filled with fearful forebodings all those who were acquainted with Stalin's method of accusing a fictitious enemy of the crime he himself was about to commit. (The best known example is of course his accusation that Tukhachevski conspired with Germany at the very moment when Stalin was contemplating an alliance with the Nazis.) Obviously, in 1952 Stalin's entourage was much wiser to what his words actually meant than they could have been in the thirties, and the very wording of the accusation must have spread panic among all higher officials of the regime. This panic may still be the most plausible explanation of Stalin's death, the mysterious circumstances surrounding it, and the swift closing of ranks in the higher echelons of the party, notoriously ridden by strife and intrigues, during the first months of the succession crisis. However little we know of the details of this story, we know more than enough to support my original conviction that such "wrecking operations" as the Great Purge were not isolated episodes, not excesses of the regime provoked by extraordinary circumstances, but that they were an institution of terror and to be expected at regular intervals—unless, of course, the nature of the regime itself was changed.

The most dramatic new element in this last purge, which Stalin planned in the last years of his life, was a decisive shift in ideology, the introduction of a Jewish world conspiracy. For years, the ground for this change had been carefully laid in a number of trials in the satellite countries—the Rajk trial in Hungary, the Ana Pauker affair in Rumania, and, in 1952, the Slansky trial in Czechoslovakia. In these preparatory measures, high party officials were singled out because of their "Jewish bourgeois" origins and accused of Zionism; this accusation was gradually changed to implicate notoriously non-Zionist agencies (especially the American Jewish Joint Distribution Committee), in order to indicate that all Jews were Zionists and all Zionist groups "hirelings of American imperialism."[32] There was of course nothing new in the "crime" of Zionism, but as the campaign progressed and began to center on Jews in the Soviet Union, another significant change took place: Jews now stood accused of "cosmopolitanism" rather than Zionism, and the pattern of accusations that developed out of this slogan followed ever more closely the Nazi pattern of a Jewish world conspiracy in the sense of the Elders of Zion. It now became startlingly clear how deep an impression this mainstay of Nazi ideology must have made on Stalin—the first indications of this had been in evidence ever since the Hitler-Stalin pact—partly, to be sure, because of its obvious propaganda value in Russia as in all of the satellite countries, where anti-Jewish feeling was widespread

[31] Fainsod, *op. cit.*, p. 56.
[32] Armstrong, *op. cit.*, p. 236.

and anti-Jewish propaganda had always enjoyed great popularity, but partly also because this type of a fictitious world conspiracy provided an ideologically more suitable background for totalitarian claims to world rule than Wall Street, capitalism, and imperialism. The open, unashamed adoption of what had become to the whole world the most prominent sign of Nazism was the last compliment Stalin paid to his late colleague and rival in total domination with whom, much to his chagrin, he had not been able to come to a lasting agreement.

Stalin, like Hitler, died in the midst of a horrifying unfinished business. And when this happened, the story this book has to tell, and the events it tries to understand and to come to terms with, came to an at least provisional end.

Hannah Arendt

June 1966

Contents

Totalitarianism

Normal men do not know that everything is possible.

DAVID ROUSSET

CHAPTER ONE:

A Classless Society

I: *The Masses*

NOTHING is more characteristic of the totalitarian movements in general and of the quality of fame of their leaders in particular than the startling swiftness with which they are forgotten and the startling ease with which they can be replaced. What Stalin accomplished laboriously over many years through bitter factional struggles and vast concessions at least to the name of his predecessor—namely, to legitimate himself as Lenin's political heir—Stalin's successors attempted to do without concessions to the name of their predecessor, even though Stalin had thirty years' time and could manipulate a propaganda apparatus, unknown in Lenin's day, to immortalize his name. The same is true for Hitler, who during his lifetime exercised a fascination to which allegedly no one was immune,[1] and who

[1] The "magic spell" that Hitler cast over his listeners has been acknowledged many times, latterly by the publishers of *Hitlers Tischgespräche*, Bonn, 1951 (*Hitler's Table Talks*, American edition, New York, 1953; quotations from the original German edition). This fascination—"the strange magnetism that radiated from Hitler in such a compelling manner"—rested indeed "on the fanatical belief of this man in himself" (introduction by Gerhard Ritter, p. 14), on his pseudo-authoritative judgments about everything under the sun, and on the fact that his opinions—whether they dealt with the harmful effects of smoking or with Napoleon's policies—could always be fitted into an all-encompassing ideology.

Fascination is a social phenomenon, and the fascination Hitler exercised over his environment must be understood in terms of the particular company he kept. Society is always prone to accept a person offhand for what he pretends to be, so that a crackpot posing as a genius always has a certain chance to be believed. In modern society, with its characteristic lack of discerning judgment, this tendency is strengthened, so that someone who not only holds opinions but also presents them in a tone of unshakable conviction will not so easily forfeit his prestige, no matter how many times he has been demonstrably wrong. Hitler, who knew the modern chaos of opinions from first-hand experience, discovered that the helpless seesawing between various opinions and "the conviction . . . that everything is balderdash" (p. 281) could best be avoided by adhering to *one* of the many current opinions with "unbending consistency." The hair-raising arbitrariness of such fanaticism holds great fascination for society because for the duration of the social gathering it is freed from the chaos of opinions that it constantly generates. This "gift" of fascination, however, has only social relevance; it is so prominent in the *Tischgespräche* because here Hitler played the game of society and was not speaking to his own kind but to the generals of the Wehrmacht, all of whom more or less belonged to "society." To believe that Hitler's successes were based on his "powers of fascination" is altogether erroneous; with those qualities alone he would have never advanced beyond the role of a prominent figure in the salons.

after his defeat and death is today so thoroughly forgotten that he scarcely plays any further role even among the neo-Fascist and neo-Nazi groups of postwar Germany. This impermanence no doubt has something to do with the proverbial fickleness of the masses and the fame that rests on them; more likely, it can be traced to the perpetual-motion mania of totalitarian movements which can remain in power only so long as they keep moving and set everything around them in motion. Therefore, in a certain sense this very impermanence is a rather flattering testimonial to the dead leaders insofar as they succeeded in contaminating their subjects with the specifically totalitarian virus; for if there is such a thing as a totalitarian personality or mentality, this extraordinary adaptability and absence of continuity are no doubt its outstanding characteristics. Hence it might be a mistake to assume that the inconstancy and forgetfulness of the masses signify that they are cured of the totalitarian delusion, which is occasionally identified with the Hitler or Stalin cult; the opposite might well be true.

It would be a still more serious mistake to forget, because of this impermanence, that the totalitarian regimes, so long as they are in power, and the totalitarian leaders, so long as they are alive, "command and rest upon mass support" up to the end.[2] Hitler's rise to power was legal in terms of majority rule[3] and neither he nor Stalin could have maintained the leadership of large populations, survived many interior and exterior crises, and braved the numerous dangers of relentless intra-party struggles if they had not had the confidence of the masses. Neither the Moscow trials nor the liquidation of the Röhm faction would have been possible if these masses had not supported Stalin and Hitler. The widespread belief that Hitler was simply an agent of German industrialists and that Stalin was victorious in the succession struggle after Lenin's death only through a sinister conspiracy are both legends which can be refuted by many facts but above all by the leaders' indisputable popularity.[4] Nor can their popularity be attributed to the victory of masterful and lying propaganda over ignorance and stupidity.

[2] See the illuminating remarks of Carlton J. H. Hayes on "The Novelty of Totalitarianism in the History of Western Civilization," in *Symposium on the Totalitarian State,* 1939. Proceedings of the American Philosophical Society, Philadelphia, 1940, Vol. LXXXII.

[3] This was indeed "the first large revolution in history that was carried out by applying the existing formal code of law at the moment of seizing power" (Hans Frank, *Recht und Verwaltung,* 1939, p. 8).

[4] The best study of Hitler and his career is the new Hitler biography by Alan Bullock, *Hitler, A Study in Tyranny,* London, 1952. In the English tradition of political biographies it makes meticulous use of all available source material and gives a comprehensive picture of the contemporary political background. By this publication the excellent books of Konrad Heiden—primarily *Der Fuehrer: Hitler's Rise to Power,* Boston, 1944—have been superseded in their details although they remain important for the general interpretation of events. For Stalin's career, Boris Souvarine, *Stalin: A Critical Survey of Bolshevism,* New York, 1939, is still a standard work. Isaac Deutscher, *Stalin: A Political Biography,* New York and London, 1949, is indispensable for its rich documentary material and great insight into the internal struggles of the Bolshevik party; it suffers from an interpretation which likens Stalin to—Cromwell, Napoleon, and Robespierre.

For the propaganda of totalitarian movements which precede and accompany totalitarian regimes is invariably as frank as it is mendacious, and would-be totalitarian rulers usually start their careers by boasting of their past crimes and carefully outlining their future ones. The Nazis "were convinced that evil-doing in our time has a morbid force of attraction,"[5] Bolshevik assurances inside and outside Russia that they do not recognize ordinary moral standards have become a mainstay of Communist propaganda, and experience has proved time and again that the propaganda value of evil deeds and general contempt for moral standards is independent of mere self-interest, supposedly the most powerful psychological factor in politics.

The attraction of evil and crime for the mob mentality is nothing new. It has always been true that the mob will greet "deeds of violence with the admiring remark: it may be mean but it is very clever."[6] The disturbing factor in the success of totalitarianism is rather the true selflessness of its adherents: it may be understandable that a Nazi or Bolshevik will not be shaken in his conviction by crimes against people who do not belong to the movement or are even hostile to it; but the amazing fact is that neither is he likely to waver when the monster begins to devour its own children and not even if he becomes a victim of persecution himself, if he is framed and condemned, if he is purged from the party and sent to a forced-labor or a concentration camp. On the contrary, to the wonder of the whole civilized world, he may even be willing to help in his own prosecution and frame his own death sentence if only his status as a member of the movement is not touched.[7] It would be naïve to consider this stubbornness of conviction which outlives all actual experiences and cancels all immediate self-interest a simple expression of fervent idealism. Idealism, foolish or heroic, always springs from some individual decision and conviction and is subject to experience and argument.[8] The fanaticism of totalitarian move-

[5] Franz Borkenau, *The Totalitarian Enemy*, London, 1940, p. 231.

[6] Quoted from the German edition of the "Protocols of the Elders of Zion," *Die Zionistischen Protokolle mit einem Vor- und Nachwort von Theodor Fritsch*, 1924, p. 29.

[7] This, to be sure, is a specialty of the Russian brand of totalitarianism. It is interesting to note that in the early trial of foreign engineers in the Soviet Union, Communist sympathies were already used as an argument for self-accusation: "All the time the authorities insisted on my admitting having committed acts of sabotage I had never done. I refused. I was told: 'If you are in favour of the Soviet Government, as you pretend you are, prove it by your actions; the Government needs your confession.'" Reported by Anton Ciliga, *The Russian Enigma*, London, 1940, p. 153.

A theoretical justification for this behavior was given by Trotsky: "We can only be right with and by the Party, for history has provided no other way of being in the right. The English have a saying, 'My country, right or wrong.' . . . We have much better historical justification in saying whether it is right or wrong in certain individual concrete cases, it is my party" (Souvarine, *op. cit.*, p. 361).

On the other hand, the Red Army officers who did not belong to the movement had to be tried behind closed doors.

[8] The Nazi author Andreas Pfenning explicitly rejects the notion that the SA were fighting for an "ideal" or were prompted by an "idealistic experience." Their "basic

ments, contrary to all forms of idealism, breaks down the moment the movement leaves its fanaticized followers in the lurch, killing in them any remaining conviction that might have survived the collapse of the movement itself.[9] But within the organizational framework of the movement, so long as it holds together, the fanaticized members can be reached by neither experience nor argument; identification with the movement and total conformism seem to have destroyed the very capacity for experience, even if it be as extreme as torture or the fear of death.

The totalitarian movements aim at and succeed in organizing masses—not classes, like the old interest parties of the Continental nation-states; not citizens with opinions about, and interests in, the handling of public affairs, like the parties of Anglo-Saxon countries. While all political groups depend upon proportionate strength, the totalitarian movements depend on the sheer force of numbers to such an extent that totalitarian regimes seem impossible, even under otherwise favorable circumstances, in countries with relatively small populations.[10] After the first World War, a deeply antidemocratic, prodictatorial wave of semitotalitarian and totalitarian movements swept Europe; Fascist movements spread from Italy to nearly all Central and Eastern European countries (the Czech part of Czechoslovakia was one of the notable exceptions); yet even Mussolini, who was so fond of the term "totalitarian state," did not attempt to establish a full-fledged totalitarian regime[11] and contented himself with dictatorship and one-party

---

experience came into existence in the course of the struggle." "Gemeinschaft und Staatswissenschaft," in *Zeitschrift für die gesamte Staatswissenschaft*, Band 96. Translation quoted from Ernst Fraenkel, *The Dual State*, New York and London, 1941. p. 192. From the extensive literature issued in pamphlet form by the main indoctrination center (*Hauptamt-Schulungsamt*) of the SS, it is quite evident that the word "idealism" has been studiously avoided. Not idealism was demanded of SS members, but "utter logical consistency in all questions of ideology and the ruthless pursuit of the political struggle" (Werner Best, *Die deutsche Polizei*, 1941, p. 99).

[9] In this respect postwar Germany offers many illuminating examples. It was astonishing enough that American Negro troops were by no means received with hostility, in spite of the massive racial indoctrination undertaken by the Nazis. But equally startling was "the fact that the Waffen-SS in the last days of German resistance against the Allies did not fight 'to the last man'" and that this special Nazi combat unit "after the enormous sacrifices of the preceding years, which far exceeded the proportionate losses of the Wehrmacht, in the last few weeks acted like any unit drawn from the ranks of civilians, and bowed to the hopelessness of the situation" (Karl O. Paetel, "Die SS," in *Vierteljahreshefte für Zeitgeschichte*, January, 1954).

[10] The Moscow-dominated Eastern European governments rule for the sake of Moscow and act as agents of the Comintern; they are examples of the spread of the Moscow-directed totalitarian movement, not of native developments. The only exception seems to be Tito of Yugoslavia, who may have broken with Moscow because he realized that the Russian-inspired totalitarian methods would cost him a heavy percentage of Yugoslavia's population.

[11] Proof of the nontotalitarian nature of the Fascist dictatorship is the surprisingly small number and the comparatively mild sentences meted out to political offenders. During the particularly active years from 1926 to 1932, the special tribunals for political offenders pronounced 7 death sentences, 257 sentences of 10 or more years imprisonment, 1,360 under 10 years, and sentenced many more to exile; 12,000, more-

rule. Similar nontotalitarian dictatorships sprang up in prewar Rumania, Poland, the Baltic states, Hungary, Portugal and Franco Spain. The Nazis, who had an unfailing instinct for such differences, used to comment contemptuously on the shortcomings of their Fascist allies while their genuine admiration for the Bolshevik regime in Russia (and the Communist Party in Germany) was matched and checked only by their contempt for Eastern European races.[12] The only man for whom Hitler had "unqualified respect" was "Stalin the genius,"[13] and while in the case of Stalin and the Russian

over, were arrested and found innocent, a procedure quite inconceivable under conditions of Nazi or Bolshevik terror. See E. Kohn-Bramstedt, *Dictatorship and Political Police: The Technique of Control by Fear,* London, 1945, pp. 51 ff.

[12] Nazi political theorists have always emphatically stated that "Mussolini's 'ethical state' and Hitler's 'ideological state' [*Weltanschauungsstaat*] cannot be mentioned in the same breath" (Gottfried Neesse, "Die verfassungsrechtliche Gestaltung der Ein-Partei," in *Zeitschrift für die gesamte Staatswissenschaft,* 1938, Band 98).

Goebbels on the difference between Fascism and National Socialism: "[Fascism] is . . . nothing like National Socialism. While the latter goes deep down to the roots, Fascism is only a superficial thing" (*The Goebbels Diaries 1942-1943,* ed. by Louis Lochner, New York, 1948, p. 71). "[The Duce] is not a revolutionary like the Führer or Stalin. He is so bound to his own Italian people that he lacks the broad qualities of a worldwide revolutionary and insurrectionist" (*ibid.,* p. 468).

Himmler expressed the same opinion in a speech delivered in 1943 at a Conference of Commanding Officers: "Fascism and National Socialism are two fundamentally different things, . . . there is absolutely no comparison between Fascism and National Socialism as spiritual, ideological movements." See Kohn-Bramstedt, *op. cit.,* Appendix A.

Hitler recognized in the early twenties the affinity between the Nazi and the Communist movements: "In our movement the two extremes come together: the Communists from the Left and the officers and the students from the Right. These two have always been the most active elements. . . . The Communists were the idealists of Socialism. . . ." See Heiden, *op. cit.,* p. 147. Röhm, the chief of the SA, only repeated a current opinion when he wrote in the late twenties: "Many things are between us and the Communists, but we respect the sincerity of their conviction and their willingness to bring sacrifices for their own cause, and this unites us with them" (Ernst Röhm, *Die Geschichte eines Hochverräters,* 1933, Volksausgabe, p. 273).

During the last war, the Nazis more readily recognized the Russians as their peers than any other nation. Hitler, speaking in May, 1943, at a conference of the Reichsleiter and Gauleiter, "began with the fact that in this war bourgeoisie and revolutionary states are facing each other. It has been an easy thing for us to knock out the bourgeois states, for they were quite inferior to us in their upbringing and attitude. Countries with an ideology have an edge on bourgois states. . . . [In the East] we met an opponent who also sponsors an ideology, even though a wrong one. . . ." (*Goebbels Diaries,* p. 355).—This estimate was based on ideological, not on military considerations. Gottfried Neesse, *Partei und Staat,* 1936, gave the official version of the movement's struggle for power when he wrote: "For us the united front of the *system* extends from the German National People's Party [*i.e.,* the extreme Right] to the Social Democrats. The Communist Party was an enemy outside of the *system.* During the first months of 1933, therefore, when the doom of the *system* was already sealed, we still had to fight a decisive battle against the Communist Party" (p. 76).

[13] *Hitlers Tischgespräche,* p. 113. There we also find numerous examples showing that, contrary to certain postwar legends, Hitler never intended to defend "the West" against Bolshevism but always remained ready to join "the Reds" for the destruction of the West, even in the middle of the struggle against Soviet Russia. See especially pp. 95, 108, 113 ff., 158, 385.

regime we do not have (and presumably never will have) the rich documentary material that is available for Germany, we nevertheless know since Khrushchev's speech before the Twentieth Party Congress that Stalin trusted only one man and that was Hitler.[14]

The point is that in all these smaller European countries nontotalitarian dictatorships were preceded by totalitarian movements, so that it appeared that totalitarianism was too ambitious an aim, that although it had served well enough to organize the masses until the movement seized power, the absolute size of the country then forced the would-be totalitarian ruler of masses into the more familiar patterns of class or party dictatorship. The truth is that these countries simply did not control enough human material to allow for total domination and its inherent great losses in population.[15] Without much hope for the conquest of more heavily populated territories, the tyrants in these small countries were forced into a certain old-fashioned moderation lest they lose whatever people they had to rule. This is also why Nazism, up to the outbreak of the war and its expansion over Europe, lagged so far behind its Russian counterpart in consistency and ruthlessness; even the German people were not numerous enough to allow for the full development of this newest form of government. Only if Germany had won the war would she have known a fully developed totalitarian rulership, and the sacrifices this would have entailed not only for the "inferior races" but for the Germans themselves can be gleaned and evaluated from the legacy of Hitler's plans.[16] In any event it was only during the war, after the conquests

[14] We now know that Stalin was warned repeatedly of the imminent attack of Hitler on the Soviet Union. Even when the Soviet military attaché in Berlin informed him of the day of the Nazi attack, Stalin refused to believe that Hitler would violate the treaty. (See Khrushchev's "Speech on Stalin," text released by the State Department, New York *Times*, June 5, 1956.)

[15] The following information reported by Souvarine, *op. cit.*, p. 669, seems to be an outstanding illustration: "According to W. Krivitsky, whose excellent confidential source of information is the GPU: 'Instead of the 171 million inhabitants calculated for 1937, only 145 million were found; thus nearly 30 million people in the USSR are missing.'" And this, it should be kept in mind, occurred after the dekulakization of the early thirties which had cost an estimated 8 million human lives. See *Communism in Action*. U. S. Government, Washington, 1946, p. 140.

[16] A large part of these plans, based on the original documents, can be found in Léon Poliakov's *Bréviaire de la Haine*, Paris, 1951, chapter 8 (American edition under the title *Harvest of Hate*, Syracuse, 1954; we quote from the original French edition), but only insofar as they referred to the extermination of non-Germanic peoples, above all those of Slavic origin. That the Nazi engine of destruction would not have stopped even before the German people is evident from a Reich health bill drafted by Hitler himself. Here he proposes to "isolate" from the rest of the population all families with cases of heart or lung ailments among them, their physical liquidation being of course the next step in this program. This as well as several other interesting projects for a victorious postwar Germany are contained in a circular letter to the district leaders (Kreisleiter) of Hesse-Nassau in the form of a report on a discussion at the Fuehrer's headquarters concerning "measures that before . . . and after victorious termination of the war" should be adopted. See the collection of documents in *Nazi Conspiracy and Aggression*, Washington, 1946, *et seq.*, Vol. VII, p. 175. In the same context belongs the planned enactment of an "over-all alien legislation," by

in the East furnished large masses of people and made the extermination camps possible, that Germany was able to establish a truly totalitarian rule. (Conversely, the chances for totalitarian rule are frighteningly good in the lands of traditional Oriental despotism, in India and China, where there is almost inexhaustible material to feed the power-accumulating and man-destroying machinery of total domination, and where, moreover, the mass man's typical feeling of superfluousness—an entirely new phenomenon in Europe, the concomitant of mass unemployment and the population growth of the last 150 years—has been prevalent for centuries in the contempt for the value of human life.) Moderation or less murderous methods of rule were hardly attributable to the governments' fear of popular rebellion; depopulation in their own country was a much more serious threat. Only where great masses are superfluous or can be spared without disastrous results of depopulation is totalitarian rule, as distinguished from a totalitarian movement, at all possible.

Totalitarian movements are possible wherever there are masses who for one reason or another have acquired the appetite for political organization. Masses are not held together by a consciousness of common interest and they lack that specific class articulateness which is expressed in determined, limited, and obtainable goals. The term masses applies only where we deal with people who either because of sheer numbers, or indifference, or a combination of both, cannot be integrated into any organization based on common interest, into political parties or municipal governments or professional organizations or trade unions. Potentially, they exist in every country and form the majority of those large numbers of neutral, politically indifferent people who never join a party and hardly ever go to the polls.

It was characteristic of the rise of the Nazi movement in Germany and of the Communist movements in Europe after 1930[17] that they recruited their members from this mass of apparently indifferent people whom all other parties had given up as too apathetic or too stupid for their attention. The result was that the majority of their membership consisted of

means of which the "institutional authority" of the police—namely, to ship persons innocent of any offenses to concentration camps—was to be legalized and expanded. (See Paul Werner, SS-Standartenführer, in *Deutsches Jugendrecht,* Heft 4, 1944.)

In connection with this "negative population policy," which in its aim at extermination decidedly matches the Bolshevist party purges, it is important to remember that "in this process of selection there can never be a standstill" (Himmler, "Die Schutzstaffel," in *Grundlagen, Aufbau und Wirtschaftsordnung des nationalsozialistischen Staates,* No. 7b). "The struggle of the Fuehrer and his party was a hitherto unattained selection. . . . This selection and this struggle were ostensibly accomplished on January 30, 1933. . . . The Fuehrer and his old guard knew that the real struggle had just begun" (Robert Ley, *Der Weg zur Ordensburg,* o.D. Verlag der Deutschen Arbeitsfront. "Not available for sale").

[17] F. Borkenau describes the situation correctly: "The Communists had only very modest successes when they tried to win influence among the masses of the working class; their mass basis, therefore, if they had it at all, moved more and more away from the proletariat" ("Die neue Komintern," in *Der Monat,* Berlin, 1949, Heft 4).

people who never before had appeared on the political scene. This permitted the introduction of entirely new methods into political propaganda, and indifference to the arguments of political opponents; these movements not only placed themselves outside and against the party system as a whole, they found a membership that had never been reached, never been "spoiled" by the party system. Therefore they did not need to refute opposing arguments and consistently preferred methods which ended in death rather than persuasion, which spelled terror rather than conviction. They presented disagreements as invariably originating in deep natural, social, or psychological sources beyond the control of the individual and therefore beyond the power of reason. This would have been a shortcoming only if they had sincerely entered into competition with other parties; it was not if they were sure of dealing with people who had reason to be equally hostile to all parties.

The success of totalitarian movements among the masses meant the end of two illusions of democratically ruled countries in general and of European nation-states and their party system in particular. The first was that the people in its majority had taken an active part in government and that each individual was in sympathy with one's own or somebody else's party. On the contrary, the movements showed that the politically neutral and indifferent masses could easily be the majority in a democratically ruled country, that therefore a democracy could function according to rules which are actively recognized by only a minority. The second democratic illusion exploded by the totalitarian movements was that these politically indifferent masses did not matter, that they were truly neutral and constituted no more than the inarticulate backward setting for the political life of the nation. Now they made apparent what no other organ of public opinion had ever been able to show, namely, that democratic government had rested as much on the silent approbation and tolerance of the indifferent and inarticulate sections of the people as on the articulate and visible institutions and organizations of the country. Thus when the totalitarian movements invaded Parliament with their contempt for parliamentary government, they merely appeared inconsistent: actually, they succeeded in convincing the people at large that parliamentary majorities were spurious and did not necessarily correspond to the realities of the country, thereby undermining the self-respect and the confidence of governments which also believed in majority rule rather than in their constitutions.

It has frequently been pointed out that totalitarian movements use and abuse democratic freedoms in order to abolish them. This is not just devilish cleverness on the part of the leaders or childish stupidity on the part of the masses. Democratic freedoms may be based on the equality of all citizens before the law; yet they acquire their meaning and function organically only where the citizens belong to and are represented by groups or form a social and political hierarchy. The breakdown of the class system, the only social and political stratification of the European nation-states, certainly was "one of the most dramatic events in recent German history"[18] and as favorable to the rise of Nazism as the absence of social stratification in Russia's immense rural population (this "great flaccid body destitute of political education, almost inaccessible to ideas capable of ennobling action"[19]) was to the Bolshevik overthrow of the democratic Kerensky government. Conditions in pre-Hitler Germany are indicative of the dangers implicit in the development of the Western part of the world since, with the end of the second World War, the same dramatic event of a breakdown of the class system repeated itself in almost all European countries, while events in Russia clearly indicate the direction which the inevitable revolutionary changes in Asia may take. Practically speaking, it will make little difference whether totalitarian movements adopt the pattern of Nazism or Bolshevism, organize the masses in the name of race or class, pretend to follow the laws of life and nature or of dialectics and economics.

Indifference to public affairs, neutrality on political issues, are in themselves no sufficient cause for the rise of totalitarian movements. The competitive and acquisitive society of the bourgeoisie had produced apathy and even hostility toward public life not only, and not even primarily, in the social strata which were exploited and excluded from active participation in the rule of the country, but first of all in its own class. The long period of false modesty, when the bourgeoisie was content with being the dominating class in society without aspiring to political rule, which it gladly left to the aristocracy, was followed by the imperialist era, during which the bourgeoisie grew increasingly hostile to existing national institutions and began to claim and to organize itself for the exercise of political power. Both the early apathy and the later demand for monopolistic dictatorial direction of the nation's foreign affairs had their roots in a way and philosophy of life so insistently and exclusively centered on the individual's success or failure in ruthless competition that a citizen's duties and responsibilities could only be felt to be a needless drain on his limited time and energy. These bourgeois attitudes are very useful for those forms of dictatorship in which a "strong man" takes upon himself the troublesome responsibility for the conduct of public affairs; they are a positive hindrance to totalitarian movements which can tolerate bourgeois individualism no more than any other kind of individualism. The apathetic sections of a bourgeois-dominated society, no matter how unwilling they may be to assume the responsibilities of citizens, keep their personalities intact if only because without them they could hardly expect to survive the competitive struggle for life.

The decisive differences between nineteenth-century mob organizations and twentieth-century mass movements are difficult to perceive because the modern totalitarian leaders do not differ much in psychology and mentality from the earlier mob leaders, whose moral standards and political devices so closely resembled those of the bourgeoisie. Yet, insofar as individualism

[18] William Ebenstein, *The Nazi State*, New York, 1943, p. 247.
[19] As Maxim Gorky had described them. See Souvarine, *op. cit.*, p. 290.

characterized the bourgeoisie's as well as the mob's attitude to life, the totalitarian movements can rightly claim that they were the first truly antibourgeois parties; none of their nineteenth-century predecessors, neither the Society of the 10th of December which helped Louis Napoleon into power, the butcher brigades of the Dreyfus Affair, the Black Hundreds of the Russian pogroms, nor the pan-movements, ever involved their members to the point of complete loss of individual claims and ambition, or had ever realized that an organization could succeed in extinguishing individual identity permanently and not just for the moment of collective heroic action.

The relationship between the bourgeois-dominated class society and the masses which emerged from its breakdown is not the same as the relationship between the bourgeoisie and the mob which was a by-product of capitalist production. The masses share with the mob only one characteristic, namely, that both stand outside all social ramifications and normal political representation. The masses do not inherit, as the mob does—albeit in a perverted form—the standards and attitudes of the dominating class, but reflect and somehow pervert the standards and attitudes toward public affairs of all classes. The standards of the mass man were determined not only and not even primarily by the specific class to which he had once belonged, but rather by all-pervasive influences and convictions which were tacitly and inarticulately shared by all classes of society alike.

Membership in a class, although looser and never as inevitably determined by social origin as in the orders and estates of feudal society, was generally by birth, and only extraordinary gifts or luck could change it. Social status was decisive for the individual's participation in politics, and except in cases of national emergency when he was supposed to act only as a *national,* regardless of his class or party membership, he never was directly confronted with public affairs or felt directly responsible for their conduct. The rise of a class to greater importance in the community was always accompanied by the education and training of a certain number of its members for politics as a job, for paid (or, if they could afford it, unpaid) service in the government and representation of the class in Parliament. That the majority of people remained outside all party or other political organization was not important to anyone, and no truer for one particular class than another. In other words, membership in a class, its limited group obligations and traditional attitudes toward government, prevented the growth of a citizenry that felt individually and personally responsible for the rule of the country. This apolitical character of the nation-state's populations came to light only when the class system broke down and carried with it the whole fabric of visible and invisible threads which bound the people to the body politic.

The breakdown of the class system meant automatically the breakdown of the party system, chiefly because these parties, being interest parties, could no longer represent class interests. Their continuance was of some importance to the members of former classes who hoped against hope to regain their old social status and who stuck together not because they had common interests any longer but because they hoped to restore them. The parties, consequently, became more and more psychological and ideological in their propaganda, more and more apologetic and nostalgic in their political approach. They had lost, moreover, without being aware of it, those neutral supporters who had never been interested in politics because they felt that no parties existed to take care of their interests. So that the first signs of the breakdown of the Continental party system were not the desertion of old party members, but the failure to recruit members from the younger generation, and the loss of the silent consent and support of the unorganized masses who suddenly shed their apathy and went wherever they saw an opportunity to voice their new violent opposition.

The fall of protecting class walls transformed the slumbering majorities behind all parties into one great unorganized, structureless mass of furious individuals who had nothing in common except their vague apprehension that the hopes of party members were doomed, that, consequently, the most respected, articulate and representative members of the community were fools and that all the powers that be were not so much evil as they were equally stupid and fraudulent. It was of no great consequence for the birth of this new terrifying negative solidarity that the unemployed worker hated the status quo and the powers that be in the form of the Social Democratic Party, the expropriated small property owner in the form of a centrist or rightist party, and former members of the middle and upper classes in the form of the traditional extreme right. The number of this mass of generally dissatisfied and desperate men increased rapidly in Germany and Austria after the first World War, when inflation and unemployment added to the disrupting consequences of military defeat; they existed in great proportion in all the succession states, and they have supported the extreme movements in France and Italy since the second World War.

In this atmosphere of the breakdown of class society the psychology of the European mass man developed. The fact that with monotonous but abstract uniformity the same fate had befallen a mass of individuals did not prevent their judging themselves in terms of individual failure or the world in terms of specific injustice. This self-centered bitterness, however, although repeated again and again in individual isolation, was not a common bond despite its tendency to extinguish individual differences, because it was based on no common interest, economic or social or political. Self-centeredness, therefore, went hand in hand with a decisive weakening of the instinct for self-preservation. Selflessness in the sense that oneself does not matter, the feeling of being expendable, was no longer the expression of individual idealism but a mass phenomenon. The old adage that the poor and oppressed have nothing to lose but their chains no longer applied to the mass men, for they lost much more than the chains of misery when they lost interest in their own well-being: the source of all the worries and cares which make human life troublesome and anguished was gone. Compared with their nonmaterialism, a Christian monk looks like a man absorbed in worldly affairs. Himmler, who knew so well the mentality of those whom he organized, described not only his SS-men, but the large strata from which he recruited them, when he said they were not interested in "everyday problems" but only "in ideological questions of importance for decades and centuries, so that the man . . . knows he is working for a great task which occurs but once in 2,000 years."[20] The gigantic massing of individuals produced a mentality which, like Cecil Rhodes some forty years before, thought in continents and felt in centuries.

Eminent European scholars and statesmen had predicted, from the early nineteenth century onward, the rise of the mass man and the coming of a mass age. A whole literature on mass behavior and mass psychology had demonstrated and popularized the wisdom, so familiar to the ancients, of the affinity between democracy and dictatorship, between mob rule and tyranny. They had prepared certain politically conscious and overconscious sections of the Western educated world for the emergence of demagogues, for gullibility, superstition, and brutality. Yet, while all these predictions in a sense came true, they lost much of their significance in view of such unexpected and unpredicted phenomena as the radical loss of self-interest,[21] the cynical or bored indifference in the face of death or other personal catastrophes, the passionate inclination toward the most abstract notions as guides for life, and the general contempt for even the most obvious rules of common sense.

The masses, contrary to prediction, did not result from growing equality of condition, from the spread of general education and its inevitable lowering of standards and popularization of content. (America, the classical land of equality of condition and of general education with all its shortcomings, knows less of the modern psychology of masses than perhaps any other country in the world.) It soon became apparent that highly cultured people were particularly attracted to mass movements and that, generally, highly differentiated individualism and sophistication did not prevent, indeed sometimes encouraged, the self-abandonment into the mass for which mass movements provided. Since the obvious fact that individualization and cultivation do not prevent the formation of mass attitudes was so unexpected, it has frequently been blamed upon the morbidity or nihilism of the modern intelligentsia, upon a supposedly typical intellectual self-hatred, upon the spirit's "hostility to life" and antagonism to vitality. Yet, the much-slandered intellectuals were only the most illustrative example and the most articulate spokesmen for a much more general phenomenon. Social atomization and extreme individualization preceded the mass movements

[20] Heinrich Himmler's speech on "Organization and Obligation of the SS and the Police," published in *National-politischer Lehrgang der Wehrmacht vom 15-23. Januar 1937*. Translation quoted from *Nazi Conspiracy and Aggression*. Office of the United States Chief of Counsel for the Prosecution of Axis Criminality. U. S. Government, Washington, 1946, IV, 616 ff.

[21] Gustave Lebon, *La Psychologie des Foules*, 1895, mentions the peculiar selflessness of the masses. See chapter ii, paragraph 5.

which, much more easily and earlier than they did the sociable, nonindividualistic members of the traditional parties, attracted the completely unorganized, the typical "nonjoiners" who for individualistic reasons always had refused to recognize social links or obligations.

The truth is that the masses grew out of the fragments of a highly atomized society whose competitive structure and concomitant loneliness of the individual had been held in check only through membership in a class. The chief characteristic of the mass man is not brutality and backwardness, but his isolation and lack of normal social relationships. Coming from the class-ridden society of the nation-state, whose cracks had been cemented with nationalistic sentiment, it is only natural that these masses, in the first helplessness of their new experience, have tended toward an especially violent nationalism, to which mass leaders have yielded against their own instincts and purposes for purely demagogic reasons.[22]

Neither tribal nationalism nor rebellious nihilism is characteristic of or ideologically appropriate to the masses as they were to the mob. But the most gifted mass leaders of our time have still risen from the mob rather than from the masses.[23] Hitler's biography reads like a textbook example in this respect, and the point about Stalin is that he comes from the conspiratory apparatus of the Bolshevik party with its specific mixture of outcasts and revolutionaries. Hitler's early party, almost exclusively composed of misfits, failures, and adventurers, indeed represented the "armed bohemians"[24] who were only the reverse side of bourgeois society and whom, consequently, the German bourgeoisie should have been able to use successfully for its own purposes. Actually, the bourgeoisie was as much taken in by the Nazis as was the Röhm-Schleicher faction in the Reichswehr, which also thought that Hitler, whom they had used as a stool-pigeon, or the SA, which they had used for militaristic propaganda and paramilitary training, would act as their agents and help in the establishment of a military dictatorship.[25] Both considered the Nazi movement in

[22] The founders of the Nazi party referred to it occasionally even before Hitler took over as a "party of the Left." An incident which occurred after the parliamentary elections of 1932 is also interesting: "Gregor Strasser bitterly pointed out to his Leader that before the elections the National Socialists in the Reichstag might have formed a majority with the Center; now this possibility was ended, the two parties were less than half of parliament; . . . But with the Communists they still had a majority, Hitler replied; no one can govern against us" (Heiden, *op. cit.*, pp. 94 and 495, respectively).

[23] Compare Carlton J. H. Hayes, *op. cit.*, who does not differentiate between the mob and the masses, thinks that totalitarian dictators "have come from the masses rather than from the classes."

[24] This is the central theory of K. Heiden, whose analyses of the Nazi movement are still outstanding. "From the wreckage of dead classes arises the new class of intellectuals, and at the head march the most ruthless, those with the least to lose, hence the strongest: the armed bohemians, to whom war is home and civil war fatherland" (*op. cit.*, p. 100).

[25] The plot between Reichswehr General Schleicher and Röhm, the chief of the SA, consisted of a plan to bring all paramilitary formations under the military authority of the Reichswehr, which at once would have added millions to the German

their own terms, in terms of the political philosophy of the mob,[26] and overlooked the independent, spontaneous support given the new mob leaders by masses as well as the mob leaders' genuine talents for creating new forms of organization. The mob as leader of these masses was no longer the agent of the bourgeoisie or of anyone else except the masses.

That totalitarian movements depended less on the structurelessness of a mass society than on the specific conditions of an atomized and individualized mass, can best be seen in a comparison of Nazism and Bolshevism which began in their respective countries under very different circumstances. To change Lenin's revolutionary dictatorship into full totalitarian rule, Stalin had first to create artificially that atomized society which had been prepared for the Nazis in Germany by historical circumstances.

The October Revolution's amazingly easy victory occurred in a country where a despotic and centralized bureaucracy governed a structureless mass population which neither the remnants of the rural feudal orders nor the weak, nascent urban capitalist classes had organized. When Lenin said that nowhere in the world would it have been so easy to win power and so difficult to keep it, he was aware not only of the weakness of the Russian working class, but of anarchic social conditions in general, which favored sudden changes. Without the instincts of a mass leader—he was no orator and had a passion for public admission and analysis of his own errors, which is against the rules of even ordinary demagogy—Lenin seized at once upon all the possible differentiations, social, national, professional, that might bring some structure into the population, and he seemed convinced that in such stratification lay the salvation of the revolution. He legalized the anarchic expropriation of the landowners by the rural masses and established thereby for the first and probably last time in Russia that emancipated peasant class which, since the French Revolution, had been

army. This, of course, would inevitably have led to a military dictatorship. In June, 1934, Hitler liquidated Röhm and Schleicher. The initial negotiations were started with the full knowledge of Hitler who used Röhm's connections with the Reichswehr to deceive German military circles about his real intentions. In April, 1932, Röhm testified in one of Hitler's lawsuits that the SA's military status had the full understanding of the Reichswehr. (For documentary evidence on the Röhm-Schleicher plan, see *Nazi Conspiracy*, V, 456 ff. See also Heiden, *op. cit.*, p. 450.) Röhm himself proudly reports his negotiations with Schleicher, which according to him were started in 1931. Schleicher had promised to put the SA under the command of Reichswehr officers in case of an emergency. (See *Die Memoiren des Stabschefs Röhm*, Saarbrücken, 1934, p. 170.) The militaristic character of the SA, shaped by Röhm and constantly fought by Hitler, continued to determine its vocabulary even after the liquidation of the Röhm faction. Contrary to the SS, the members of the SA always insisted on being the "representatives of Germany's military will," and for them the Third Reich was a "military community [supported by] two pillars: Party and Wehrmacht" (see *Handbuch der SA*, Berlin, 1939, and Victor Lutze, "Die Sturmabteilungen," in *Grundlagen, Aufbau und Wirtschaftsordnung des nationalsozialistischen Staates*, No. 7a).

[26] Röhm's autobiography especially is a veritable classic in this kind of literature.

the firmest supporter of the Western nation-states. He tried to strengthen the working class by encouraging independent trade unions. He tolerated the timid appearance of a new middle class which resulted from the NEP policy after the end of the civil war. He introduced further distinguishing features by organizing, and sometimes inventing, as many nationalities as possible, furthering national consciousness and awareness of historical and cultural differences even among the most primitive tribes in the Soviet Union. It seems clear that in these purely practical political matters Lenin followed his great instincts for statesmanship rather than his Marxist convictions; his policy, at any rate, proves that he was more frightened by the absence of social and other structure than by the possible development of centrifugal tendencies in the newly emancipated nationalities or even by the growth of a new bourgeoisie out of the newly established middle and peasant classes. There is no doubt that Lenin suffered his greatest defeat when, with the outbreak of the civil war, the supreme power that he originally planned to concentrate in the Soviets definitely passed into the hands of the party bureaucracy; but even this development, tragic as it was for the course of the revolution, would not necessarily have led to totalitarianism. A one-party dictatorship added only one more class to the already developing social stratification of the country, *i.e.*, bureaucracy, which, according to socialist critics of the revolution, "possessed the State as private property" (Marx).[27] At the moment of Lenin's death the roads were still open. The formation of workers, peasants, and middle classes need not necessarily have led to the class struggle which had been characteristic of European capitalism. Agriculture could still be developed on a collective, co-operative, or private basis, and the national economy was still free to follow a socialist, state-capitalist, or a free-enterprise pattern. None of these alternatives would have automatically destroyed the new structure of the country.

All these new classes and nationalities were in Stalin's way when he began to prepare the country for totalitarian government. In order to fabricate an atomized and structureless mass, he had first to liquidate the remnants of power in the Soviets which, as the chief organ of national representation, still played a certain role and prevented absolute rule by the party hierarchy.

[27] It is well known that the anti-Stalinist splinter groups have based their criticism of the development of the Soviet Union on this Marxist formulation, and have actually never outgrown it. The repeated "purges" of Soviet bureaucracy, which were tantamount to a liquidation of bureaucracy as a class, have never prevented them from seeing in it the dominating and ruling class of the Soviet Union. The following is the estimate of Rakovsky, writing in 1930 from his exile in Siberia: "Under our eyes has formed and is being formed a great class of directors which has its internal subdivisions and which increases through calculated co-option and direct or indirect nominations. . . . The element which unites this original class is a form, also original, of private property, to wit, the State power" (quoted from Souvarine, *op. cit.*, p. 564). This analysis is indeed quite accurate for the development of the pre-Stalinist era. For the development of the relationship between party and Soviets, which is of decisive importance for the course of the October revolution, see I. Deutscher, *The Prophet Armed: Trotsky 1879-1921*, 1954.

Therefore he first undermined the national Soviets through the introduction of Bolshevik cells from which alone the higher functionaries to the central committees were appointed.[28] By 1930, the last traces of former communal institutions had disappeared and had been replaced by a firmly centralized party bureaucracy whose tendencies toward Russification were not too different from those of the Czarist regime, except that the new bureaucrats were no longer afraid of literacy.

The Bolshevik government then proceeded to the liquidation of classes and started, for ideological and propaganda reasons, with the property-owning classes, the new middle class in the cities, and the peasants in the country. Because of the combination of numbers and property, the peasants up to then had been potentially the most powerful class in the Union; their liquidation, consequently, was more thorough and more cruel than that of any other group and was carried through by artificial famine and deportation under the pretext of expropriation of the kulaks and collectivization. The liquidation of the middle and peasant classes was completed in the early thirties; those who were not among the many millions of dead or the millions of deported slave laborers had learned "who is master here," had realized that their lives and the lives of their families depended not upon their fellow-citizens but exclusively on the whims of the government which they faced in complete loneliness without any help whatsoever from the group to which they happened to belong. The exact moment when collectivization produced a new peasantry bound by common interests, which owing to its numerical and economic key position in the country's economy again presented a potential danger to totalitarian rule, cannot be determined either from statistics or documentary sources. But for those who know how to read totalitarian "source material" this moment had come two years before Stalin died, when he proposed to dissolve the collectives and transform them into larger units. He did not live to carry out this plan; this time the sacrifices would have been still greater and the chaotic consequences for the total economy still more catastrophic than the liquidation of the first peasant class, but there is no reason to doubt that he might have succeeded; there is no class that cannot be wiped out if a sufficient number of its members are murdered.

The next class to be liquidated as a group were the workers. As a class they were much weaker and offered much less resistance than the peasants because their spontaneous expropriation of factory owners during the revolution, unlike the peasants' expropriation of landowners, had been frus-

[28] In 1927, 90 per cent of the village Soviets and 75 per cent of their chairmen were non-party members; the executive committees of the counties were made up of 50 per cent party members and 50 per cent non-party members, while in the Central Committee 75 per cent of the delegates were party members. See the article on "Bolshevism" by Maurice Dobb in the *Encyclopedia of Social Sciences.*

How the party members of the Soviets, by voting "in conformity with the instructions they received from the permanent officials of the Party," destroyed the Soviet system from within is described in detail in A. Rosenberg, *A History of Bolshevism,* London, 1934, chapter vi.

trated at once by the government which confiscated the factories as state property under the pretext that the state belonged to the proletariat in any event. The Stakhanov system, adopted in the early thirties, broke up all solidarity and class consciousness among the workers, first by the ferocious competition and second by the temporary solidification of a Stakhanovite aristocracy whose social distance from the ordinary worker naturally was felt more acutely than the distance between the workers and the management. This process was completed in 1938 with the introduction of the labor book which transformed the whole Russian worker class officially into a gigantic forced-labor force.

On top of these measures came the liquidation of that bureaucracy which had helped to carry out the previous liquidation measures. It took Stalin about two years, from 1936 to 1938, to rid himself of the whole administrative and military aristocracy of the Soviet society; nearly all offices, factories, economic and cultural bodies, government, party, and military bureaus came into new hands, when "nearly half the administrative personnel, party and nonparty, had been swept out," and more than 50 per cent of all party members and "at least eight million more" were liquidated.[29] Again the introduction of an interior passport, on which all departures from one city to another have to be registered and authorized, completed the destruction of the party bureaucracy as a class. As for its juridical status, the bureaucracy along with the party functionaries was now on the same level with the workers; it, too, had now become a part of the vast multitude of Russian forced laborers and its status as a privileged class in Soviet society was a thing of the past. And since this general purge ended with the liquidation of the highest police officials—the same who had organized the general purge in the first place—not even the cadres of the GPU which had carried out the terror could any longer delude themselves that as a group they represented anything at all, let alone power.

None of these immense sacrifices in human life was motivated by a *raison d'état* in the old sense of the term. None of the liquidated social strata was hostile to the regime or likely to become hostile in the foreseeable future. Active organized opposition had ceased to exist by 1930 when Stalin, in his speech to the Sixteenth Party Congress, outlawed the rightist and leftist deviations inside the Party, and even these feeble oppositions had hardly been able to base themselves on any of the existing classes.[30]

[29] These figures are taken from Victor Kravchenko's Book *I Chose Freedom: The Personal and Political Life of a Soviet Official,* New York, 1946, pp. 278 and 303. This is of course a highly questionable source. But since in the case of Soviet Russia we basically have nothing but questionable sources to resort to—meaning that we have to rely altogether on news stories, reports and evaluations of one kind or another—all we can do is use whatever information at least appears to have a high degree of probability. Some historians seem to think that the opposite method—namely, to use exclusively whatever material is furnished by the Russian government—is more reliable, but this is the not the case. It is precisely the official material that is nothing but propaganda.

[30] Stalin's Report to the Sixteenth Congress denounced the devations as the "reflection" of the resistance of the peasant and petty bourgeois classes in the ranks of the

Dictatorial terror—distinguished from totalitarian terror insofar as it threatens only authentic opponents but not harmless citizens without political opinions—had been grim enough to suffocate all political life, open or clandestine, even before Lenin's death. Intervention from abroad, which might ally itself with one of the dissatisfied sections in the population, was no longer a danger when, by 1930, the Soviet regime had been recognized by a majority of governments and concluded commercial and other international agreements with many countries. (Nor did Stalin's government eliminate such a possibility as far as the people themselves were concerned: we know now that Hitler, if he had been an ordinary conqueror and not a rival totalitarian ruler, might have had an extraordinary chance to win for his cause at least the people of the Ukraine.)

If the liquidation of classes made no political sense, it was positively disastrous for the Soviet economy. The consequences of the artificial famine in 1933 were felt for years throughout the country; the introduction of the Stakhanov system in 1935, with its arbitrary speed-up of individual output and its complete disregard of the necessities for teamwork in industrial production, resulted in a "chaotic imbalance" of the young industry.[31] The liquidation of the bureaucracy, that is, of the class of factory managers and engineers, finally deprived industrial enterprises of what little experience and know-how the new Russian technical intelligentsia had been able to acquire.

Equality of condition among their subjects has been one of the foremost concerns of despotisms and tyrannies since ancient times, yet such equalization is not sufficient for totalitarian rule because it leaves more or less intact certain nonpolitical communal bonds between the subjects, such as family ties and common cultural interests. If totalitarianism takes its own claim seriously, it must come to the point where it has "to finish once and for all with the neutrality of chess," that is, with the autonomous existence of any activity whatsoever. The lovers of "chess for the sake of chess," aptly compared by their liquidator with the lovers of "art for art's sake,"[32] are not yet absolutely atomized elements in a mass society whose completely heterogeneous uniformity is one of the primary conditions for totalitarianism. From the point of view of totalitarian rulers, a society devoted to chess for the sake of chess is only in degree different and less dangerous than a class of farmers for the sake of farming. Himmler quite aptly defined the SS member as the new type of man who under no circumstances will ever do "a thing for its own sake."[33]

Party. (See *Leninism*, 1933, Vol. II, chapter iii.) Against this attack the opposition was curiously defenseless because they too, and especially Trotsky, were "always anxious to discover a struggle of classes behind the struggles of cliques" (Souvarine, *op. cit.*, p. 440).

[31] Kravchenko, *op. cit.*, p. 187.

[32] Souvarine, *op. cit.*, p. 575.

[33] The watchword of the SS as formulated by Himmler himself begins with the words: "There is no task that exists for its own sake." See Gunter d'Alquen, "Die SS," in *Schriften der Hochschule für Politik*, 1939. The pamphlets issued by the SS solely

Mass atomization in Soviet society was achieved by the skillful use of repeated purges which invariably precede actual group liquidation. In order to destroy all social and family ties, the purges are conducted in such a way as to threaten with the same fate the defendant and all his ordinary relations, from mere acquaintances up to his closest friends and relatives. The consequence of the simple and ingenious device of "guilt by association" is that as soon as a man is accused, his former friends are transformed immediately into his bitterest enemies; in order to save their own skins, they volunteer information and rush in with denunciations to corroborate the nonexistent evidence against him; this obviously is the only way to prove their own trustworthiness. Retrospectively, they will try to prove that their acquaintance or friendship with the accused was only a pretext for spying on him and revealing him as a saboteur, a Trotskyite, a foreign spy, or a Fascist. Merit being "gauged by the number of your denunciations of close comrades,"[34] it is obvious that the most elementary caution demands that one avoid all intimate contacts, if possible—not in order to prevent discovery of one's secret thoughts, but rather to eliminate, in the almost certain case of future trouble, all persons who might have not only an ordinary cheap interest in your denunciation but an irresistible need to bring about your ruin simply because they are in danger of their own lives. In the last analysis, it has been through the development of this device to its farthest and most fantastic extremes that Bolshevik rulers have succeeded in creating an atomized and individualized society the like of which we have never seen before and which events or catastrophes alone would hardly have brought about.

Totalitarian movements are mass organizations of atomized, isolated individuals. Compared with all other parties and movements, their most conspicuous external characteristic is their demand for total, unrestricted, unconditional, and unalterable loyalty of the individual member. This demand is made by the leaders of totalitarian movements even before they seize power. It usually precedes the total organization of the country under their actual rule and it follows from the claim of their ideologies that their organization will encompass, in due course, the entire human race. Where, however, totalitarian rule has not been prepared by a totalitarian movement (and this, in contradistinction to Nazi Germany, was the case in Russia), the movement has to be organized afterward and the conditions for its growth have artificially to be created in order to make total loyalty—the psychological basis for total domination—at all possible. Such loyalty can be expected only from the completely isolated human being who, without any other social ties to family, friends, comrades, or even mere acquaint-

for internal consumption emphasize time and again "the absolute necessity for understanding the futility of everything that is an end in itself" (see *Der Reichsführer SS und Chef der deutschen Polizei*, undated, "only for internal use within the police").

[34] The practice itself has been abundantly documented. W. Krivitsky, in his book *In Stalin's Secret Services* (New York, 1939), traces it directly to Stalin.

ances, derives his sense of having a place in the world only from his belonging to a movement, his membership in the party.

Total loyalty is possible only when fidelity is emptied of all concrete content, from which changes of mind might naturally arise. The totalitarian movements, each in its own way, have done their utmost to get rid of the party programs which specified concrete content and which they inherited from earlier, nontotalitarian stages of development. No matter how radically they might have been phrased, every definite political goal which does not simply assert or circumscribe the claim to world rule, every political program which deals with issues more specific than "ideological questions of importance for centuries" is an obstruction to totalitarianism. Hitler's greatest achievement in the organization of the Nazi movement, which he gradually built up from the obscure crackpot membership of a typically nationalistic little party, was that he unburdened the movement of the party's earlier program, not by changing or officially abolishing it, but simply by refusing to talk about it or discuss its points, whose relative moderateness of content and phraseology were very soon outdated.[35] Stalin's task in this as in other respects was much more formidable; the socialist program of the Bolshevik party was a much more troublesome burden[36] than the 25 points of an amateur economist and a crackpot politician.[37] But Stalin achieved eventually, after having abolished the factions of the Russian party, the same result through the constant zigzag of the Communist Party lines, and the constant reinterpretation and application of Marxism which voided the doctrine of all its content because it was no longer possible to predict what course or action it would inspire. The fact that the most perfect education in Marxism and Leninism was no guide whatsoever for political behavior—that, on the contrary, one could follow the party line only if one repeated each morning what Stalin had announced the night before—naturally resulted in the same state of mind, the same concentrated obedience, undivided by any attempt to understand what one was doing, that Himmler's ingenious watchword for his SS-men expressed: "My honor is my loyalty."[38]

[35] Hitler stated in *Mein Kampf* (2 vols., 1st German ed., 1925 and 1927 respectively. Unexpurgated translation, New York, 1939) that it was better to have an antiquated program than to allow a discussion of program (Book II, chapter v). Soon he was to proclaim publicly: "Once we take over the government, the program will come of itself. . . . The first thing must be an inconceivable wave of propaganda. That is a political action which would have little to do with the other problems of the moment." See Heiden, *op. cit.*, p. 203.

[36] Souvarine, in our opinion wrongly, suggests that Lenin had already abolished the role of a party program: "Nothing could show more clearly the non-existence of Bolshevism as a doctrine except in Lenin's brain; every Bolshevik left to himself wandered from 'the line' of his faction . . . for these men were bound together by their temperament and by the ascendancy of Lenin rather than by ideas" (*op. cit.*, p. 85).

[37] Gottfried Feder's Program of the Nazi Party with its famous 25 points has played a greater role in the literature about the movement than in the movement itself.

[38] The impact of the watchword, formulated by Himmler himself, is difficult to render. Its German equivalent: "*Meine Ehre heisst Treue,*" indicates an absolute devotion and obedience which transcends the meaning of mere discipline or personal

Lack of or ignoring of a party program is by itself not necessarily a sign of totalitarianism. The first to consider programs and platforms as needless scraps of paper and embarrassing promises, inconsistent with the style and impetus of a movement, was Mussolini with his Fascist philosophy of activism and inspiration through the historical moment itself.[39] Mere lust for power combined with contempt for "talkative" articulation of what they intend to do with it is characteristic of all mob leaders, but does not come up to the standards of totalitarianism. The true goal of Fascism was only to seize power and establish the Fascist "elite" as uncontested ruler over the country. Totalitarianism is never content to rule by external means, namely, through the state and a machinery of violence; thanks to its peculiar ideology and the role assigned to it in this apparatus of coercion, totalitarianism has discovered a means of dominating and terrorizing human beings from within. In this sense it eliminates the distance between the rulers and the ruled and achieves a condition in which power and the will to power, as we understand them, play no role, or at best, a secondary role. In substance, the totalitarian leader is nothing more nor less than the functionary of the masses he leads; he is not a power-hungry individual imposing a tyrannical and arbitrary will upon his subjects. Being a mere functionary, he can be replaced at any time, and he depends just as much on the "will" of the masses he embodies as the masses depend on him. Without him they would lack external representation and remain an amorphous horde; without the masses the leader is a nonentity. Hitler, who was fully aware of this interdependence, expressed it once in a speech addressed to the SA: "All that you are, you are through me; all that I am, I am through you alone."[40] We are only too inclined to belittle such statements or to misunderstand them in the sense that acting is defined here in terms of giving and executing orders, as has happened too often in the political tradition and history of the West.[41] But this idea has always presupposed someone in command who thinks and wills, and then imposes his thought and will on a thought- and will-deprived group—be it by persuasion, authority, or violence. Hitler, however, was of the opinion that even "thinking . . . [exists] only by virtue of giving or executing orders,"[42]

faithfulness. *Nazi Conspiracy*, whose translations of German documents and Nazi literature are indispensable source material but, unfortunately, are very uneven, renders the SS watchword: "My honor signifies faithfulness" (V, 346).

[39] Mussolini was probably the first party leader who consciously rejected a formal program and replaced it with inspired leadership and action alone. Behind this act lay the notion that the actuality of the moment itself was the chief element of inspiration, which would only be hampered by a party program. The philosophy of Italian Fascism has been expressed by Gentile's "actualism" rather than by Sorel's "myths." Compare also the article "Fascism" in the *Encyclopedia of the Social Sciences*. The Program of 1921 was formulated when the movement had been in existence two years and contained, for the most part, its nationalist philosophy.

[40] Ernst Bayer, *Die SA*, Berlin, 1938. Translation quoted from *Nazi Conspiracy*, IV, 783.

[41] For the first time in Plato's *Statesman*, 305, where acting is interpreted in terms of *archein* and *prattein*—of ordering the start of an action and of executing this order.

[42] *Hitlers Tischgespräche*, p. 198.

and thereby eliminated even theoretically the distinction between thinking and acting on one hand, and between the rulers and the ruled on the other.

Neither National Socialism nor Bolshevism has ever proclaimed a new form of government or asserted that its goals were reached with the seizure of power and the control of the state machinery. Their idea of domination was something that no state and no mere apparatus of violence can ever achieve, but only a movement that is constantly kept in motion: namely, the permanent domination of each single individual in each and every sphere of life.[43] The seizure of power through the means of violence is never an end in itself but only the means to an end, and the seizure of power in any given country is only a welcome transitory stage but never the end of the movement. The practical goal of the movement is to organize as many people as possible within its framework and to set and keep them in motion; a political goal that would constitute the end of the movement simply does not exist.

II: *The Temporary Alliance Between the Mob and the Elite*

WHAT IS MORE disturbing to our peace of mind than the unconditional loyalty of members of totalitarian movements, and the popular support of totalitarian regimes, is the unquestionable attraction these movements exert on the elite, and not only on the mob elements in society. It would be rash indeed to discount, because of artistic vagaries or scholarly naïveté, the terrifying roster of distinguished men whom totalitarianism can count among its sympathizers, fellow-travelers, and inscribed party members.

This attraction for the elite is as important a clue to the understanding of totalitarian movements (though hardly of totalitarian regimes) as their more obvious connection with the mob. It indicates the specific atmosphere, the general climate in which the rise of totalitarianism takes place. It should be remembered that the leaders of totalitarian movements and their sympathizers are, so to speak, older than the masses which they organize so that chronologically speaking the masses do not have to wait helplessly for the rise of their own leaders in the midst of a decaying class society, of which they are the most outstanding product. Those who voluntarily left society before the wreckage of classes had come about, along with the mob, which was an earlier by-product of the rule of the bourgeoisie, stand ready to welcome them. The present totalitarian rulers and the leaders of totalitarian movements still bear the characteristic traits of the mob, whose psychology

[43] *Mein Kampf*, Book I, chapter xi. See also, for example, Dieter Schwarz, *Angriffe auf die nationalsozialistische Weltanschauung:* Aus dem Schwarzen Korps, No. 2, 1936, who answers the obvious criticism that National Socialists after their rise to power continued to talk about "a struggle": "National Socialism as an ideology *[Weltanschauung]* will not abandon its struggle until . . . the way of life of each individual German has been shaped by its fundamental values and these are realized every day anew."

and political philosophy are fairly well known; what will happen once the authentic mass man takes over, we do not know yet, although it may be a fair guess that he will have more in common with the meticulous, calculated correctness of Himmler than with the hysterical fanaticism of Hitler, will more resemble the stubborn dullness of Molotov than the sensual vindictive cruelty of Stalin.

In this respect, the situation after the second World War in Europe does not differ essentially from that after the first; just as in the twenties the ideologies of Fascism, Bolshevism, and Nazism were formulated and the movements led by the so-called front generation, by those who had been brought up and still remembered distinctly the times before the war, so the present general political and intellectual climate of postwar totalitarianism is being determined by a generation which knew intimately the time and life which preceded the present. This is specifically true for France, where the breakdown of the class system came after the second instead of after the first War. Like the mob men and the adventurers of the imperialist era, the leaders of totalitarian movements have in common with their intellectual sympathizers the fact that both had been outside the class and national system of respectable European society even before this system broke down.

This breakdown, when the smugness of spurious respectability gave way to anarchic despair, seemed the first great opportunity for the elite as well as the mob. This is obvious for the new mass leaders whose careers reproduce the features of earlier mob leaders: failure in professional and social life, perversion and disaster in private life. The fact that their lives prior to their political careers had been failures, naïvely held against them by the more respectable leaders of the old parties, was the strongest factor in their mass appeal. It seemed to prove that individually they embodied the mass destiny of the time and that their desire to sacrifice everything for the movement, their assurance of devotion to those who had been struck by catastrophe, their determination never to be tempted back into the security of normal life, and their contempt for respectability were quite sincere and not just inspired by passing ambitions.

The postwar elite, on the other hand, was only slightly younger than the generation which had let itself be used and abused by imperialism for the sake of glorious careers outside of respectability, as gamblers and spies and adventurers, as knights in shining armor and dragon-killers. They shared with Lawrence of Arabia the yearning for "losing their selves" and the violent disgust with all existing standards, with every power that be. If they still remembered the "golden age of security," they also remembered how they had hated it and how real their enthusiasm had been at the outbreak of the first World War. Not only Hitler and not only the failures thanked God on their knees when mobilization swept Europe in 1914.[44] They did not even have to reproach themselves with having been an easy prey for chauvinist propaganda or lying explanations about the purely defensive

[44] See Hitler's description of his reaction to the outbreak of the first World War in *Mein Kampf*, Book I, chapter v.

character of the war. The elite went to war with an exultant hope that everything they knew, the whole culture and texture of life, might go down in its "storms of steel" (Ernst Jünger). In the carefully chosen words of Thomas Mann, war was "chastisement" and "purification"; "war in itself, rather than victories, inspired the poet." Or in the words of a student of the time, "what counts is always the readiness to make a sacrifice, not the object for which the sacrifice is made"; or in the words of a young worker, "it doesn't matter whether one lives a few years longer or not. One would like to have something to show for one's life."[45] And long before one of Nazism's intellectual sympathizers announced, "When I hear the word culture, I draw my revolver," poets had proclaimed their disgust with "rubbish culture" and called poetically on "ye Barbarians, Scythians, Negroes, Indians, to trample it down."[46]

Simply to brand as outbursts of nihilism this violent dissatisfaction with the prewar age and subsequent attempts at restoring it (from Nietzsche and Sorel to Pareto, from Rimbaud and T. E. Lawrence to Jünger, Brecht, and Malraux, from Bakunin and Nechayev to Alexander Blok) is to overlook how justified disgust can be in a society wholly permeated with the ideological outlook and moral standards of the bourgeoisie. Yet it is also true that the "front generation," in marked contrast to their own chosen spiritual fathers, were completely absorbed by their desire to see the ruin of this whole world of fake security, fake culture, and fake life. This desire was so great that it outweighed in impact and articulateness all earlier attempts at a "transformation of values," such as Nietzsche had attempted, or a reorganization of political life as indicated in Sorel's writings, or a revival of human authenticity in Bakunin, or a passionate love of life in the purity of exotic adventures in Rimbaud. Destruction without mitigation, chaos and ruin as such assumed the dignity of supreme values.[47]

The genuineness of these feelings can be seen in the fact that very few of this generation were cured of their war enthusiasm by actual experience of its horrors. The survivors of the trenches did not become pacifists. They cherished an experience which, they thought, might serve to separate them

[45] See the collection of material on the "inner chronicle of the first World War" by Hanna Hafkesbrink, *Unknown Germany*, New Haven, 1948, pp. 43, 45, 81, respectively. The great value of this collection for the imponderables of historical atmosphere makes the lack of similar studies for France, England, and Italy all the more deplorable.

[46] *Ibid.*, pp. 20-21.

[47] This started with a feeling of complete alienation from normal life. Wrote Rudolf Binding, for instance: "More and more we are to be counted among the dead, among the estranged—because the greatness of the occurrence estranges and separates us—rather than among the banished whose return is possible" (*ibid.*, p. 160). A curious reminiscence of the front generation's elite claim can still be found in Himmler's account of how he finally hit upon his "form of selection" for the reorganization of the SS: ". . . the most severe selection procedure is brought about by war, the struggle for life and death. In this procedure the value of blood is shown through achievement. . . . War, however, is an exceptional circumstance, and a way had to be found to make selections in peace time" (*op. cit.*).

definitely from the hated surroundings of respectability. They clung to their memories of four years of life in the trenches as though they constituted an objective criterion for the establishment of a new elite. Nor did they yield to the temptation to idealize this past; on the contrary, the worshipers of war were the first to concede that war in the era of machines could not possibly breed virtues like chivalry, courage, honor, and manliness,[48] that it imposed on men nothing but the experience of bare destruction together with the humiliation of being only small cogs in the majestic wheel of slaughter.

This generation remembered the war as the great prelude to the breakdown of classes and their transformation into masses. War, with its constant murderous arbitrariness, became the symbol for death, the "great equalizer"[49] and therefore the true father of a new world order. The passion for equality and justice, the longing to transcend narrow and meaningless class lines, to abandon stupid privileges and prejudices, seemed to find in war a way out of the old condescending attitudes of pity for the oppressed and disinherited. In times of growing misery and individual helplessness, it seems as difficult to resist pity when it grows into an all-devouring passion as it is not to resent its very boundlessness, which seems to kill human dignity with a more deadly certainty than misery itself.

In the early years of his career, when a restoration of the European status quo was still the most serious threat to the ambitions of the mob,[50] Hitler appealed almost exclusively to these sentiments of the front generation. The peculiar selflessness of the mass man appeared here as yearning for anonymity, for being just a number and functioning only as a cog, for every transformation, in brief, which would wipe out the spurious identifications with specific types or predetermined functions within society. War had been experienced as that "mightiest of all mass actions" which obliterated individual differences so that even suffering, which traditionally had marked off individuals through unique unexchangeable destinies, could now be interpreted as "an instrument of historical progress."[51] Nor did national distinctions limit the masses into which the postwar elite wished to be immersed. The first World War, somewhat paradoxically, had almost extinguished genuine national feelings in Europe where, between the wars, it was far more important to have belonged to the generation of the trenches, no matter on which side, than to be a German or a Frenchman.[52] The Nazis based their

[48] See, for instance, Ernst Jünger, *The Storm of Steel*, London, 1929.

[49] Hafkesbrink, *op. cit.*, p. 156.

[50] Heiden, *op. cit.*, shows how consistently Hitler sided with catastrophe in the early days of the movement, how he feared a possible recovery of Germany. "Half a dozen times [*i.e.*, during the Ruhrputsch], in different terms, he declared to his storm troops that Germany was going under. 'Our job is to insure the success of our movement'" (p. 167)—a success which at that moment depended upon the collapse of the fight in the Ruhr.

[51] Hafkesbrink, *op. cit.*, pp. 156-157.

[52] This feeling was already widespread during the war when Rudolf Binding wrote: "[This war] is not to be compared with a campaign. For there one leader pits his

whole propaganda on this indistinct comradeship, this "community of fate," and won over a great number of veteran organizations in all European countries, thereby proving how meaningless national slogans had become even in the ranks of the so-called Right, which used them for their connotation of violence rather than for their specific national content.

No single element in this general intellectual climate in postwar Europe was very new. Bakunin had already confessed, "I do not want to be *I*, I want to be *We*,"[53] and Nechayev had preached the evangel of the "doomed man" with "no personal interests, no affairs, no sentiments, attachments, property, not even a name of his own."[54] The antihumanist, antiliberal, anti-individualist, and anticultural instincts of the front generation, their brilliant and witty praise of violence, power, and cruelty, was preceded by the awkward and pompous "scientific" proofs of the imperialist elite that a struggle of all against all is the law of the universe, that expansion is a psychological necessity before it is a political device, and that man has to behave by such universal laws.[55] What was new in the writings of the front generation was their high literary standard and great depth of passion. The postwar writers no longer needed the scientific demonstrations of genetics, and they made little if any use of the collected works of Gobineau or Houston Stewart Chamberlain, which belonged already to the cultural household of the philistines. They read not Darwin but the Marquis de Sade.[56] If they believed at all in universal laws, they certainly did not particularly care to conform to them. To them, violence, power, cruelty, were the supreme capacities of men who had definitely lost their place in the universe and were much too proud to long for a power theory that would safely bring them back and re-

will against that of another. But in this War both adversaries lie on the ground, and only the War has its will" (*ibid.*, p. 67).

[53] Bakunin in a letter written on February 7, 1870. See Max Nomad, *Apostles of Revolution*, Boston, 1939, p. 180.

[54] The "Catechism of the Revolutionist" was either written by Bakunin himself or by his disciple Nechayev. For the question of authorship and a translation of the complete text, see Nomad, *op. cit.*, p. 227 ff. In any event, the "system of complete disregard for any tenets of simple decency and fairness in [the revolutionist's] attitude towards other human beings . . . went down in Russian revolutionary history under the name of 'Nechayevshchina' " (*ibid.*, p. 224).

[55] Outstanding among these political theorists of imperialism is Ernest Seillière, *Mysticisme et Domination: Essais de Critique Impérialiste*, 1913. See also Cargill Sprietsma, *We Imperialists: Notes on Ernest Seillière's Philosophy of Imperialism*, New York, 1931; G. Monod in *La Revue Historique*, January, 1912; and Louis Estève, *Une nouvelle Psychologie de l'Impérialisme: Ernest Seillière*, 1913.

[56] In France, since 1930, the Marquis de Sade has become one of the favored authors of the literary avant-garde. Jean Paulhan, in his Introduction to a new edition of Sade's *Les Infortunes de la Vertu*, Paris, 1946, remarks: "When I see so many writers today consciously trying to deny artifice and the literary game for the sake of the inexpressible [*un évènement indicible*] . . . , anxiously looking for the sublime in the infamous, for the great in the subversive . . . , I ask myself . . . if our modern literature, in those parts which appear to us most vital—or at any rate most aggressive—has not turned entirely toward the past, and if it was not precisely Sade who determined it." See also Georges Bataille, "Le Secret de Sade," in *La Critique*, Tome III, Nos. 15-16, 17, 1947.

integrate them into the world. They were satisfied with blind partisanship in anything that respectable society had banned, regardless of theory or content, and they elevated cruelty to a major virtue because it contradicted society's humanitarian and liberal hypocrisy.

If we compare this generation with the nineteenth-century ideologists, with whose theories they sometimes seem to have so much in common, their chief distinction is their greater authenticity and passion. They had been more deeply touched by misery, they were more concerned with the perplexities and more deadly hurt by hypocrisy than all the apostles of good will and brotherhood had been. And they could no longer escape into exotic lands, could no longer afford to be dragon-slayers among strange and exciting people. There was no escape from the daily routine of misery, meekness, frustration, and resentment embellished by a fake culture of educated talk; no conformity to the customs of fairy tale lands could possibly save them from the rising nausea that this combination continuously inspired.

This inability to escape into the wide world, this feeling of being caught again and again in the trappings of society—so different from the conditions which had formed the imperialist character—added a constant strain and the yearning for violence to the older passion for anonymity and losing oneself. Without the possibility of a radical change of role and character, such as the identification with the Arab national movement or the rites of an Indian village, the self-willed immersion in the suprahuman forces of destruction seemed to be a salvation from the automatic identification with pre-established functions in society and their utter banality, and at the same time to help destroy the functioning itself. These people felt attracted to the pronounced activism of totalitarian movements, to their curious and only seemingly contradictory insistence on both the primacy of sheer action and the overwhelming force of sheer necessity. This mixture corresponded precisely to the war experience of the "front generation," to the experience of constant activity within the framework of overwhelming fatality.

Activism, moreover, seemed to provide new answers to the old and troublesome question, "Who am I?" which always appears with redoubled persistence in times of crisis. If society insisted, "You are what you appear to be," postwar activism replied: "You are what you have done"—for instance, the man who for the first time had crossed the Atlantic in an airplane (as in Brecht's *Der Flug der Lindberghs*)—an answer which after the second World War was repeated and slightly varied by Sartre's "You are your life" (in *Huis Clos*). The pertinence of these answers lies less in their validity as redefinitions of personal identity than in their usefulness for an eventual escape from social identification, from the multiplicity of interchangeable roles and functions which society had imposed. The point was to do something, heroic or criminal, which was unpredictable and undetermined by anybody else.

The pronounced activism of the totalitarian movements, their preference for terrorism over all other forms of political activity, attracted the intellectual elite and the mob alike, precisely because this terrorism was so utterly different from that of the earlier revolutionary societies. It was no longer a matter of calculated policy which saw in terrorist acts the only means to eliminate certain outstanding personalities who, because of their policies or position, had become the symbol of oppression. What proved so attractive was that terrorism had become a kind of philosophy through which to express frustration, resentment, and blind hatred, a kind of political expressionism which used bombs to express oneself, which watched delightedly the publicity given to resounding deeds and was absolutely willing to pay the price of life for having succeeded in forcing the recognition of one's existence on the normal strata of society. It was still the same spirit and the same game which made Goebbels, long before the eventual defeat of Nazi Germany, announce with obvious delight that the Nazis, in case of defeat, would know how to slam the door behind them and not to be forgotten for centuries.

Yet it is here if anywhere that a valid criterion may be found for distinguishing the elite from the mob in the pretotalitarian atmosphere. What the mob wanted, and what Goebbels expressed with great precision, was access to history even at the price of destruction. Goebbels' sincere conviction that "the greatest happiness that a contemporary can experience today" is either to be a genius or to serve one,[57] was typical of the mob but neither of the masses nor the sympathizing elite. The latter, on the contrary, took anonymity seriously to the point of seriously denying the existence of genius; all the art theories of the twenties tried desperately to prove that the excellent is the product of skill, craftsmanship, logic, and the realization of the potentialities of the material.[58] The mob, and not the elite, was charmed by the "radiant power of fame" (Stefan Zweig) and accepted enthusiastically the genius idolatry of the late bourgeois world. In this the mob of the twentieth century followed faithfully the pattern of earlier parvenus who also had discovered the fact that bourgeois society would rather open its doors to the fascinating "abnormal," the genius, the homosexual, or the Jew, than to simple merit. The elite's contempt for the genius and its yearning for anonymity was still witness of a spirit which neither the masses nor the mob were in a position to understand, and which, in the words of Robespierre, strove to assert the grandeur of man against the pettiness of the great.

This difference between the elite and the mob notwithstanding, there is no doubt that the elite was pleased whenever the underworld frightened respectable society into accepting it on an equal footing. The members of the elite did not object at all to paying a price, the destruction of civilization, for the fun of seeing how those who had been excluded unjustly in the past forced their way into it. They were not particularly outraged at the monstrous forgeries in historiography of which all totalitarian regimes are guilty and which announce themselves clearly enough in totalitarian propaganda. They had convinced themselves that traditional historiography was a forgery

[57] Goebbels, *op. cit.*, p. 139.

[58] The art theories of the Bauhaus were characteristic in this respect. See also Bertolt Brecht's remarks on the theater, *Gesammelte Werke*, London, 1938.

in any case, since it had excluded the underprivileged and oppressed from the memory of mankind. Those who were rejected by their own time were usually forgotten by history, and insult added to injury had troubled all sensitive consciences ever since faith in a hereafter where the last would be the first had disappeared. Injustices in the past as well as the present became intolerable when there was no longer any hope that the scales of justice eventually would be set right. Marx's great attempt to rewrite world history in terms of class struggles fascinated even those who did not believe in the correctness of his thesis, because of his original intention to find a device by which to force the destinies of those excluded from official history into the memory of posterity.

The temporary alliance between the elite and the mob rested largely on this genuine delight with which the former watched the latter destroy respectability. This could be achieved when the German steel barons were forced to deal with and to receive socially Hitler the housepainter and self-admitted former derelict, as it could be with the crude and vulgar forgeries perpetrated by the totalitarian movements in all fields of intellectual life, insofar as they gathered all the subterranean, nonrespectable elements of European history into one consistent picture. From this viewpoint it was rather gratifying to see that Bolshevism and Nazism began even to eliminate those sources of their own ideologies which had already won some recognition in academic or other official quarters. Not Marx's dialectical materialism, but the conspiracy of 300 families; not the pompous scientificality of Gobineau and Chamberlain, but the "Protocols of the Elders of Zion"; not the traceable influence of the Catholic Church and the role played by anticlericalism in Latin countries, but the backstairs literature about the Jesuits and the Freemasons became the inspiration for the rewriters of history. The object of the most varied and variable constructions was always to reveal official history as a joke, to demonstrate a sphere of secret influences of which the visible, traceable, and known historical reality was only the outward façade erected explicitly to fool the people.

To this aversion of the intellectual elite for official historiography, to its conviction that history, which was a forgery anyway, might as well be the playground of crackpots, must be added the terrible, demoralizing fascination in the possibility that gigantic lies and monstrous falsehoods can eventually be established as unquestioned facts, that man may be free to change his own past at will, and that the difference between truth and falsehood may cease to be objective and become a mere matter of power and cleverness, of pressure and infinite repetition. Not Stalin's and Hitler's skill in the art of lying but the fact that they were able to organize the masses into a collective unit to back up their lies with impressive magnificence, exerted the fascination. Simple forgeries from the viewpoint of scholarship appeared to receive the sanction of history itself when the whole marching reality of the movements stood behind them and pretended to draw from them the necessary inspiration for action.

The attraction which the totalitarian movements exert on the elite, so long as and wherever they have not seized power, has been perplexing because the patently vulgar and arbitrary, positive doctrines of totalitarianism are more conspicuous to the outsider and mere observer than the general mood which pervades the pretotalitarian atmosphere. These doctrines were so much at variance with generally accepted intellectual, cultural, and moral standards that one could conclude that only an inherent fundamental shortcoming of character in the intellectual, *"la trahison des clercs"* (J. Benda), or a perverse self-hatred of the spirit, accounted for the delight with which the elite accepted the "ideas" of the mob. What the spokesmen of humanism and liberalism usually overlook, in their bitter disappointment and their unfamiliarity with the more general experiences of the time, is that an atmosphere in which all traditional values and propositions had evaporated (after the nineteenth-century ideologies had refuted each other and exhausted their vital appeal) in a sense made it easier to accept patently absurd propositions than the old truths which had become pious banalities, precisely because nobody could be expected to take the absurdities seriously. Vulgarity with its cynical dismissal of respected standards and accepted theories carried with it a frank admission of the worst and a disregard for all pretenses which were easily mistaken for courage and a new style of life. In the growing prevalence of mob attitudes and convictions—which were actually the attitudes and convictions of the bourgeoisie cleansed of hypocrisy—those who traditionally hated the bourgeoisie and had voluntarily left respectable society saw only the lack of hypocrisy and respectability, not the content itself.[59]

Since the bourgeoisie claimed to be the guardian of Western traditions and confounded all moral issues by parading publicly virtues which it not only did not possess in private and business life, but actually held in contempt, it seemed revolutionary to admit cruelty, disregard of human values, and general amorality, because this at least destroyed the duplicity upon which the existing society seemed to rest. What a temptation to flaunt extreme attitudes in the hypocritical twilight of double moral standards, to wear publicly the mask of cruelty if everybody was patently inconsiderate and pretended to be gentle, to parade wickedness in a world, not of wickedness, but of meanness! The intellectual elite of the twenties who knew little of the earlier connections between mob and bourgeoisie was certain that the old game of *épater le bourgeois* could be played to perfection if one started to shock society with an ironically exaggerated picture of its own behavior.

At that time, nobody anticipated that the true victims of this irony would

[59] The following passage by Röhm is typical of the feeling of almost the whole younger generation and not only of an elite: "Hypocrisy and Pharisaism rule. They are the most conspicuous characteristics of society today. . . . Nothing could be more lying than the so-called morals of society." These boys "don't find their way in the philistine world of bourgeois double morals and don't know any longer how to distinguish between truth and error" (*Die Geschichte eines Hochverräters,* pp. 267 and 269). The homosexuality of these circles was also at least partially an expression of their protest against society.

be the elite rather than the bourgeoisie. The avant-garde did not know they were running their heads not against walls but against open doors, that a unanimous success would belie their claim to being a revolutionary minority, and would prove that they were about to express a new mass spirit or the spirit of the time. Particularly significant in this respect was the reception given Brecht's *Dreigroschenoper* in pre-Hitler Germany. The play presented gangsters as respectable businessmen and respectable businessmen as gangsters. The irony was somewhat lost when respectable businessmen in the audience considered this a deep insight into the ways of the world and when the mob welcomed it as an artistic sanction of gangsterism. The theme song in the play, *"Erst kommt das Fressen, dann kommt die Moral,"* was greeted with frantic applause by exactly everybody, though for different reasons. The mob applauded because it took the statement literally; the bourgeoisie applauded because it had been fooled by its own hypocrisy for so long that it had grown tired of the tension and found deep wisdom in the expression of the banality by which it lived; the elite applauded because the unveiling of hypocrisy was such superior and wonderful fun. The effect of the work was exactly the opposite of what Brecht had sought by it. The bourgeoisie could no longer be shocked; it welcomed the exposure of its hidden philosophy, whose popularity proved they had been right all along, so that the only political result of Brecht's "revolution" was to encourage everyone to discard the uncomfortable mask of hypocrisy and to accept openly the standards of the mob.

A reaction similar in its ambiguity was aroused some ten years later in France by Céline's *Bagatelles pour un Massacre,* in which he proposed to massacre all the Jews. André Gide was publicly delighted in the pages of the *Nouvelle Revue Française,* not of course because he wanted to kill the Jews of France, but because he rejoiced in the blunt admission of such a desire and in the fascinating contradiction between Céline's bluntness and the hypocritical politeness which surrounded the Jewish question in all respectable quarters. How irresistible the desire for the unmasking of hypocrisy was among the elite can be gauged by the fact that such delight could not even be spoiled by Hitler's very real persecution of the Jews, which at the time of Céline's writing was already in full swing. Yet aversion against the philosemitism of the liberals had much more to do with this reaction than hatred of Jews. A similar frame of mind explains the remarkable fact that Hitler's and Stalin's widely publicized opinions about art and their persecution of modern artists have never been able to destroy the attraction which the totalitarian movements had for avant-garde artists; this shows the elite's lack of a sense of reality, together with its perverted selflessness, both of which resemble only too closely the fictitious world and the absence of self-interest among the masses. It was the great opportunity of the totalitarian movements, and the reason why a temporary alliance between the intellectual elite and the mob could come about, that in an elementary and undifferentiated way their problems had become the same and foreshadowed the problems and mentality of the masses.

Closely related to the attraction which the mob's lack of hypocrisy and the masses' lack of self-interest exerted on the elite was the equally irresistible appeal of the totalitarian movements' spurious claim to have abolished the separation between private and public life and to have restored a mysterious irrational wholeness in man. Since Balzac revealed the private lives of the public figures of French society and since Ibsen's dramatization of the "Pillars of Society" had conquered the Continental theater, the issue of double morality was one of the main topics for tragedies, comedies, and novels. Double morality as practiced by the bourgeoisie became the outstanding sign of that *esprit de sérieux,* which is always pompous and never sincere. This division between private and public or social life had nothing to do with the justified separation between the personal and public spheres, but was rather the psychological reflection of the nineteenth-century struggle between *bourgeois* and *citoyen,* between the man who judged and used all public institutions by the yardstick of his private interests and the responsible citizen who was concerned with public affairs as the affairs of all. In this connection, the liberals' political philosophy, according to which the mere sum of individual interests adds up to the miracle of the common good, appeared to be only a rationalization of the recklessness with which private interests were pressed regardless of the common good.

Against the class spirit of the Continental parties, which had always admitted they represented certain interests, and against the "opportunism" resulting from their conception of themselves as only parts of a total, the totalitarian movements asserted their "superiority" in that they carried a *Weltanschauung* by which they would take possession of man as a whole.[60] In this claim to totality the mob leaders of the movements again formulated and only reversed the bourgeoisie's own political philosophy. The bourgeois class, having made its way through social pressure and, frequently, through an economic blackmail of political institutions, always believed that the public and visible organs of power were directed by their own secret, nonpublic interests and influence. In this sense, the bourgeoisie's political philosophy was always "totalitarian"; it always assumed an identity of politics, economics and society, in which political institutions served only as the façade for private interests. The bourgeoisie's double standard, its differentiation between public and private life, were a concession to the nation-state which had desperately tried to keep the two spheres apart.

What appealed to the elite was radicalism as such. Marx's hopeful predictions that the state would wither away and a classless society emerge were no longer radical, no longer Messianic enough. If Berdyaev is right in stating that "Russian revolutionaries . . . had always been totalitarian," then the attraction which Soviet Russia exerted almost equally on Nazi and Communist intellectual fellow-travelers lay precisely in the fact that in Russia

[60] The role of the *Weltanschauung* in the formation of the Nazi movement has been stressed many times by Hitler himself. In *Mein Kampf,* it is interesting to note that he pretends to have understood the necessity of basing a party on a *Weltanschauung* through the superiority of the Marxist parties. Book II, chapter i: "*Weltanschauung* and Party."

"the revolution was a religion and a philosophy, not merely a conflict concerned with the social and political side of life."[61] The truth was that the transformation of classes into masses and the breakdown of the prestige and authority of political institutions had brought to Western European countries conditions which resembled those prevalent in Russia, so that it was no accident that their revolutionaries also began to take on the typically Russian revolutionary fanaticism which looked forward, not to change in social or political conditions, but to the radical destruction of every existing creed, value, and institution. The mob merely took advantage of this new mood and brought about a short-lived alliance of revolutionaries and criminals, which also had been present in many revolutionary sects in Czarist Russia but conspicuously absent from the European scene.

The disturbing alliance between the mob and the elite, and the curious coincidence of their aspirations, had their origin in the fact that these strata had been the first to be eliminated from the structure of the nation-state and the framework of class society. They found each other so easily, if only temporarily, because they both sensed that they represented the fate of the time, that they were followed by unending masses, that sooner or later the majority of European peoples might be with them—as they thought, ready to make their revolution.

It turned out that they were both mistaken. The mob, the underworld of the bourgeois class, hoped that the helpless masses would help them into power, would support them when they attempted to forward their private interests, that they would be able simply to replace the older strata of bourgeois society and to instill into it the more enterprising spirit of the underworld. Yet totalitarianism in power learned quickly that enterprising spirit was not restricted to the mob strata of the population and that, in any event, such initiative could only be a threat to the total domination of man. Absence of scruple, on the other hand, was not restricted to the mob either and, in any event, could be taught in a relatively short time. For the ruthless machines of domination and extermination, the masses of co-ordinated philistines provided much better material and were capable of even greater crimes than so-called professional criminals, provided only that these crimes were well organized and assumed the appearance of routine jobs.

It is not fortuitous, then, that the few protests against the Nazis' mass atrocities against the Jews and Eastern European peoples were voiced not by the military men nor by any other part of the co-ordinated masses of respectable philistines, but precisely by those early comrades of Hitler who were typical representatives of the mob.[62] Nor was Himmler, the most power-

[61] Nicolai Berdyaev, *The Origin of Russian Communism*, 1937, pp. 124-125.

[62] There is, for instance, the curious intervention of Welhelm Kube, General Commissar in Minsk and one of the oldest members of the Party, who in 1941, *i.e.*, at the beginning of the mass murder, wrote to his chief: "I certainly am tough and willing to co-operate in the solution of the Jewish question, but people who have been brought up in our own culture are, after all, different from the local bestial hordes. Are we to assign the task of slaughtering them to the Lithuanians and Letts who are dis-

ful man in Germany after 1936, one of those "armed bohemians" (Heiden) whose features were distressingly similar to those of the intellectual elite. Himmler was himself "more normal," that is, more of a philistine, than any of the original leaders of the Nazi movement.[63] He was not a bohemian like Goebbels, or a sex criminal like Streicher, or a crackpot like Rosenberg, or a fanatic like Hitler, or an adventurer like Göring. He proved his supreme ability for organizing the masses into total domination by assuming that most people are neither bohemians, fanatics, adventurers, sex maniacs, crackpots, nor social failures, but first and foremost job holders and good family men.

The philistine's retirement into private life, his single-minded devotion to matters of family and career was the last, and already degenerated, product of the bourgeoisie's belief in the primacy of private interest. The philistine is the bourgeois isolated from his own class, the atomized individual who is produced by the breakdown of the bourgeois class itself. The mass man whom Himmler organized for the greatest mass crimes ever committed in history bore the features of the philistine rather than of the mob man, and was the bourgeois who in the midst of the ruins of his world worried about nothing so much as his private security, was ready to sacrifice everything—belief, honor, dignity—on the slightest provocation. Nothing proved easier to destroy than the privacy and private morality of people who thought of nothing but safeguarding their private lives. After a few years of power and

---

criminated against even by the indigenous population? I could not do it. I ask you to give me clear-cut instructions to take care of the matter in the most humane way for the sake of the prestige of our Reich and our Party." This letter is published in Max Weinreich, *Hitler's Professors*, New York, 1946, pp. 153-154. Kube's intervention was quickly overruled, yet an almost identical attempt to save the lives of Danish Jews, made by W. Best, the Reich's plenipotentiary in Denmark, and a well-known Nazi, was more successful. See *Nazi Conspiracy*, V, 2.

Similarly Alfred Rosenberg, who had preached the inferiority of the Slav peoples, obviously never realized that his theories might one day mean their liquidation. Charged with the administration of the Ukraine, he wrote outraged reports about conditions there during the fall of 1942 after he had tried earlier to get direct intervention from Hitler himself. See *Nazi Conspiracy*, III, 83 ff., and IV, 62.

There are of course some exceptions to this rule. The man who saved Paris from destruction was General von Choltitz who, however, still "feared that he would be deprived of his command as he had not executed his orders" even though he knew that the "war had been lost for several years." That he would have had the courage to resist the order "to turn Paris into a mass of ruins" without the energetic support of a Nazi of old standing, Otto Abetz the Ambassador to France, appears dubious according to his own testimony during the trial of Abetz in Paris. See New York *Times*, July 21, 1949.

[63] An Englishman, Stephen H. Roberts, *The House that Hitler Built*, London, 1939, describes Himmler as "a man of exquisite courtesy and still interested in the simple things of life. He has none of the pose of those Nazis who act as demigods. . . . No man looks less like his job than this police dictator of Germany, and I am convinced that nobody I met in Germany is more normal. . . ." (pp. 89-90)—This reminds one in a curious way of the remark of Stalin's mother who according to Bolshevik propaganda said of him: "An exemplary son. I wish everybody were like him" (Souvarine, *op. cit.*, p. 656).

systematic co-ordination, the Nazis could rightly announce: "The only person who is still a private individual in Germany is somebody who is asleep."[64]

In all fairness to those among the elite, on the other hand, who at one time or another have let themselves be seduced by totalitarian movements, and who sometimes, because of their intellectual abilities, are even accused of having inspired totalitarianism, it must be stated that what these desperate men of the twentieth century did or did not do had no influence on totalitarianism whatsoever, although it did play some part in earlier, successful, attempts of the movements to force the outside world to take their doctrines seriously. Wherever totalitarian movements seized power, this whole group of sympathizers was shaken off even before the regimes proceeded toward their greatest crimes. Intellectual, spiritual, and artistic initiative is as dangerous to totalitarianism as the gangster initiative of the mob, and both are more dangerous than mere political opposition. The consistent persecution of every higher form of intellectual activity by the new mass leaders springs from more than their natural resentment against everything they cannot understand. Total domination does not allow for free initiative in any field of life, for any activity that is not entirely predictable. Totalitarianism in power invariably replaces all first-rate talents, regardless of their sympathies, with those crackpots and fools whose lack of intelligence and creativity is still the best guarantee of their loyalty.[65]

[64] The remark was made by Robert Ley. See Kohn-Bramstedt, *op. cit.*, p. 178.

[65] Bolshevik policy, in this respect surprisingly consistent, is well known and hardly needs further comment. Picasso, to take the most famous instance, is not liked in Russia even though he has become a Communist. It is possible that André Gide's sudden reversal of attitude after seeing the Bolshevik reality in Soviet Russia (*Retour de l'URSS*) in 1936, definitely convinced Stalin of the uselessness of creative artists even as fellow-travelers. Nazi policy was distinguished from Bolshevik measures only insofar as it did not yet kill its first-rate talents.

It would be worthwhile to study in detail the careers of those comparatively few German scholars who went beyond mere co-operation and volunteered their services because they were convinced Nazis. (Weinreich, *op. cit.*, the only available study, and misleading because he does not distinguish between professors who adopted the Nazi creed and those who owed their careers exclusively to the regime, omits the earlier careers of the concerned scholars and thus indiscriminately puts well-known men of great achievement into the same category as crackpots.) Most interesting is the example of the jurist Carl Schmitt, whose very ingenious theories about the end of democracy and legal government still make arresting reading; as early as the middle thirties, he was replaced by the Nazis' own brand of political and legal theorists, such as Hans Frank, the later governor of Poland, Gottfried Neesse, and Reinhard Hoehn. The last to fall into disgrace was the historian Walter Frank, who had been a convinced antisemite and member of the Nazi party before it came to power, and who, in 1933, became director of the newly founded Reichsinstitut für Geschichte des Neuen Deutschlands with its famous Forschungsabteilung Judenfrage, and editor of the nine-volume *Forschungen zur Judenfrage* (1937-1944). In the early forties, Frank had to cede his position and influence to the notorious Alfred Rosenberg, whose *Der Mythos des 20. Jahrhunderts* certainly shows no aspiration whatsoever to "scholarship." Frank clearly was mistrusted for no other reason than that he was not a charlatan.

What neither the elite nor the mob that "embraced" National Socialism with such fervor could understand was that "one cannot embrace this Order . . . by accident. Above and beyond the willingness to serve stands the unrelenting necessity of selection that knows neither extenuating circumstances nor clemency" (*Der Weg der SS,* issued by the SS Hauptamt-Schulungsamt, n.d., p. 4). In other words, concerning the selection of those who would belong to them the Nazis intended to make their own decisions, regardless of the "accident" of any opinions. The same appears to be true for the selection of Bolshevists for the secret police. F. Beck and W. Godin report in *Russian Purge and the Extraction of Confession,* 1951, p. 160, that the members of the NKVD are claimed from the ranks of party members without having the slightest opportunity to volunteer for this "career."

CHAPTER TWO:

The Totalitarian Movement

I: *Totalitarian Propaganda*

ONLY THE MOB and the elite can be attracted by the momentum of totalitarianism itself; the masses have to be won by propaganda. Under conditions of constitutional government and freedom of opinion, totalitarian movements struggling for power can use terror to a limited extent only and share with other parties the necessity of winning adherents and of appearing plausible to a public which is not yet rigorously isolated from all other sources of information.

It was recognized early and has frequently been asserted that in totalitarian countries propaganda and terror present two sides of the same coin.[1] This, however, is only partly true. Wherever totalitarianism possesses absolute control, it replaces propaganda with indoctrination and uses violence not so much to frighten people (this is done only in the initial stages when political opposition still exists) as to realize constantly its ideological doctrines and its practical lies. Totalitarianism will not be satisfied to assert, in the face of contrary facts, that unemployment does not exist; it will abolish unemployment benefits as part of its propaganda.[2] Equally important is the fact that the refusal to acknowledge unemployment realized—albeit in a rather unexpected way—the old socialist doctrine: He who does not work shall not eat. Or when, to take another instance, Stalin decided to rewrite

[1] See, for instance, E. Kohn-Bramstedt, *Dictatorship and Political Police: The Technique of Control by Fear,* London, 1945, p. 164 ff. The explanation is that "terror without propaganda would lose most of its psychological effect, whereas propaganda without terror does not contain its full punch" (p. 175). What is overlooked in these and similar statements, which mostly go around in circles, is the fact that not only political propaganda but the whole of modern mass publicity contains an element of threat; that terror, on the other hand, can be fully effective without propaganda, so long as it is only a question of conventional political terror of tyranny. Only when terror is intended to coerce not merely from without but, as it were, from within, when the political regime wants more than power, is terror in need of propaganda. In this sense the Nazi theorist, Eugen Hadamovsky, could say in *Propaganda und nationale Macht,* 1933: "Propaganda and violence are never contradictions. Use of violence can be part of the propaganda" (p. 22).

[2] "At that time, it was officially announced that unemployment was 'liquidated' in Soviet Russia. The result of the announcement was that all unemployment benefits were equally 'liquidated'" (Anton Ciliga, *The Russian Enigma,* London, 1940, p. 109).

the history of the Russian Revolution, the propaganda of his new version consisted in destroying, together with the older books and documents, their authors and readers: the publication in 1938 of a new official history of the Communist Party was the signal that the superpurge which had decimated a whole generation of Soviet intellectuals had come to an end. Similarly, the Nazis in the Eastern occupied territories at first used chiefly antisemitic propaganda to win firmer control of the population. They neither needed nor used terror to support this propaganda. When they liquidated the greater part of the Polish intelligentsia, they did it not because of its opposition, but because according to their doctrine Poles had no intellect, and when they planned to kidnap blue-eyed and blond-haired children, they did not intend to frighten the population but to save "Germanic blood.[3]

Since totalitarian movements exist in a world which itself is nontotalitarian, they are forced to resort to what we commonly regard as propaganda. But such propaganda always makes its appeal to an external sphere—be it the nontotalitarian strata of the population at home or the nontotalitarian countries abroad. This external sphere to which totalitarian propaganda makes its appeal may vary greatly; even after the seizure of power totalitarian propaganda may address itself to those segments of its own population whose co-ordination was not followed by sufficient indoctrination. In this respect Hitler's speeches to his generals during the war are veritable models of propaganda, characterized mainly by the monstrous lies with which the Fuehrer entertained his guests in an attempt to win them over.[4] The external sphere can also be represented by groups of sympathizers who

[3] The so-called "Operation Hay" began with a decree dated February 16, 1942, by Himmler "concerning [individuals] of German stock in Poland," stipulating that their children should be sent to families "that are willing [to accept them] without reservations, out of love for the good blood in them" (Nuremberg Document R 135, photostated by the Centre de Documentation Juive, Paris). It seems that in June, 1944, the Ninth Army actually kidnapped 40,000 to 50,000 children and subsequently transported them to Germany. A report on this matter, sent to the General Staff of the Wehrmacht in Berlin by a man called Brandenburg, mentions similar plans for the Ukraine (Document PS 031, published by Léon Poliakov in *Bréviaire de la Haine*, p. 317). Himmler himself made several references to this plan. (See *Nazi Conspiracy and Aggression*, Office of the United States Chief of Counsel for the Prosecution of Axis Criminality, U.S. Government, Washington, 1946, III, 640, which contains excerpts from Himmler's speech at Cracow in March, 1942; see also the comments on Himmler's speech at Bad Schachen in 1943 in Kohn-Bramstedt, *op. cit.*, p. 244.) How the selection of these children was arrived at can be gathered from medical certificates made out by Medical Section II at Minsk on August 10, 1942: "The racial examination of Natalie Harpf, born August 14, 1922, showed a normally developed girl of predominantly East Baltic type with Nordic features."—"Examination of Arnold Cornies, born February 19, 1930, showed a normally developed boy, twelve years old, of predominantly Eastern type with Nordic features." Signed: N. Wc. (Document in the archives of the Yiddish Scientific Institute, New York, No. Occ E 3a-17.)

For the extermination of the Polish intelligentsia, which, in Hitler's opinion, could be "wiped out without qualms," see Poliakov, *op. cit.*, p. 321, and Document NO 2472.

[4] See *Hitlers Tischgespräche*. In the summer of 1942, he still talks about "[kicking] even the last Jew out of Europe" (p. 113) and resettling the Jews in Siberia or Africa (p. 311), or Madagascar, while in reality he had already decided on the "final solution" prior to the Russian invasion, probably in 1940, and ordered the gas ovens to

are not yet ready to accept the true aims of the movement; finally, it often happens that even party members are regarded by the Fuehrer's inner circle or the members of the elite formations as belonging to such an external sphere, and in this case they, too, are still in need of propaganda because they cannot yet be reliably dominated. In order not to overestimate the importance of the propaganda lies one should recall the much more numerous instances in which Hitler was completely sincere and brutally unequivocal in the definition of the movement's true aims, but they were simply not acknowledged by a public unprepared for such consistency.[5] But, basically speaking, totalitarian domination strives to restrict propaganda methods solely to its foreign policy or to the branches of the movement abroad for the purpose of supplying them with suitable material. Whenever totalitarian indoctrination at home comes into conflict with the propaganda line for consumption abroad (which happened in Russia during the war, not when Stalin had concluded his alliance with Hitler, but when the war with Hitler brought him into the camp of the democracies), the propaganda is explained at home as a "temporary tactical maneuver."[6] As far as possible, this distinction between ideological doctrine for the initiated in the movement, who are no longer in need of propaganda, and unadulterated propaganda for the outside world is already established in the prepower existence of the movements. The relationship between propaganda and indoctrination usually depends upon the size of the movements on one hand, and upon outside pressure on the other. The smaller the movement, the more energy it will expend in mere propaganda; the greater the pressure on totalitarian regimes from the outside world—a pressure that even behind iron curtains cannot be ignored entirely—the more actively will the totalitarian dictators

---

be set up in the fall of 1941 (see *Nazi Conspiracy and Aggression*, II, pp. 265 ff.; III, pp. 783 ff. Document PS 1104; V. pp. 322 ff. Document PS 2605). Himmler already knew in the spring of 1941 that "the Jews [must be] exterminated to the last man by the end of the war. This is the unequivocal desire and command of the Fuehrer" (Dossier Kersten in the Centre de Documentation Juive).

[5] In this connection there is a very interesting report, dated July 16, 1940, on a discussion at the Fuehrer's headquarters, in the presence of Rosenberg, Lammers and Keitel, which Hitler began by stating the following "basic principles": "It was now essential not to parade our ultimate goal before the entire world; . . . Hence it must not be obvious that [the decrees for maintaining peace and order in the occupied territories] point to a final settlement. All necessary measures—executions, resettlements —can, and will be, carried out in spite of this." This is followed by a discussion which makes no reference whatever to Hitler's words and in which Hitler no longer participates. He quite obviously had not been "understood" (Document L 221 in the Centre de Documentation Juive).

[6] For Stalin's confidence that Hitler would not attack Russia, see Isaac Deutscher, *Stalin: a Political Biography*, New York and London, 1949, pp. 454 ff., and especially the footnote on p. 458: "It was only in 1948 that the Chief of the State Planning Commission, Vice-Premier N. Voznesensky, disclosed that the economic plans for the third quarter of 1941 had been based on the assumption of peace and that a new plan, suited for war, had been drafted only after the outbreak of hostilities." Deutscher's estimate has now been solidly confirmed by Khrushchev's report on Stalin's reaction to the German attack on the Soviet Union. See his "Speech on Stalin" at the Twentieth Congress as released by the State Department, New York *Times*, June 5, 1956.

engage in propaganda. The essential point is that the necessities for propaganda are always dictated by the outside world and that the movements themselves do not actually propagate but indoctrinate. Conversely, indoctrination, inevitably coupled with terror, increases with the strength of the movements or the totalitarian governments' isolation and security from outside interference.

Propaganda is indeed part and parcel of "psychological warfare"; but terror is more. Terror continues to be used by totalitarian regimes even when its psychological aims are achieved: its real horror is that it reigns over a completely subdued population. Where the rule of terror is brought to perfection, as in concentration camps, propaganda disappears entirely; it was even expressly prohibited in Nazi Germany.[7] Propaganda, in other words, is one, and possibly the most important, instrument of totalitarianism for dealing with the nontotalitarian world; terror, on the contrary, is the very essence of its form of government. Its existence depends as little on psychological or other subjective factors as the existence of laws in a constitutionally governed country depends upon the number of people who transgress them.

Terror as the counterpart of propaganda played a greater role in Nazism than in Communism. The Nazis did not strike at prominent figures as had been done in the earlier wave of political crimes in Germany (the murder of Rathenau and Erzberger); instead, by killing small socialist functionaries or influential members of opposing parties, they attempted to prove to the population the dangers involved in mere membership. This kind of mass terror, which still operated on a comparatively small scale, increased steadily because neither the police nor the courts seriously prosecuted political offenders on the so-called Right. It was valuable as what a Nazi publicist has aptly called "power propaganda": [8] it made clear to the population at large that the power of the Nazis was greater than that of the authorities and that it was safer to be a member of a Nazi paramilitary organization than a loyal Republican. This impression was greatly strengthened by the specific use the Nazis made of their political crimes. They always admitted them publicly, never apologized for "excesses of the lower ranks"—such apologies were used only by Nazi sympathizers—and impressed the population as being very different from the "idle talkers" of other parties.

The similarities between this kind of terror and plain gangsterism are too

[7] "Education [in the concentration camps] consists of discipline, never of any kind of instruction on an ideological basis, for the prisoners have for the most part slave-like souls" (Heinrich Himmler, *Nazi Conspiracy*, IV, 616 ff.).

[8] Eugen Hadamovsky, *op. cit.*, is outstanding in the literature on totalitarian propaganda. Without explicitly stating it, Hadamovsky offers an intelligent and revealing pro-Nazi interpretation of Hitler's own exposition on the subject in "Propaganda and Organization," in Book II, chapter xi of *Mein Kampf* (2 vols., 1st German edition, 1925 and 1927 respectively. Unexpurgated translation, New York, 1939).—See also F. A. Six, *Die politische Propaganda der NSDAP im Kampf um die Macht*, 1936, pp. 21 ff.

obvious to be pointed out. This does not mean that Nazism was gangsterism, as has sometimes been concluded, but only that the Nazis, without admitting it, learned as much from American gangster organizations as their propaganda, admittedly, learned from American business publicity.

More specific in totalitarian propaganda, however, than direct threats and crimes against individuals is the use of indirect, veiled, and menacing hints against all who will not heed its teachings and, later, mass murder perpetrated on "guilty" and "innocent" alike. People are threatened by Communist propaganda with missing the train of history, with remaining hopelessly behind their time, with spending their lives uselessly, just as they were threatened by the Nazis with living against the eternal laws of nature and life, with an irreparable and mysterious deterioration of their blood. The strong emphasis of totalitarian propaganda on the "scientific" nature of its assertions has been compared to certain advertising techniques which also address themselves to masses. And it is true that the advertising columns of every newspaper show this "scientificality," by which a manufacturer proves with facts and figures and the help of a "research" department that his is the "best soap in the world."[9] It is also true that there is a certain element of violence in the imaginative exaggerations of publicity men, that behind the assertion that girls who do not use this particular brand of soap may go through life with pimples and without a husband, lies the wild dream of monopoly, the dream that one day the manufacturer of the "only soap that prevents pimples" may have the power to deprive of husbands all girls who do not use his soap. Science in the instances of both business publicity and totalitarian propaganda is obviously only a surrogate for power. The obsession of totalitarian movements with "scientific" proofs ceases once they are in power. The Nazis dismissed even those scholars who were willing to serve them, and the Bolsheviks use the reputation of their scientists for entirely unscientific purposes and force them into the role of charlatans.

But there is nothing more to the frequently overrated similarities between mass advertisement and mass propaganda. Businessmen usually do not pose as prophets and they do not constantly demonstrate the correctness of their predictions. The scientificality of totalitarian propaganda is characterized by its almost exclusive insistence on scientific prophecy as distinguished from the more old-fashioned appeal to the past. Nowhere does the ideological origin, of socialism in one instance and racism in the other, show more clearly than when their spokesmen pretend that they have discovered the hidden forces that will bring them good fortune in the chain of fatality. There is of course a great appeal to the masses in "absolutist systems which represent all the events of history as depending upon the great first causes linked by the chain of fatality, and which, as it were, suppress men from the history of the human race" (in the words of Tocqueville). But it cannot

[9] Hitler's analysis of "War Propaganda" (*Mein Kampf*, Book I, chapter vi) stresses the business angle of propaganda and uses the example of publicity for soap. Its importance has been generally overestimated, while his later positive ideas on "Propaganda and Organization" were neglected.

be doubted either that the Nazi leadership actually believed in, and did not merely use as propaganda, such doctrines as the following: "The more accurately we recognize and observe the laws of nature and life, . . . so much the more do we conform to the will of the Almighty. The more insight we have into the will of the Almighty, the greater will be our successes."[10] It is quite apparent that very few changes are needed to express Stalin's creed in two sentences which might run as follows: "The more accurately we recognize and observe the laws of history and class struggle, so much the more do we conform to dialectic materialism. The more insight we have into dialectic materialism, the greater will be our success." Stalin's notion of "correct leadership,"[11] at any rate, could hardly be better illustrated.

Totalitarian propaganda raised ideological scientificality and its technique of making statements in the form of predictions to a height of efficiency of method and absurdity of content because, demagogically speaking, there is hardly a better way to avoid discussion than by releasing an argument from the control of the present and by saying that only the future can reveal its merits. However, totalitarian ideologies did not invent this procedure, and were not the only ones to use it. Scientificality of mass propaganda has indeed been so universally employed in modern politics that it has been interpreted as a more general sign of that obsession with science which has characterized the Western world since the rise of mathematics and physics in the sixteenth century; thus totalitarianism appears to be only the last stage in a process during which "science [has become] an idol that will magically cure the evils of existence and transform the nature of man."[12] And there was, indeed, an early connection between scientificality and the rise of the masses. The "collectivism" of masses was welcomed by those who hoped for the appearance of "natural laws of historical development" which would eliminate the unpredictability of the individual's actions and behavior.[13] There has been cited the example of Enfantin who could already "see the time approaching when the 'art of moving the masses' will be so perfectly developed that the painter, the musician, and the poet will possess the power to please and to move with the same certainty as the mathematician solves a geometrical problem or the chemist analyses any substance,"

[10] See Martin Bormann's important memorandum on the "Relationship of National Socialism and Christianity" in *Nazi Conspiracy*, VI, 1036 ff. Similar formulations can be found time and again in the pamphlet literature issued by the SS for the "ideological indoctrination" of its cadets. "The laws of nature are subject to an unchangeable will that cannot be influenced. Hence it is necessary to recognize these laws" ("SS-Mann und Blutsfrage," *Schriftenreihe für die weltanschauliche Schulung der Ordnungspolizei*, 1942). All these are nothing but variations of certain phrases taken from Hitler's *Mein Kampf*, of which the following is quoted as the motto for the pamphlet just mentioned: "While man attempts to struggle against the iron logic of nature, he comes into conflict with the basic principles to which alone he owes his very existence as man."

[11] J. Stalin, *Leninism* (1933), Vol. II, chapter iii.

[12] Eric Voegelin, "The Origins of Scientism," in *Social Research*, December, 1948.

[13] See F. A. v. Hayek, "The Counter-Revolution of Science," in *Economica*, Vol. VIII (February, May, August, 1941), p. 13.

and it has been concluded that modern propaganda was born then and there.[14]

Yet whatever the shortcomings of positivism, pragmatism, and behaviorism, and however great their influence on the formation of the nineteenth-century brand of common sense, it is not at all "the cancerous growth of the utilitarian segment of existence"[15] which characterizes the masses to whom totalitarian propaganda and scientificality appeal. The positivists' conviction, as we know it from Comte, that the future is eventually scientifically predictable, rests on the evaluation of interest as an all-pervasive force in history and the assumption that objective laws of power can be discovered. Rohan's political theory that "the kings command the peoples and the interest commands the king," that objective interest is the rule "that alone can never fail," that "rightly or wrongly understood, the interest makes governments live or die" is the traditional core of modern utilitarianism, positivist or socialist, but none of these theories assumes that it is possible "to transform the nature of man" as totalitarianism indeed tries to do. On the contrary, they all implicitly or explicitly assume that human nature is always the same, that history is the story of changing objective circumstances and the human reactions to them, and that interest, rightly understood, may lead to a change of circumstances, but not to a change of human reactions as such. "Scientism" in politics still presupposes that human welfare is its object, a concept which is utterly alien to totalitarianism.[16]

It is precisely because the utilitarian core of ideologies was taken for granted that the anti-utilitarian behavior of totalitarian governments, their complete indifference to mass interest, has been such a shock. This introduced into contemporary politics an element of unheard-of unpredictability. Totalitarian propaganda, however—although in the form of shifted emphasis—indicated even before totalitarianism could seize power how far the masses had drifted from mere concern with interest. Thus the suspicion of the Allies that the murder of the insane which Hitler ordered at the beginning of the war should be attributed to the desire to get rid of unnecessary mouths to feed was altogether unjustified.[17] Hitler was not forced by the war

[14] *Ibid.*, p. 137. The quotation is from the Saint-Simonist magazine *Producteur*, I, 399.

[15] Voegelin, *op. cit.*

[16] William Ebenstein, *The Nazi State*, New York, 1943, in discussing the "Permanent War Economy" of the Nazi state is almost the only critic who has realized that "the endless discussion . . . as to the socialist or capitalist nature of the German economy under the Nazi regime is largely artificial . . . [because it] tends to overlook the vital fact that capitalism and socialism are categories which relate to Western welfare economics" (p. 239).

[17] The testimony of Karl Brandt, one of the physicians charged by Hitler with carrying out the program of euthanasia, is characteristic in this context (*Medical Trial. US against Karl Brandt et al. Hearing of May 14, 1947*). Brandt vehemently protested against the suspicion that the project was initiated to eliminate superfluous food consumers; he emphasized that party members who brought up such arguments in the discussion had always been sharply rebuked. In his opinion, the measures were dictated solely by "ethical considerations." The same is, of course, true for the deporta-

to throw all ethical considerations overboard, but regarded the mass slaughter of war as an incomparable opportunity to start a murder program which, like all other points of his program, was calculated in terms of millennia.[18] Since virtually all of European history through many centuries had taught people to judge each political action by its *cui bono* and all political events by their particular underlying interests, they were suddenly confronted with an element of unprecedented unpredictability. Because of its demagogic qualities, totalitarian propaganda, which long before the seizure of power clearly indicated how little the masses were driven by the famous instinct of self-preservation, was not taken seriously. The success of totalitarian propaganda, however, does not rest so much on its demagoguery as on the knowledge that interest as a collective force can be felt only where stable social bodies provide the necessary transmission belts between the individual and the group; no effective propaganda based on mere interest can be carried on among masses whose chief characteristic is that they belong to no social or political body, and who therefore present a veritable chaos of individual interests. The fanaticism of members of totalitarian movements, so clearly different in quality from the greatest loyalty of members of ordinary parties, is produced by the lack of self-interest of masses who are quite prepared to sacrifice themselves. The Nazis have proved that one can lead a whole people into war with the slogan "or else we shall go down" (something which the war propaganda of 1914 would have avoided carefully), and this is not in times of misery, unemployment, or frustrated national ambitions. The same spirit showed itself during the last months of a war that was obviously lost, when Nazi propaganda consoled an already badly frightened population with the promise that the Fuehrer "in his wisdom had prepared an easy death for the German people by gassing them in case of defeat."[19]

Totalitarian movements use socialism and racism by emptying them of their utilitarian content, the interests of a class or nation. The form of infallible prediction in which these concepts were presented has become more important than their content.[20] The chief qualification of a mass leader has

tions. The files are filled with desperate memoranda written by the military complaining that the deportations of millions of Jews and Poles completely disregarded all "military and economic necessities." See Poliakov, *op. cit.*, p. 321, as well as the documentary material published there.

[18] The decisive decree starting all subsequent mass murders was signed by Hitler on September 1, 1939—the day the war broke out—and referred not merely to the insane (as is often erroneously assumed) but to all those who were "incurably sick." The insane were only the first to go.

[19] See Friedrich Percyval Reck-Malleczewen, *Tagebuch eines Verzweifelten*, Stuttgart, 1947, p. 190.

[20] Hitler based the superiority of ideological movements over political parties on the fact that ideologies (*Weltanschauungen*) always "proclaim their infallibility" (*Mein Kampf*, Book II, chapter v, "*Weltanschauung* and Organization").—The first pages of the official handbook for the Hitler Youth, *The Nazi Primer*, New York, 1938, consequently emphasize that all questions of *Weltanschauung*, formerly deemed "unrealistic" and "ununderstandable," "have become so clear, simple and *definite* [my italics] that every comrade can understand them and co-operate in their solution."

become unending infallibility; he can never admit an error.[21] The assumption of infallibility, moreover, is based not so much on superior intelligence as on the correct interpretation of the essentially reliable forces in history or nature, forces which neither defeat nor ruin can prove wrong because they are bound to assert themselves in the long run.[22] Mass leaders in power have one concern which overrules all utilitarian considerations: to make their predictions come true. The Nazis did not hesitate to use, at the end of the war, the concentrated force of their still intact organization to bring about as complete a destruction of Germany as possible, in order to make true their prediction that the German people would be ruined in case of defeat.

The propaganda effect of infallibility, the striking success of posing as a mere interpreting agent of predictable forces, has encouraged in totalitarian dictators the habit of announcing their political intentions in the form of prophecy. The most famous example is Hitler's announcement to the German Reichstag in January, 1939: "I want today once again to make a prophecy: In case the Jewish financiers . . . succeed once more in hurling the peoples into a world war, the result will be . . . the annihilation of the Jewish race in Europe."[23] Translated into nontotalitarian language, this meant: I intend to make war and I intend to kill the Jews of Europe. Similarly Stalin, in the great speech before the Central Committee of the Communist Party in 1930 in which he prepared the physical liquidation of intraparty right and left deviationists, described them as representatives of "dying classes."[24] This definition not only gave the argument its specific sharpness but also announced, in totalitarian style, the physical destruction of those whose "dying out" had just been prophesied. In both instances the same objective is accomplished: the liquidation is fitted into a historical process in which man only does or suffers what, according to immutable laws, is bound to happen anyway. As soon as the execution of the victims has been carried out, the "prophecy" becomes a retrospective alibi: nothing happened but what had already been predicted.[25] It does not matter

[21] The first among the "pledges of the Party member," as enumerated in the *Organisationsbuch der NSDAP*, reads: "The Führer is always right." Edition published in 1936, p. 8. But the *Dienstvorschrift für die P.O. der NSDAP*, 1932, p. 38, puts it this way: "Hitler's decision is final!" Note the remarkable difference in phraseology.

"Their claim to be infallible, [that] neither of them has ever sincerely admitted an error" is in this respect the decisive difference between Stalin and Trotsky on one hand, and Lenin on the other. See Boris Souvarine, *Stalin: A Critical Survey of Bolshevism*, New York, 1939, p. 583.

[22] That Hegelian dialectics should provide a wonderful instrument for always being right, because they permit the interpretation of all defeats as the beginning of victory, is obvious. One of the most beautiful examples of this kind of sophistry occurred after 1933 when the German Communists for nearly two years refused to recognize that Hitler's victory had been a defeat for the German Communist Party.

[23] Quoted from Goebbels: *The Goebbels Diaries (1942-1943)*, ed. by Louis Lochner, New York, 1948, p. 148.

[24] Stalin, *op. cit., loc. cit.*

[25] In a speech he made in September, 1942, when the extermination of the Jews was in full swing, Hitler explicitly referred to his speech of January 30, 1939 (published

whether the "laws of history" spell the "doom" of the classes and their representatives, or whether the "laws of nature . . . exterminate" all those elements—democracies, Jews, Eastern subhumans (*Untermenschen*), or the incurably sick—that are not "fit to live" anyway. Incidentally, Hitler too spoke of "dying classes" that ought to be "eliminated without much ado."[26]

This method, like other totalitarian propaganda methods, is foolproof only after the movements have seized power. Then all debate about the truth or falsity of a totalitarian dictator's prediction is as weird as arguing with a potential murderer about whether his future victim is dead or alive—since by killing the person in question the murderer can promptly provide proof of the correctness of his statement. The only valid argument under such conditions is promptly to rescue the person whose death is predicted. Before mass leaders seize the power to fit reality to their lies, their propaganda is marked by its extreme contempt for facts as such,[27] for in their opinion fact depends entirely on the power of man who can fabricate it. The assertion that the Moscow subway is the only one in the world is a lie only so long as the Bolsheviks have not the power to destroy all the others. In other words, the method of infallible prediction, more than any other totalitarian propaganda device, betrays its ultimate goal of world conquest, since only in a world completely under his control could the totalitarian ruler possibly realize all his lies and make true all his prophecies.

The language of prophetic scientificality corresponded to the needs of masses who had lost their home in the world and now were prepared to be reintegrated into eternal, all-dominating forces which by themselves would bear man, the swimmer on the waves of adversity, to the shores of safety. "We shape the life of our people and our legislation according to the verdicts of genetics,"[28] said the Nazis, just as the Bolsheviks assure their followers that economic forces have the power of a verdict of history. They thereby promise a victory which is independent of "temporary" defeats and failures in specific enterprises. For masses, in contrast to classes, want victory and success as such, in their most abstract form; they are not bound together by those special collective interests which they feel to be essential to their survival as a group and which they therefore may assert even in

---

as a booklet titled *Der Führer vor dem ersten Reichstag Grossdeutschlands*, 1939), and to the Reichstag session of September 1, 1939, when he had announced that "if Jewry should instigate an international world war to exterminate the Aryan peoples of Europe, not the Aryan peoples but Jewry will [rest of sentence drowned by applause]" (see *Der Führer zum Kriegswinterhilfswerk*, Schriften NSV, No. 14, p. 33).

[26] In the speech of January 30, 1939, p. 19, as quoted above.

[27] Konrad Heiden, *Der Fuehrer: Hitler's Rise to Power*, Boston, 1944, underlines Hitler's "phenomenal untruthfulness," "the lack of demonstrable reality in nearly all his utterances," his "indifference to facts which he does not regard as vitally important" (pp. 368, 374).—In almost identical terms, Khrushchev describes "Stalin's reluctance to consider life's realities" and his indifference to "the real state of affairs," *op. cit.* Stalin's opinion of the importance of facts is best expressed in his periodic revisions of Russian history.

[28] *Nazi Primer*.

the face of overwhelming odds. More important t[...] may be victorious, or the particular enterprise that [...] victory of no matter what cause, and success in no m[...]

Totalitarian propaganda perfects the techniques of mass [...] it neither invents them nor originates their themes. These we[...] them by fifty years of the rise of imperialism and disintegration o[...] state, when the mob entered the scene of European politics. Like [...] mob leaders, the spokesmen for totalitarian movements possessed an [...] instinct for anything that ordinary party propaganda or public opinio[...] not care or dare to touch. Everything hidden, everything passed over [...] silence, became of major significance, regardless of its own intrinsic importance. The mob really believed that truth was whatever respectable society had hypocritically passed over, or covered up with corruption.

Mysteriousness as such became the first criterion for the choice of topics. The origin of mystery did not matter; it could lie in a reasonable, politically comprehensible desire for secrecy, as in the case of the British Secret Services or the French Deuxième Bureau; or in the conspiratory need of revolutionary groups, as in the case of anarchist and other terrorist sects; or in the structure of societies whose original secret content had long since become well known and where only the formal ritual still retained the former mystery, as in the case of the Freemasons; or in age-old superstitions which had woven legends around certain groups, as in the case of the Jesuits and the Jews. The Nazis were undoubtedly superior in the selection of such topics for mass propaganda; but the Bolsheviks have gradually learned the trick, although they rely less on traditionally accepted mysteries and prefer their own inventions—since the middle thirties, one mysterious world conspiracy has followed another in Bolshevik propaganda, starting with the plot of the Trotskyites, followed by the rule of the 300 families, to the sinister imperialist (*i.e.*, global) machinations of the British or American Secret Services.[29]

The effectiveness of this kind of propaganda demonstrates one of the chief characteristics of modern masses. They do not believe in anything visible, in the reality of their own experience; they do not trust their eyes and ears but only their imaginations, which may be caught by anything that is at once universal and consistent in itself. What convinces masses are not facts, and not even invented facts, but only the consistency of the system of which they are presumably part. Repetition, somewhat overrated in importance because of the common belief in the masses' inferior capacity to grasp and remember, is important only because it convinces them of consistency in time.

What the masses refuse to recognize is the fortuitousness that pervades

[29] It is interesting to note that the Bolsheviks during the Stalin era somehow accumulated conspiracies, that the discovery of a new one did not mean they would discard the former. The Trotskyite conspiracy started around 1930, the 300 families were added during the Popular Front period, from 1935 onward, British imperialism became an actual conspiracy during the Stalin-Hitler alliance, the "American Secret Service" followed soon after the close of the war; the last, Jewish cosmopolitanism, had an obvious and disquieting resemblance to Nazi propaganda.

...ies because they explain facts as ...incidences by inventing an all- ... to be at the root of every acci- ...s escape from reality into fiction, ...anda is that it cannot fulfill this ...istent, comprehensible, and pre- ...g with common sense. If, for ...ponents in the Soviet Union are ... same motives, the consistency- ...eme proof of their truthfulness; ...ecisely their consistency which ...fabrication. Figuratively speak- ...nstant repetition of the miracle ... legend, seventy isolated trans- ...Greek version of the Old Testament. Common sense can accept this tale only as a legend or a miracle; yet it could also be adduced as proof of the absolute faithfulness of every single word in the translated text.

In other words, while it is true that the masses are obsessed by a desire to escape from reality because in their essential homelessness they can no longer bear its accidental, incomprehensible aspects, it is also true that their longing for fiction has some connection with those capacities of the human mind whose structural consistency is superior to mere occurrence. The masses' escape from reality is a verdict against the world in which they are forced to live and in which they cannot exist, since coincidence has become  its supreme master and human beings need the constant transformation of chaotic and accidental conditions into a man-made pattern of relative consistency. The revolt of the masses against "realism," common sense, and all "the plausibilities of the world" (Burke) was the result of their atomization, of their loss of social status along with which they lost the whole sector of communal relationships in whose framework common sense makes sense. In their situation of spiritual and social homelessness, a measured insight into the interdependence of the arbitrary and the planned, the accidental and the necessary, could no longer operate. Totalitarian propaganda can outrageously insult common sense only where common sense has lost its validity. Before the alternative of facing the anarchic growth and total arbitrariness of decay or bowing down before the most rigid, fantastically fictitious consistency of  an ideology, the masses probably will always choose the latter and be ready to pay for it with individual sacrifices—and this not because they are stupid or wicked, but because in the general disaster this escape grants them a minimum of self-respect.

While it has been the specialty of Nazi propaganda to profit from the longing of the masses for consistency, Bolshevik methods have demonstrated, as though in a laboratory, its impact on the isolated mass man. The Soviet secret police, so eager to convince its victims of their guilt for crimes they never committed, and in many instances were in no position to commit, completely isolates and eliminates all real factors, so that the very logic, the very consistency of "the story" contained in the prepared confession becomes overwhelming. In a situation where the dividing line between fiction and reality is blurred by the monstrosity and the inner consistency of the accusation, not only the strength of character to resist constant threats but great confidence in the existence of fellow human beings—relatives or friends or neighbors—who will never believe "the story" are required to resist the temptation to yield to the mere abstract possibility of guilt.

To be sure, this extreme of an artificially fabricated insanity can be achieved only in a totalitarian world. Then, however, it is part of the propaganda apparatus of the totalitarian regimes to which confessions are not indispensable for punishment. "Confessions" are as much a specialty of Bolshevik propaganda as the curious pedantry of legalizing crimes by retrospective and retroactive legislation was a specialty of Nazi propaganda. The aim in both cases is consistency.

Before they seize power and establish a world according to their doctrines, totalitarian movements conjure up a lying world of consistency which is more adequate to the needs of the human mind than reality itself; in which, through sheer imagination, uprooted masses can feel at home and are spared the never-ending shocks which real life and real experiences deal to human beings and their expectations. The force possessed by totalitarian propaganda—before the movements have the power to drop iron curtains to prevent anyone's disturbing, by the slightest reality, the gruesome quiet of an entirely imaginary world—lies in its ability to shut the masses off from the real world. The only signs which the real world still offers to the understanding of the unintegrated and disintegrating masses—whom every new stroke of ill luck makes more gullible—are, so to speak, its lacunae, the questions it does not care to discuss publicly, or the rumors it does not dare to contradict because they hit, although in an exaggerated and deformed way, some sore spot.

From these sore spots the lies of totalitarian propaganda derive the element of truthfulness and real experience they need to bridge the gulf between reality and fiction. Only terror could rely on mere fiction, and even the terror-sustained lying fictions of totalitarian regimes have not yet become entirely arbitrary, although they are usually cruder, more impudent, and, so to speak, more original than those of the movements. (It takes power, not propaganda skill, to circulate a revised history of the Russian Revolution in which no man by the name of Trotsky was ever commander-in-chief of the Red Army.) The lies of the movements, on the other hand, are much subtler. They attach themselves to every aspect of social and political life that is hidden from the public eye. They succeed best where the official authorities have surrounded themselves with an atmosphere of secrecy. In the eyes of the masses, they then acquire the reputation of superior "realism" because they touch upon real conditions whose existence is being hidden. Revelations of scandals in high society, of corruption of politicians, everything that belongs to yellow journalism, becomes in their hands a weapon of more than sensational importance.

The most efficient fiction of Nazi propaganda was the story of a Jewish world conspiracy. Concentration on antisemitic propaganda had been a common device of demagogues ever since the end of the nineteenth century, and was widespread in the Germany and Austria of the twenties. The more consistently a discussion of the Jewish question was avoided by all parties and organs of public opinion, the more convinced the mob became that Jews were the true representatives of the powers that be, and that the Jewish issue was the symbol for the hypocrisy and dishonesty of the whole system.

The actual content of postwar antisemitic propaganda was neither a monopoly of the Nazis nor particularly new and original. Lies about a Jewish world conspiracy had been current since the Dreyfus Affair and based themselves on the existing international interrelationship and interdependence of a Jewish people dispersed all over the world. Exaggerated notions of Jewish world power are even older; they can be traced back to the end of the eighteenth century, when the intimate connection betwen Jewish business and the nation-states had become visible. The representation of *the* Jew as the incarnation of evil is usually blamed on remnants and superstitious memories from the Middle Ages, but is actually closely connected with the more recent ambiguous role which Jews played in European society since their emancipation. One thing was undeniable: in the postwar period Jews had become more prominent than ever before.

The point about the Jews themselves is that they grew prominent and conspicuous in inverse proportion to their real influence and position of power. Every decrease in the stability and force of the nation-states was a direct blow to Jewish positions. The partially successful conquest of the state by the nation made it impossible for the government machine to maintain its position above all classes and parties, and thereby nullified the value of alliances with the Jewish sector of the population, which was supposed also to stay outside the ranks of society and to be indifferent to party politics. The growing concern with foreign policy of the imperialist-minded bourgeoisie and its growing influence on the state machinery was accompanied by the steadfast refusal of the largest segment of Jewish wealth to engage itself in industrial enterprises and to leave the tradition of capital trading. All this taken together almost ended the economic usefulness to the state of the Jews as a group, and the advantages to themselves of social separation. After the first World War, Central European Jewries became as assimilated and nationalized as French Jewry had become during the first decades of the Third Republic.

How conscious the concerned states were of the changed situation came to light when, in 1917, the German government, following a long-established tradition, tried to use its Jews for tentative peace negotiations with the Allies. Instead of addressing itself to the established leaders of German

Jewry, it went to the small and comparatively uninfluential Zionist minority which were still trusted in the old way precisely because they insisted on the existence of a Jewish people independent of citizenship, and could therefore be expected to render services which depended upon international connections and an international point of view. The step, however, turned out to have been a mistake for the German government. The Zionists did something that no Jewish banker had ever done before; they set their own conditions and told the government that they would only negotiate a peace without annexations and reparations.[30] The old Jewish indifference to political issues was gone; the majority could no longer be used, since it was no longer aloof from the nation, and the Zionist minority was useless because it had political ideas of its own.

The replacement of monarchical governments by republics in Central Europe completed the disintegration of Central European Jewries, just as the establishment of the Third Republic had done it in France some fifty years earlier. The Jews had already lost much of their influence when the new governments established themselves under conditions in which they lacked the power as well as the interest to protect their Jews. During the peace negotiations in Versailles, Jews were used chiefly as experts, and even antisemites admitted that the petty Jewish swindlers in the postwar era, mostly new arrivals (behind whose fraudulent activities, which distinguished them sharply from their native coreligionists, lay an attitude which oddly resembled the old indifference to the standards of their environment), had no connections with the representatives of a supposed Jewish international.[31]

Among a host of competing antisemitic groups and in an atmosphere rife with antisemitism, Nazi propaganda developed a method of treating this subject which was different from and superior to all others. Still, not one Nazi slogan was new—not even Hitler's shrewd picture of a class struggle caused by the Jewish businessman who exploits his workers, while at the same time his brother in the factory courtyard incites them to strike.[32] The only new element was that the Nazi party demanded proof of non-Jewish descent for membership and that it remained, the Feder program notwithstanding, extremely vague about the actual measures to be taken against Jews once it came to power.[33] The Nazis placed the Jewish issue at the center

[30] See Chaim Weizmann's autobiography, *Trial and Error,* New York, 1949, p. 185.

[31] See, for instance, Otto Bonhard, *Jüdische Geld- und Weltherrschaft?*, 1926, p. 57.

[32] Hitler used this picture for the first time in 1922: "Moses Kohn on the one side encourages his association to refuse the workers' demands, while his brother Isaac in the factory invites the masses . . ." to strike. (*Hitler's Speeches: 1922-1939,* ed. Baynes, London, 1942, p. 29.) It is noteworthy that no complete collection of Hitler's speeches was ever published in Nazi Germany, so that one is forced to resort to the English edition. That this was no accident can be seen from a bibliography compiled by Philipp Bouhler, *Die Reden des Führer's nach der Machtübernahme,* 1940: only the public speeches were printed verbatim in the *Völkischer Beobachter;* as for speeches to the Fuehrerkorps and other party units, they were merely "referred to" in that newspaper. They were not at any time meant for publication.

[33] Feder's 25 points contain only standard measures demanded by all antisemitic

of their propaganda in the sense that antisemitism was no longer a question of opinions about people different from the majority, or a concern of national politics,[34] but the intimate concern of every individual in his personal existence; no one could be a member whose "family tree" was not in order, and the higher the rank in the Nazi hierarchy, the farther back the family tree had to be traced.[35] By the same token, though less consistently, Bolshevism changed the Marxist doctrine of the inevitable final victory of the proletariat by organizing its members as "born proletarians" and making other class origins shameful and scandalous.[36]

Nazi propaganda was ingenious enough to transform antisemitism into a principle of self-definition, and thus to eliminate it from the fluctuations of mere opinion. It used the persuasion of mass demagogy only as a preparatory step and never overestimated its lasting influence, whether in oratory or in print.[37] This gave the masses of atomized, undefinable, unstable and futile individuals a means of self-definition and identification which not only restored some of the self-respect they had formerly derived from their function in society, but also created a kind of spurious stability which made them better candidates for an organization. Through this kind of propaganda, the movement could set itself up as an artificial extension of the mass meeting and rationalize the essentially futile feelings of self-importance and hysterical

---

groups: expulsion of naturalized Jews, and treatment of native Jews as aliens. Nazi antisemitic oratory was always much more radical than its program.

Waldemar Gurian, "Antisemitism in Modern Germany," in *Essays on Antisemitism*, ed. by Koppel S. Pinson, New York, 1946, p. 243, stresses the lack of originality in Nazi antisemitism: "All these demands and views were not remarkable for their originality—they were self-evident in all nationalistic circles; what was remarkable was the demagogic and oratorical skill with which they were presented."

[34] A typical example of mere nationalistic antisemitism within the Nazi movement itself is Röhm who writes: "And here again, my opinion differs from that of the national philistine. Not: the Jew is to be blamed for everything! We are to be blamed for the fact that the Jew can rule today" (Ernst Röhm, *Die Geschichte eines Hochverräters*, 1933, Volksausgabe, p. 284).

[35] SS applicants had to trace their ancestry back to 1750. Applicants for leading positions in the party were asked only three questions: 1. What have you done for the party? 2. Are you absolutely sound, physically, mentally, morally? 3. Is your family tree in order? See *Nazi Primer*.

It is characteristic for the affinity between the two systems that the elite and police formations of the Bolsheviks—the NKVD— also demanded proof of ancestry from their members. See F. Beck and W. Godin, *Russian Purge and the Extraction of Confession*, 1951.

[36] Thus the totalitarian tendencies of McCarthyism in the United States showed most glaringly in the attempt not merely to persecute Communists, but to force every citizen to furnish proof of not being a Communist.

[37] "One should not overestimate the influence of the press . . . , it decreases in general while the influence of the organization increases" (Hadamovsky, *op. cit.*, p. 64). "The newspapers are helpless when they are supposed to fight against the aggressive force of a living organization" (*ibid.*, p. 65). "Power formations which have their origin in mere propaganda are fluctuating and can disappear quickly unless the violence of an organization supports the propaganda" (*ibid.*, p. 21).

security that it offered to the isolated individuals of an atomized society.[38]

The same ingenious application of slogans, coined by others and tried out before, was apparent in the Nazis' treatment of other relevant issues. When public attention was equally focused on nationalism on one hand and socialism on the other, when the two were thought to be incompatible and actually constituted the ideological watershed between the Right and the Left, the "National Socialist German Workers' Party" (Nazi) offered a synthesis supposed to lead to national unity, a semantic solution whose double trademark of "German" and "Worker" connected the nationalism of the Right with the internationalism of the Left. The very name of the Nazi movement stole the political contents of all other parties and pretended implicitly to incorporate them all. Combinations of supposedly antagonistic political doctrines (national-socialist, christian-social, etc.) had been tried, and successfully, before; but the Nazis realized their own combination in such a way that the whole struggle in Parliament between the socialists and the nationalists, between those who pretended to be workers first of all and those who were Germans first, appeared as a sham designed to hide ulterior sinister motives—for was not a member of the Nazi movement all these things at once?

It is interesting that even in their beginnings the Nazis were prudent enough never to use slogans which, like democracy, republic, dictatorship, or monarchy, indicated a specific form of government.[39] It is as though, in this one matter, they had always known that they would be entirely original. Every discussion about the actual form of their future government could be dismissed as empty talk about mere formalities—the state, according to Hitler, being only a "means" for the conservation of the race, as the state, according to Bolshevik propaganda, is only an instrument in the struggle of classes.[40]

[38] "The mass-meeting is the strongest form of propaganda . . . [because] each individual feels more self-confident and more powerful in the unity of a mass" (*ibid*, p. 47). "The enthusiasm of the moment becomes a principle and a spiritual attitude through organization and systematic training and discipline" (*ibid.*, p. 21-22).

[39] In the isolated instances in which Hitler concerned himself with this question at all, he used to emphasize: "Incidentally, I am not the head of a state in the sense of a dictator or monarch, but I am a leader of the German people" (see *Ausgewählte Reden des Führers*, 1939, p. 114).—Hans Frank expresses himself in the same spirit: "The National Socialist Reich is not a dictatorial, let alone an arbitrary, regime. Rather, the National Socialist Reich rests on the mutual loyalty of the Führer and the people" (in *Recht und Verwaltung*, Munich, 1939, p. 15).

[40] Hitler repeated many times: "The state is only the means to an end. The end is: Conservation of race" (*Reden*, 1939, p. 125). He also stressed that his movement "does not rest on the state idea, but is primarily based on the closed *Volksgemeinschaft*" (see *Reden*, 1933, p. 125, and the speech before the new generation of political leaders [*Führernachwuchs*], 1937, which is printed as an addendum in *Hitlers Tischgespräche*, p. 446). This, *mutatis mutandis*, is also the core of the complicated double talk which is Stalin's so-called "state theory": "We are in favor of the State dying out, and at the same time we stand for the strengthening of the dictatorship of the proletariat which represents the most powerful and mighty authority of all forms of

In another curious and roundabout way, however, the Nazis gave a propaganda answer to the question of what their future role would be, and that was in their use of the "Protocols of the Elders of Zion" as a model for the future organization of the German masses for "world empire." The use of the Protocols was not restricted to the Nazis; hundreds of thousands of copies were sold in postwar Germany, and even their open adoption as a handbook of politics was not new.[41] Nevertheless, this forgery was mainly used for the purpose of denouncing the Jews and arousing the mob to the dangers of Jewish domination.[42] In terms of mere propaganda, the discovery of the Nazis was that the masses were not so frightened by Jewish world rule as they were interested in how it could be done, that the popularity of the Protocols was based on admiration and eagerness to learn rather than on hatred, and that it would be wise to stay as close as possible to certain of their outstanding formulas, as in the case of the famous slogan: "Right is what is good for the German people," which was copied from the Protocols' "Everything that benefits the Jewish people is morally right and sacred."[43]

The Protocols are a very curious and noteworthy document in many respects. Apart from their cheap Machiavellianism, their essential political characteristic is that in their crackpot manner they touch on every important political issue of the time. They are antinational in principle and picture the nation-state as a colossus with feet of clay. They discard national sovereignty

---

State which have existed up to the present day. The highest possible development of the power of the State with the object of preparing the conditions for the dying out of the State; that is the Marxist formula" (*op. cit., loc. cit.*).

[41] Alexander Stein, *Adolf Hitler, Schüler der "Weisen von Zion,"* Karlsbad, 1936, was the first to analyze by philological comparison the ideological identity of the teachings of the Nazis with that of the "Elders of Zion." See also R. M. Blank, *Adolf Hitler et les "Protocoles des Sages de Sion,"* 1938.

The first to admit indebtedness to the teachings of the Protocols was Theodor Fritsch, the "grand old man" of German postwar antisemitism. He writes in the epilogue to his edition of the *Protocols*, 1924: "Our future statesmen and diplomats will have to learn from the oriental masters of villainy even the ABC of government, and for this purpose, the 'Zionist Protocols' offer an excellent preparatory schooling."

[42] On the history of the Protocols, see John S. Curtiss, *An Appraisal of the Protocols of Zion*, 1942.

The fact that the Protocols were a forgery was irrelevant for propaganda purposes. The Russian publicist S. A. Nilus who published the second Russian edition in 1905 was already well aware of the doubtful character of this "document" and added the obvious: "But if it were possible to show its authenticity by documents or by the testimony of trustworthy witnesses, if it were possible to disclose the persons standing at the head of the world-wide plot . . . then . . . 'the secret iniquity' could be broken. . . ." Translation in Curtiss, *op. cit.*

Hitler did not need Nilus to use the same trick: the best proof of their authenticity is that they have been proved to be a forgery. And he also adds the argument of their "plausibility": "What many Jews may do unconsciously is here consciously made clear. And that is what counts" (*Mein Kampf*, Book I, chapter xi).

[43] Fritsch, *op. cit.*, "[*Der Juden*] *oberster Grundsatz lautet: 'Alles, was dem Volke Juda nützt, ist moralisch und ist heilig.'*"

and believe, as Hitler once put it, in a world empire on a national basis.[44] They are not satisfied with revolution in a particular country, but aim at the conquest and rule of the world. They promise the people that, regardless of superiority in numbers, territory, and state power, they will be able to achieve world conquest through organization alone. To be sure, part of their persuasive strength derives from very old elements of superstition. The notion of the uninterrupted existence of an international sect that has pursued the same revolutionary aims since antiquity is very old[45] and has played a role in political backstairs literature ever since the French Revolution, even though it did not occur to anyone writing at the end of the eighteenth century that the "revolutionary sect," this "peculiar nation . . . in the midst of all civilized nations," could be the Jews.[46]

It was the motif of a global conspiracy in the Protocols which appealed most to the masses, for it corresponded so well to the new power situation. (Hitler very early promised that the Nazi movement would "transcend the narrow limits of modern nationalism,"[47] and during the war attempts were

[44] "World Empires spring from a national basis, but they expand soon far beyond it" (*Reden*).

[45] Henri Rollin, *L'Apocalypse de Notre Temps*, Paris, 1939, who considers the popularity of the Protocols to be second only to the Bible (p. 40), shows the similarity between them and the *Monita Secreta*, first published in 1612 and still sold in 1939 on the streets of Paris, which claim to reveal a Jesuit conspiracy "that justifies all villainies and all uses of violence. . . . This is a real campaign against the established order" (p. 32).

[46] This whole literature is well represented by the Chevalier de Malet, *Recherches politiques et historiques qui prouvent l'existence d'une secte révolutionnaire*, 1817, who quotes extensively from earlier authors. The heroes of the French Revolution are to him "*mannequins*" of an "*agence secrète*," the agents of the Freemasons. But Freemasonry is only the name which his contemporaries have given to a "revolutionary sect" which has existed at all times and whose policy always has been to attack "remaining behind the scenes, manipulating the strings of the marionettes it thought convenient to put on the scene." He starts by saying: "Probably, it will be difficult to believe in a plan which was formed in antiquity and always followed with the same constancy: . . . the authors of the Revolution are no more French than they are German, Italian, English, etc. They constitute a peculiar nation which was born and has grown in darkness, in the midst of all civilized nations, with the aim of subduing them all to its domination."

For an extensive discussion of this literature, see E. Lesueur, *La Franc-Maçonnerie Artésienne au 18e siècle*, Bibliothèque d'Histoire Révolutionnaire, 1914. How persistent these conspiracy legends are in themselves, even under normal circumstances, can be seen by the enormous anti-Freemason crackpot literature in France, which is hardly less extensive than its antisemitic counterpart. A kind of compendium of all theories which saw in the French Revolution the product of secret conspiracy societies can be found in G. Bord, *La Franc-Maçonnerie en France dès origines à 1815*, 1908.

[47] *Reden*.—See the transcript of a session of the SS Committee on Labor Questions at SS headquarters in Berlin on January 12, 1943, where it was suggested that the word "nation," a concept being burdened with connotations of liberalism, should be eliminated as it was inadequate for the Germanic peoples (Document 705—PS in *Nazi Conspiracy and Aggression*, V, 515).

made within the SS to erase the word "nation" from the National Socialist vocabulary altogether.) Only world powers seemed still to have a chance of independent survival and only global politics a chance of lasting results. That this situation should frighten the smaller nations which are not world powers is only too understandable. The Protocols seemed to show a way out that did not depend upon objective unalterable conditions, but only on the power of organization.

Nazi propaganda, in other words, discovered in "the supranational because intensely national Jew"[48] the forerunner of the German master of the world and assured the masses that "the nations that have been the first to see through the Jew and have been the first to fight him are going to take his place in the domination of the world."[49] The delusion of an already existing Jewish world domination formed the basis for the illusion of future German world domination. This was what Himmler had in mind when he stated that "we owe the art of government to the Jews," namely, to the Protocols which "the Führer [had] learned by heart."[50] Thus the Protocols presented world conquest as a practical possibility, implied that the whole affair was only a question of inspired or shrewd know-how, and that nobody stood in the way of a German victory over the entire world but a patently small people, the Jews, who ruled it without possessing instruments of violence—an easy opponent, therefore, once their secret was discovered and their method emulated on a larger scale.

Nazi propaganda concentrated all these new and promising vistas in one concept which it labeled *Volksgemeinschaft*. This new community, tentatively realized in the Nazi movement in the pretotalitarian atmosphere, was based on the absolute equality of all Germans, an equality not of rights but of nature, and their absolute difference from all other people.[51] After the Nazis came to power, this concept gradually lost its importance and gave way to a general contempt for the German people (which the Nazis had always harbored but could not very well show publicly before) on one hand,[52] and a great eagerness, on the other, to enlarge their own ranks from

[48] *Hitler's Speeches*, ed. Baynes, p. 6.

[49] Goebbels, *op. cit.* p. 377. This promise, implied in all antisemitic propaganda of the Nazi type, was prepared by Hitler's "The most extreme contrast to the Aryan is the Jew" (*Mein Kampf*, Book I, chapter xi).

[50] Dossier Kersten, in the Centre de Documentation Juive.

[51] Hitler's early promise (*Reden*), "I shall never recognize that other nations have the same right as the German," became official doctrine: "The foundation of the national socialist outlook in life is the perception of the unlikeness of men" (*Nazi Primer*, p. 5).

[52] For instance, Hitler in 1923: "The German people consists for one third of heroes, for another third, of cowards, while the rest are traitors" (*Hitler's Speeches*, ed. Baynes, p. 76).

After the seizure of power this trend became more brutally outspoken. See, for instance, Goebbels in 1934: "Who are the people to criticize? Party members? No. The rest of the German people? They should consider themselves lucky to be still alive. It would be too much of a good thing altogether, if those who live at our mercy should be allowed to criticize." Quoted from Kohn-Bramstedt, *op. cit.*, pp. 178-179.—During the war Hitler declared: "I am nothing but a magnet constantly moving across the

"Aryans" of other nations, an idea which had played only a small role in the prepower stage of Nazi propaganda.[53] The *Volksgemeinschaft* was merely the propagandistic preparation for an "Aryan" racial society which in the end would have doomed all peoples, including the Germans.

To a certain extent, the *Volksgemeinschaft* was the Nazis' attempt to counter the Communist promise of a classless society. The propaganda appeal of the one over the other seems obvious if we disregard all ideological implications. While both promised to level all social and property differences, the classless society had the obvious connotation that everybody would be leveled to the status of a factory worker, while the *Volksgemeinschaft*, with its connotation of conspiracy for world conquest, held out a reasonable hope that every German could eventually become a factory owner. The even greater advantage of the *Volksgemeinschaft*, however, was that its establishment did not have to wait for some future time and did not depend upon objective conditions: it could be realized immediately in the fictitious world of the movement.

The true goal of totalitarian propaganda is not persuasion but organization—the "accumulation of power without the possession of the means of violence."[54] For this purpose, originality in ideological content can only be considered an unnecessary obstacle. It is no accident that the two totalitarian movements of our time, so frightfully "new" in methods of rule and ingenious in forms of organization, have never preached a new doctrine, have never invented an ideology which was not already popular.[55] Not the passing successes of demagogy win the masses, but the visible reality and power of a "living organization."[56] Hitler's brilliant gifts as a mass orator did not win him his position in the movement but rather misled his opponents into underestimating him as a simple demagogue, and Stalin was able to defeat the greater orator of the Russian Revolution.[57] What distin-

German nation and extracting the steel from this people. And I have often stated that the time will come when all worth-while men in Germany are going to be in my camp. And those who will not be in my camp are worthless anyway." Even then it was clear to Hitler's immediate environment what would happen to those who "are worthless anyway" (see *Der grossdeutsche Freiheitskampf. Reden Hitlers vom 1. 9. 1939—10. 3. 1940*, p. 174).—Himmler meant the same when he said: "The Führer does not think in German, but in Germanic terms" (Dossier Kersten, cf. above), except that we know from *Hitlers Tischgespräche* (p. 315 ff.) that in those days he was already making fun even of the Germanic "clamor" and thought in "Aryan terms."

[53] Himmler in a speech to SS leaders at Kharkov in April, 1943 (*Nazi Conspiracy*, IV, 572 ff.): "I very soon formed a Germanic SS in the various countries. . . ." An early prepower indication of this non-national policy was given by Hitler (*Reden*): "We shall certainly also receive into the new master class representatives of other nations, *i.e.*, those who deserve it because of their participation in our fight."

[54] Hadamovsky, *op. cit.*

[55] Heiden, *op. cit.*, p. 139: Propaganda is not "the art of instilling an opinion in the masses. Actually it is the art of receiving an opinion from the masses."

[56] Hadamovsky, *op. cit.*, *passim*. The term is taken from Hitler, *Mein Kampf* (Book II, chapter xi), where the "living organization" of a movement is contrasted with the "dead mechanism" of a bureaucratic party.

[57] It would be a serious error to interpret totalitarian leaders in terms of Max

guishes the totalitarian leaders and dictators is rather the simple-minded, single-minded purposefulness with which they choose those elements from existing ideologies which are best fitted to become the fundaments of another, entirely fictitious world. The fiction of the Protocols was as adequate as the fiction of a Trotskyite conspiracy, for both contained an element of plausibility—the nonpublic influence of the Jews in the past; the struggle for power between Trotsky and Stalin—which not even the fictitious world of totalitarianism can safely do without. Their art consists in using, and at the same time transcending, the elements of reality, of verifiable experiences, in the chosen fiction, and in generalizing them into regions which then are definitely removed from all possible control by individual experience. With such generalizations, totalitarian propaganda establishes a world fit to compete with the real one, whose main handicap is that it is not logical, consistent, and organized. The consistency of the fiction and strictness of the organization make it possible for the generalization eventually to survive the explosion of more specific lies—the power of the Jews after their helpless slaughter, the sinister global conspiracy of Trotskyites after their liquidation in Soviet Russia and the murder of Trotsky.

The stubbornness with which totalitarian dictators have clung to their original lies in the face of absurdity is more than superstitious gratitude to what turned the trick, and, at least in the case of Stalin, cannot be explained by the psychology of the liar whose very success may make him his own last victim. Once these propaganda slogans are integrated into a "living organization," they cannot be safely eliminated without wrecking the whole structure. The assumption of a Jewish world conspiracy was transformed by totalitarian propaganda from an objective, arguable matter into the chief element of the Nazi reality; the point was that the Nazis *acted* as though the world were dominated by the Jews and needed a counterconspiracy to defend itself. Racism for them was no longer a debatable theory of dubious scientific value, but was being realized every day in the functioning hierarchy of a political organization in whose framework it would have been very "unrealistic" to question it. Similarly, Bolshevism no longer needs to win an argument about class struggle, internationalism, and unconditional dependence of the welfare of the proletariat on the welfare of the Soviet Union; the functioning organization of the Comintern is more convincing than any argument or mere ideology can ever be.

Weber's category of the "charismatic leadership." See Hans Gerth, "The Nazi Party," in *American Journal of Sociology*, 1940, Vol. XLV. (A similar misunderstanding is also the shortcoming of Heiden's biography, *op. cit.*) Gerth describes Hitler as the charismatic leader of a bureaucratic party. This alone, in his opinion, can account for the fact that "however flagrantly actions may have contradicted words, nothing could disrupt the firmly disciplinary organization." (This contradiction, by the way, is much more characteristic of Stalin who "took care always to say the opposite of what he did, and to do the opposite of what he said." Souvarine, *op. cit.*, p. 431.)

For the source of this misunderstanding see Alfred von Martin, "Zur Soziologie der Gegenwart," in *Zeitschrift für Kulturgeschichte*, Band 27, and Arnold Koettgen, "Die Gesetzmässigkeit der Verwaltung im Führerstaat," in *Reichsverwaltungsblatt*, 1936, both of whom characterize the Nazi state as a bureaucracy with charismatic leadership.

The fundamental reason for the superiority of totalitarian propaganda over the propaganda of other parties and movements is that its content, for the members of the movement at any rate, is no longer an objective issue about which people may have opinions, but has become as real and untouchable an element in their lives as the rules of arithmetic. The organization of the entire texture of life according to an ideology can be fully carried out only under a totalitarian regime. In Nazi Germany, questioning the validity of racism and antisemitism when nothing mattered but race origin, when a career depended upon an "Aryan" physiognomy (Himmler used to select the applicants for the SS from photographs) and the amount of food upon the number of one's Jewish grandparents, was like questioning the existence of the world.

The advantages of a propaganda that constantly "adds the power of organization"[58] to the feeble and unreliable voice of argument, and thereby realizes, so to speak, on the spur of the moment, whatever it says, are obvious beyond demonstration. Foolproof against arguments based on a reality which the movements promised to change, against a counterpropaganda disqualified by the mere fact that it belongs to or defends a world which the shiftless masses cannot and will not accept, it can be disproved only by another, a stronger or better, reality.

It is in the moment of defeat that the inherent weakness of totalitarian propaganda becomes visible. Without the force of the movement, its members cease at once to believe in the dogma for which yesterday they still were ready to sacrifice their lives. The moment the movement, that is, the fictitious world which sheltered them, is destroyed, the masses revert to their old status of isolated individuals who either happily accept a new function in a changed world or sink back into their old desperate superfluousness. The members of totalitarian movements, utterly fanatical as long as the movement exists, will not follow the example of religious fanatics and die the death of martyrs (even though they were only too willing to die the death of robots).[59] Rather they will quietly give up the movement as a bad bet and look around for another promising fiction or wait until the former fiction regains enough strength to establish another mass movement.

The experience of the Allies who vainly tried to locate one self-confessed and convinced Nazi among the German people, 90 per cent of whom probably had been sincere sympathizers at one time or another, is not to be taken simply as a sign of human weakness or gross opportunism. Nazism as an ideology had been so fully "realized" that its content ceased to exist

[58] Hadamovsky, *op. cit.*, p. 21. For totalitarian purposes it is a mistake to propagate their ideology through teaching or persuasion. In the words of Robert Ley, it can be neither "taught" nor "learned," but only "exercised" and "practiced" (see *Der Weg zur Ordensburg*, undated).

[59] R. Hoehn, one of the outstanding Nazi political theorists, interpreted this lack of a doctrine or even a common set of ideals and beliefs in the movement in his *Reichsgemeinschaft und Volksgemeinschaft*, Hamburg, 1935: "From the point of view of a folk community, every community of values is destructive" (p. 83).

as an independent set of doctrines, lost its intellectual existence, so to speak; destruction of the reality therefore left almost nothing behind, least of all the fanaticism of believers.

II: *Totalitarian Organization*

THE FORMS OF totalitarian organization, as distinguished from their ideological content and propaganda slogans, are completely new.[60] They are designed to translate the propaganda lies of the movement, woven around a central fiction—the conspiracy of the Jews, or the Trotskyites, or 300 families, etc.—into a functioning reality, to build up, even under nontotalitarian circumstances, a society whose members act and react according to the rules of a fictitious world. In contrast with seemingly similar parties and movements of Fascist or Socialist, nationalist or Communist orientation, all of which back up their propaganda with terrorism as soon as they have reached a certain stage of extremism (which mostly depends on the stage of desperation of their members), the totalitarian movement is really in earnest about its propaganda, and this earnestness is expressed much more frighteningly in the organization of its followers than in the physical liquidation of its opponents. Organization and propaganda (rather than terror and propaganda) are two sides of the same coin.[61]

The most strikingly new organizational device of the movements in their prepower stage is the creation of front organizations, the distinction drawn between party members and sympathizers. Compared to this invention, other typically totalitarian features, such as the appointment of functionaries from above and the eventual monopolization of appointments by one man are secondary in importance. The so-called "leader principle" is in itself not totalitarian; it has borrowed certain features from authoritarianism and military dictatorship which have greatly contributed toward obscuring and belittling the essentially totalitarian phenomenon. If the functionaries appointed from above possessed real authority and responsibility, we would have to do with a hierarchical structure in which authority and power are delegated and governed by laws. Much the same is true for the organization of an army and the military dictatorship established after its model; here, absolute power of command from the top down and absolute obedience from the bottom up correspond to the situation of extreme danger in combat, which is precisely why they are not totalitarian. A hierarchically organized chain of command means that the commander's power is dependent on the whole hierarchic system in which he operates. Every hierarchy, no matter

[60] Hitler, discussing the relationship between *Weltanschauung* and organization, admits as a matter of course that the Nazis took over from other groups and parties the "racial idea" (*die völkische Idee*) and acted as though they were its only representatives because they were the first to base a fighting organization on it and to formulate it for practical purposes. *Op. cit.*, Book II, chapter v.

[61] See Hitler, "Propaganda and Organization," in *op. cit.*, Book II, chapter xi.

how authoritarian in its direction, and every chain of command, no matter how arbitrary or dictatorial the content of orders, tends to stabilize and would have restricted the total power of the leader of a totalitarian movement.[62] In the language of the Nazis, the never-resting, dynamic "will of the Fuehrer"—and not his orders, a phrase that might imply a fixed and circumscribed authority—becomes the "supreme law" in a totalitarian state.[63] It is only from the position in which the totalitarian movement, thanks to its unique organization, places the leader—only from his functional importance for the movement—that the leader principle develops its totalitarian character. This is also borne out by the fact that both in Hitler's and Stalin's case the actual leader principle crystallized only rather slowly, and parallel with the progressive "totalitarianization" of the movement.[64]

An anonymity which contributes greatly to the weirdness of the whole phenomenon clouds the beginnings of this new organizational structure. We do not know who first decided to organize fellow-travelers into front organizations, who first saw in vaguely sympathizing masses—upon whom all parties used to count at election day but whom they considered to be too fluctuating for membership—not only a reservoir from which to draw party members, but a decisive force in itself. The early Communist-inspired or-

[62] Himmler's vehemently urgent request "not to issue any decree concerning the definition of the term 'Jew' " is a case in point; for "with all these foolish commitments we will only be tying our hands" (Nuremberg Document No. 626, letter to Berger dated July 28, 1942, photostatic copy at the Centre de Documentation Juive).

[63] The formulation "The will of the Fuehrer is the supreme law" is found in all official rules and regulations governing the conduct of the Party and the SS. The best source on this subject is Otto Gauweiler, *Rechtseinrichtungen und Rechtsaufgaben der Bewegung*, 1939.

[64] Heiden, *op. cit.*, p. 292, reports the following difference between the first and the following editions of *Mein Kampf*: The first edition proposes the election of party officials who only after their election are vested with "unlimited power and authority"; all following editions establish appointment of party officials from above by the next higher leader. Naturally, for the stability of totalitarian regimes the appointment from above is a much more important principle than the "unlimited authority" of the appointed official. In practice, the subleaders' authority was decisively limited through the Leader's absolute sovereignty. See below.

Stalin, coming from the conspiratory apparatus of the Bolshevik party, probably never thought this a problem. To him, appointments in the party machine were a question of accumulation of personal power. (Yet, it was only in the thirties, after he had studied Hitler's example, that he let himself be addressed as "leader.") It must be admitted, however, that he could easily justify these methods by quoting Lenin's theory that "the history of all countries shows that the working class, exclusively by its own effort, is able to develop only trade-union consciousness," and that its leadership therefore necessarily comes from without. (See *What is to be done?*, first published in 1902, in *Collected Works*, Vol. IV, Book II.) The point is that Lenin considered the Communist Party as the "most progressive" part of the working class and at the same time "the lever of political organization" which "directs the whole mass of the proletariat," *i.e.*, an organization outside and above the class. (See W. H. Chamberlin, *The Russian Revolution, 1917-1921*, New York, 1935, II, 361.) Nevertheless, Lenin did not question the validity of inner-party democracy, though he was inclined to restrict democracy to the working class itself.

ganizations of sympathizers, such as the Friends of the Soviet Union or the Red Relief associations, developed into front organizations but were originally nothing more or less than what their names indicated: a gathering of sympathizers for financial or other (for instance, legal) help. Hitler was the first to say that each movement should divide the masses which have been won through propaganda into two categories, sympathizers and members. This in itself is interesting enough; even more significant is that he based this division upon a more general philosophy according to which most people are too lazy and cowardly for anything more than mere theoretical insight, and only a minority want to fight for their convictions.[65] Hitler, consequently, was the first to devise a conscious policy of constantly enlarging the ranks of sympathizers while at the same time keeping the number of party members strictly limited.[66] This notion of a minority of party members surrounded by a majority of sympathizers comes very close to the later reality of front organizations—a term which indeed expresses most aptly their eventual function, and indicates the relationship between members and sympathizers within the movement itself. For the front organizations of sympathizers are no less essential to the functioning of the movement than its actual membership.

The front organizations surround the movements' membership with a protective wall which separates them from the outside, normal world; at the same time, they form a bridge back into normalcy, without which the members in the prepower stage would feel too sharply the differences between their beliefs and those of normal people, between the lying fictitiousness of their own and the reality of the normal world. The ingeniousness of this device during the movements' struggle for power is that the front organizations not only isolate the members but offer them a semblance of outside normalcy which wards off the impact of true reality more effectively than mere indoctrination. It is the difference between his own and the fellow-traveler's attitudes which confirms a Nazi or Bolshevik in his belief in the fictitious explanation of the world, for the fellow-traveler has the same convictions, after all, albeit in a more "normal," *i.e.*, less fanatic, more confused form; so that to the party member it appears that anyone whom the movement has not expressly singled out as an enemy (a Jew, a capitalist, etc.) is on his side, that the world is full of secret allies who merely cannot, as yet, summon up the necessary strength of mind and character to draw the logical conclusions from their own convictions.[67]

[65] Hitler, *op. cit.*, Book II, chapter xi.

[66] *Ibid.* This principle was strictly enforced as soon as the Nazis seized power. Of 7 million members of the Hitler youth only 50,000 were accepted for party membership in 1937. See the preface by H. L. Childs to *The Nazi Primer.*—Compare also Gottfried Neesse, "Die verfassungsrechtliche Gestaltung der Ein-Partei," in *Zeitschift für die gesamte Staatswissenschaft*, 1938, Band 98, p. 678: "Even the One-Party must never grow to the point where it would embrace the whole population. It is 'total' because of its ideological influence on the nation."

[67] See Hitler's differentiation between the "radical people" who alone were prepared to become members of the party and hundreds of thousands of sympathizers who were too "cowardly" to make the necessary sacrifice. *Op. cit., loc. cit.*

The world at large, on the other side, usually gets its first glimpse of a totalitarian movement through its front organizations. The sympathizers, who are to all appearances still innocuous fellow-citizens in a nontotalitarian society, can hardly be called single-minded fanatics; through them, the movements make their fantastic lies more generally acceptable, can spread their propaganda in milder, more respectable forms, until the whole atmosphere is poisoned with totalitarian elements which are hardly recognizable as such but appear to be normal political reactions or opinions. The fellow-traveler organizations surround the totalitarian movements with a mist of normality and respectability that fools the membership about the true character of the outside world as much as it does the outside world about the true character of the movement. The front organization functions both ways: as the façade of the totalitarian movement to the nontotalitarian world, and as the façade of this world to the inner hierarchy of the movement.

Even more striking than this relationship is the fact that it is repeated on different levels within the movement itself. As party members are related to and separated from the fellow-travelers, so are the elite formations of the movement related to and separated from the ordinary members. If the fellow-traveler still appears to be a normal inhabitant of the outside world who has adopted the totalitarian creed as one may adopt the program of an ordinary party, the ordinary member of the Nazi or Bolshevik movement still belongs, in many respects, to the surrounding world: his professional and social relationships are not yet absolutely determined by his party membership, although he may realize—as distinguished from the mere sympathizer—that in case of conflict between his party allegiance and his private life, the former is supposed to be decisive. The member of a militant group, on the other hand, is wholly identified with the movement; he has no profession and no private life independent of it. Just as the sympathizers constitute a protective wall around the members of the movement and represent the outside world to them, so the ordinary membership surrounds the militant groups and represents the normal outside world to them.

A definite advantage of this structure is that it blunts the impact of one of the basic totalitarian tenets—that the world is divided into two gigantic hostile camps, one of which is the movement, and that the movement can and must fight the whole world—a claim which prepares the way for the indiscriminate aggressiveness of totalitarian regimes in power. Through a carefully graduated hierarchy of militancy in which each rank is the higher level's image of the nontotalitarian world because it is less militant and its members less totally organized, the shock of the terrifying and monstrous totalitarian dichotomy is vitiated and never full realized; this type of organization prevents its members' ever being directly confronted with the outside world, whose hostility remains for them a mere ideological assumption. They are so well protected against the reality of the nontotalitarian world that they constantly underestimate the tremendous risks of totalitarian politics.

There is no doubt that the totalitarian movements attack the status quo more radically than did any of the earlier revolutionary parties. They can afford this radicalism, apparently so unsuited to mass organizations, because their organization offers a temporary substitute for ordinary, nonpolitical life, which totalitarianism actually seeks to abolish. The whole world of nonpolitical social relationships, from which the "professional revolutionary" had to cut himself off or had to accept as they were, exists in the form of less militant groups in the movement; within this hierarchically organized world the fighters for world conquest and world revolution are never exposed to the shock inevitably generated by the discrepancy between "revolutionary" beliefs and the "normal" world. The reason why the movements in their prepower, revolutionary stage can attract so many ordinary philistines is that their members live in a fool's paradise of normalcy; the party members are surrounded by the normal world of sympathizers and the elite formations by the normal world of ordinary members.

Another advantage of the totalitarian pattern is that it can be repeated indefinitely and keeps the organization in a state of fluidity which permits it constantly to insert new layers and define new degrees of militancy. The whole history of the Nazi party can be told in terms of new formations within the Nazi movement. The SA, the stormtroopers (founded in 1922), were the first Nazi formation which was supposed to be more militant than the party itself;[68] in 1926, the SS was founded as the elite formation of the SA; after three years, the SS was separated from the SA and put under Himmler's command; it took Himmler only a few more years to repeat the same game within the SS. One after the other, and each more militant than its predecessor, there now came into being, first, the Shock Troops,[69] then the Death Head units (the "guard units for the concentration camps"), which later were merged to form the Armed SS (*Waffen-SS*), finally the Security Service (the "ideological intelligence service of the Party," and its executive arm for the "negative population policy") and the Office for Questions of Race and Resettlement (*Rasse- und Siedlungswesen*), whose tasks were of a "positive kind"—all of them developing out of the General SS, whose members, except for the higher Fuehrer Corps, remained in their civilian occupations. To all these new formations the member of the General SS now stood in the same relationship as the SA-man to the SS-man, or the party member to the SA-man, or the member of a front organization to a party member.[70] Now the General SS was charged not only with "safe-

[68] See Hitler: chapter on the SA in *op. cit.*, Book II, chapter ix, second part.

[69] In translating *Verfügungstruppe*, *i.e.*, the special units of the SS which originally were supposed to be at Hitler's special disposal, as shock troops, I follow O. C. Giles, *The Gestapo*. Oxford Pamphlets on World Affairs, No. 36, 1940.

[70] The most important source for the organization and history of the SS is Himmler's "Wesen und Aufgabe der SS und der Polizei," in *Sammelhefte ausgewählter Vorträge und Reden*, 1939. In the course of the war, when the ranks of the *Waffen-SS* had to be filled with enlistments owing to losses at the front, the *Waffen-SS* lost its elite character within the SS to such an extent that now the General SS, *i.e.*, the higher Fuehrer Corps, once again represented the real nuclear elite of the movement.

Very revealing documentary material for this last phase of the SS can be found in the archives of the Hoover Library, Himmler File, Folder 278. It shows that the SS

guarding the . . . embodiments of the National Socialist idea," but also with "protecting the members of all special SS cadres from becoming detached from the movement itself."[71]

This fluctuating hierarchy, with its constant addition of new layers and shifts in authority, is well known from secret control bodies, the secret police or espionage services, where new controls are always needed to control the controllers. In the prepower stage of the movements, total espionage is not yet possible; but the fluctuating hierarchy, similar to that of secret services, makes it possible, even without actual power, to degrade any rank or group that wavers or shows signs of decreasing radicalism by the mere insertion of a new more radical layer, hence driving the older group automatically in the direction of the front organization and away from the center of the movement. Thus, the Nazi elite formations were primarily inner-party organizations: the SA rose to the position of a superparty when the party appeared to lose in radicality and was then in turn and for similar reasons superseded by the SS.

The military value of the totalitarian elite formations, especially of the SA and the SS, are frequently overrated, while their purely inner-party significance has been somewhat neglected.[72] None of the Fascist Shirt-organizations was founded for specific defensive or aggressive purposes, though defense of the leaders or the ordinary party members usually was cited as a

---

went about its recruiting both among foreign workers and the native population by deliberately imitating the methods and rules of the French Foreign Legion. Enlistment among the Germans was based on an order by Hitler (never published) dated December, 1942, according to which "the 1925 class [should] be drafted into the *Waffen-SS*" (Himmler in a letter to Bormann). Conscription and enlistment were handled ostensibly on a voluntary basis. Precisely what this amounted to can be seen from numerous reports of SS leaders entrusted with this assignment. A report dated July 21, 1943, describes how the police surround the hall in which French workers are to be enlisted, how the French first sing the *Marseillaise* and then try to jump out of the windows. Attempts among German youth were scarcely more encouraging. Although they were put under extraordinary pressure and told that "they certainly would not want to join the 'dirty gray hordes'" of the army, only 18 out of 220 members of the Hitler youth reported for duty (according to a report of April 30, 1943, submitted by Häussler, head of Conscription Center Southwest of the *Waffen-SS*); all others preferred to join the Wehrmacht. It is possible that the greater losses of the SS, as compared with those of the Wehrmacht, entered into their decisions (see Karl O. Paetel, "Die SS," in *Vierteljahreshefte für Zeitgeschichte*, January, 1954). But that this factor alone could not have been decisive is proved by the following: As early as January, 1940, Hitler had ordered the drafting of SA-men into the *Waffen-SS*, and the results for Koenigsberg, based on a report that has been preserved, were listed as follows: 1807 SA-men were called up "for police service"; of these, 1094 failed to report; 631 were found to be unfit; 82 were fit for service in the SS.

[71] Werner Best, *op. cit.*, 1941, p. 99.

[72] This, however, was not the fault of Hitler, who always insisted that the very name of the SA (*Sturmabteilung*) indicated that it was only "a section of the movement" just like other party formations such as the propaganda department, the newspaper, the scientific institutes, etc. He also tried to dispel the illusions of the possible military value of a paramilitary formation and wanted training to be carried through according to the needs of the party and not according to the principles of an army. *Op. cit., loc. cit.*

pretext.[73] The paramilitary form of Nazi and Fascist elite groups was the result of their being founded as "instruments of the ideological fight of the movement"[74] against the widespread pacifism in Europe after the first World War. For totalitarian purposes it was much more important to set up, as "the expression of an aggressive attitude,"[75] a fake army which resembled as closely as possible the bogus army of the pacifists (unable to understand the constitutional place of an army within the political body, the pacifists had denounced all military institutions as bands of willful murderers), than to have a troop of well-trained soldiers. The SA and the SS were certainly model organizations for arbitrary violence and murder; they were hardly as well trained as the Black Reichswehr, and they were not equipped for a fight against regular troops. Militaristic propaganda was more popular in postwar Germany than military training, and uniforms did not enhance the military value of paramilitary troops, though they were useful as a clear indication of the abolition of civilian standards and morals; somehow these uniforms eased considerably the consciences of the murderers and also made them even more receptive to unquestioning obedience and unquestioned authority. Despite these militaristic trappings, the inner-party faction of the Nazis, which was primarily nationalistic and militaristic and therefore viewed the paramilitary troops not as mere party formations but as an illegal enlargement of the Reichswehr (which had been limited by the terms of the Versailles Peace Treaty), was the first to be liquidated. Röhm, the leader of the SA stormtroopers, had indeed dreamed of and negotiated for incorporation of his SA into the Reichswehr after the Nazis seized power. He was killed by Hitler because he tried to transform the new Nazi regime into a military dictatorship.[76] Hitler had made it clear several

[73] The official reason for the foundation of the SA was protection of Nazi meetings, while the original task of the SS was protection of Nazi leaders.

[74] Hitler, *op. cit., loc. cit.*

[75] Ernst Bayer, *Die SA*, Berlin, 1938. Translation quoted from *Nazi Conspiracy*, IV.

[76] Röhm's autobiography shows clearly how little his political convictions agreed with those of the Nazis. He always desired a *"Soldatenstaat"* and always insisted on the *"Primat des Soldaten vor dem Politiker"* (*op. cit.*, p. 349). Especially telling for his nontotalitarian attitude, or rather for his inability even to understand totalitarianism and its "total" claim, is the following passage: "I don't see why the following three things should not be compatible: my loyalty to the hereditary prince of the house of Wittelsbach and heir to Bavaria's crown; my admiration for the quartermaster-general of the World War [*i.e.*, Ludendorff], who today embodies the conscience of the German people; and my comradeship with the harbinger and bearer of the political struggle, Adolf Hitler" (p. 348). What ultimately cost Röhm his head was that after the seizure of power he envisioned a Fascist dictatorship patterned after the Italian regime, in which the Nazi party would "break the chains of the party" and "itself become the state," which was exactly what Hitler meant to avoid under all circumstances. See Ernst Röhm, *Warum SA?*, speech before the diplomatic corps, December, 1933, Berlin, undated.

Within the Nazi party, the possibility of an SA-Reichswehr plot against the rule of the SS and the police apparently never was quite forgotten. Hans Frank, Governor General of Poland, in 1942, eight years after the murder of Röhm and General Schleicher, was suspected of wishing "after the war . . . to inaugurate the greatest fight for justice [against the SS] with the assistance of the Armed Forces and the SA" (*Nazi Conspiracy*, VI, 747).

years before that such a development was not desired by the Nazi movement when he dismissed Röhm—a real soldier whose experience in the war and in the organization of the Black Reichswehr would have made him indispensable to a serious military training program—from his position as chief of the SA and chose Himmler, a man without the slightest knowledge of military matters, as reorganizer of the SS.

Apart from the importance of the elite formations to the organizational structure of the movement, where they comprised the changing nuclei of militancy, their paramilitary character must be understood in connection with other professional party organizations, such as those for teachers, lawyers, physicians, students, university professors, technicians, and workers. All these were primarily duplicates of existing nontotalitarian professional societies, paraprofessional as the stormtroopers were paramilitary. It was characteristic that the more clearly the European Communist parties became branches of a Moscow-directed Bolshevik movement, the more they, too, used their front organizations to compete with existing purely professional groups. The difference between the Nazis and the Bolsheviks in this respect was only that the Nazis had a pronounced tendency to consider these paraprofessional formations as part of the party elite, while the Communists preferred to recruit from them the material for their front organizations. The important factor for the movements is that, even before they seize power, they give the impression that all elements of society are embodied in their ranks. (The ultimate goal of Nazi propaganda was to organize the whole German people as sympathizers.[77]) The Nazis went one step further in this game and set up a series of fake departments which were modeled after the regular state administration, such as their own department of foreign affairs, education, culture, sport, etc. None of these institutions had more professional value than the imitation of the army represented by the stormtroopers, but together they created a perfect world of appearances in which every reality in the nontotalitarian world was slavishly duplicated in the form of humbug.

This technique of duplication, certainly useless for the direct overthrow of government, proved extremely fruitful in the work of undermining actively existing institutions and in the "decomposition of the status quo"[78] which totalitarian organizations invariably prefer to an open show of force. If it is the task of movements "to bore their way like polyps into all positions of power,"[79] then they must be ready for any specific social and political position. In accordance with their claim to total domination, every single organized group in the nontotalitarian society is felt to present a specific challenge to the movement to destroy it; every one needs, so to speak, a specific instrument of destruction. The practical value of the fake organizations came to light when the Nazis seized power and were ready

[77] Hitler, *op. cit.*, Book II, chapter xi, states that propaganda attempts to force a doctrine on the whole people while the organization incorporates only a comparatively small proportion of its more militant members.—Compare also G. Neesse, *op. cit.*

[78] Hitler, *op. cit.*, *loc. cit.*

[79] Hadamovsky, *op. cit.*, p. 28.

at once to destroy the existing teachers' organizations with another teachers' organization, the existing lawyers' clubs with a Nazi-sponsored lawyers' club, etc. They could change overnight the whole structure of German society—and not just political life—precisely because they had prepared its exact counterpart within their own ranks. In this respect, the task of the paramilitary formations was finished when the regular military hierarchy could be placed, during the last stages of the war, under the authority of SS generals. The technique of this "co-ordination" was as ingenious and irresistible as the deterioration of professional standards was swift and radical, although these results were more immediately felt in the highly technical and specialized field of warfare than anywhere else.

If the importance of paramilitary formations for totalitarian movements is not to be found in their doubtful military value, neither is it wholly in their fake imitation of the regular army. As elite formations they are more sharply separated from the outside world than any other group. The Nazis realized very early the intimate connection between total militancy and total separation from normality; the stormtroopers were never assigned to duty in their home communities, and the active cadres of the SA in the prepower stage, and of the SS under the Nazi regime, were so mobile and so frequently exchanged that they could not possibly get used to and take root in any other part of the ordinary world.[80] They were organized after the model of criminal gangs and used for organized murder.[81] These murders were publicly paraded and officially admitted by the upper Nazi hierarchy, so that open complicity made it well-nigh impossible for members to quit the movement even under the nontotalitarian government and even if they were not threatened, as they actually were, by their former comrades. In this respect, the function of the elite formations is the very opposite of that of the front organizations: while the latter lend the movement an air of respectability and inspire confidence, the former, by extending complicity, make every party member aware that he has left for good the normal world which outlaws murder and that he will be held accountable for all crimes committed by the elite.[82] This is achieved even in the

[80] The Death Head units of the SS were placed under the following rules: 1. No brigade is called for duty in its native district. 2. Every unit is to change after three weeks' service. 3. Members are never to be sent into the streets alone or ever to display their Death Head insignia in public. See: *Secret Speech by Himmler to the German Army General Staff 1938* (the speech, however, was delivered in 1937, see *Nazi Conspiracy*, IV, 616, where only excerpts are published). Published by the American Committee for Anti-Nazi Literature.

[81] Heinrich Himmler, *Die Schutzstaffel als antibolschewistische Kampforganisation:* Aus dem Schwarzen Korps, No. 3, 1936, said publicly: "I know that there are people in Germany who get sick when they see this black coat. We understand that and don't expect to be loved by too many people."

[82] In his speeches to the SS Himmler always stressed committed crimes, underlining their gravity. About the liquidation of the Jews, for instance, he would say: "I also want to talk to you quite frankly on a very grave matter. Among ourselves it should be mentioned quite frankly, and yet we will never speak of it publicly." On the liquidation of the Polish intelligentsia: ". . . you should hear this but also forget it immediately . . ." (*Nazi Conspiracy*, IV, 558 and 553, respectively).

prepower stage, when the leadership systematically claims responsibility for all crimes and leaves no doubt that they are committed for the ultimate good of the movement.

The artificial creation of civil-war conditions by which the Nazis blackmailed their way into power has more than the obvious advantage of stirring up trouble. For the movement, organized violence is the most efficient of the many protective walls which surround its fictitious world, whose "reality" is proved when a member fears leaving the movement more than he fears the consequences of his complicity in illegal actions, and feels more secure as a member than as an opponent. This feeling of security, resulting from the organized violence with which the elite formations protect the party members from the outside world, is as important to the integrity of the fictitious world of the organization as the fear of its terror.

In the center of the movement, as the motor that swings it into motion, sits the Leader. He is separated from the elite formation by an inner circle of the initiated who spread around him an aura of impenetrable mystery which corresponds to his "intangible preponderance."[83] His position within this intimate circle depends upon his ability to spin intrigues among its members and upon his skill in constantly changing its personnel. He owes his rise to leadership to an extreme ability to handle inner-party struggles for power rather than to demagogic or bureaucratic-organizational qualities. He is distinguished from earlier types of dictators in that he hardly wins through simple violence. Hitler needed neither the SA nor the SS to secure his position as leader of the Nazi movement; on the contrary, Röhm, the chief of the SA and able to count upon its loyalty to his own person, was one of Hitler's inner-party enemies. Stalin won against Trotsky, who not only had a far greater mass appeal but, as chief of the Red Army, held in his hands the greatest power potential in Soviet Russia at the time.[84] Not Stalin, but Trotsky, moreover, was the greatest organizational talent, the ablest bureaucrat of the Russian Revolution.[85] On the other hand, both Hitler and Stalin were masters of detail and devoted themselves in the early stages of

---

Goebbels, *op. cit.*, p. 266, notes in a similar vein: "On the Jewish question, especially, we have taken a position from which there is no escape. . . . Experience teaches that a movement and a people who have burned their bridges fight with much greater determination than those who are still able to retreat."

[83] Souvarine, *op. cit.*, p. 648.—The way the totalitarian movements have kept the private lives of their leaders (Hitler and Stalin) absolutely secret contrasts with the publicity value which all democracies find in parading the private lives of Presidents, Kings, Prime Ministers, etc., in public. Totalitarian methods do not allow for an identification based on the conviction: Even the highest of us is only human.

Souvarine, *op. cit.*, p. xiii, quotes the most frequently used tags to describe Stalin: "Stalin, the mysterious host of the Kremlin"; "Stalin, impenetrable personality"; "Stalin, the Communist Sphinx"; "Stalin, the Enigma," the "insoluble mystery," etc.

[84] "If [Trotsky] had chosen to stage a military *coup d'état* he might perhaps have defeated the triumvirs. But he left office without the slightest attempt at rallying in his defence the army he had created and led for seven years" (Isaac Deutscher, *op. cit.*, p. 297).

[85] The Commissariat for War under Trotsky "was a model institution" and Trotsky was called in in all cases of disorder in other departments. Souvarine, *op. cit.*, p. 288.

their careers almost entirely to questions of personnel, so that after a few years hardly any man of importance remained who did not owe his position to them.[86]

Such personal abilities, however, though an absolute prerequisite for the first stages of such a career and even later far from insignificant, are no longer decisive when a totalitarian movement has been built up, has established the principle that "the will of the Fuehrer is the Party's law," and when its whole hierarchy has been efficiently trained for a single purpose—swiftly to communicate the will of the Leader to all ranks. When this has been achieved, the Leader is irreplaceable because the whole complicated structure of the movement would lose its *raison d'être* without his commands. Now, despite eternal cabals in the inner clique and unending shifts of personnel, with their tremendous accumulation of hatred, bitterness, and personal resentment, the Leader's position can remain secure against chaotic palace revolutions not because of his superior gifts, about which the men in his intimate surroundings frequently have no great illusions, but because of these men's sincere and sensible conviction that without him everything would be immediately lost.

The supreme task of the Leader is to impersonate the double function characteristic of each layer of the movement—to act as the magic defense of the movement against the outside world; and at the same time, to be the direct bridge by which the movement is connected with it. The Leader represents the movement in a way totally different from all ordinary party leaders; he claims personal responsibility for every action, deed, or misdeed, committed by any member or functionary in his official capacity. This total responsibility is the most important organizational aspect of the so-called Leader principle, according to which every functionary is not only appointed by the Leader but is his walking embodiment, and every order is supposed to emanate from this one ever-present source. This thorough identification of the Leader with every appointed subleader and this monopoly of responsibility for everything which is being done are also the most conspicuous signs of the decisive difference between a totalitarian leader and an ordinary dictator or despot. A tyrant would never identify himself with his subordinates, let alone with every one of their acts;[87] he might use them as scape-

[86] The circumstances surrounding Stalin's death seem to contradict the infallibility of these methods. There is the possibility that Stalin, who, before he died, undoubtedly planned still another general purge, was killed by someone in his environment because no one felt safe any longer, but despite a great deal of circumstantial evidence this cannot be proved.

[87] Thus Hitler personally cabled his responsibility for the Potempa murder to the SA assassins in 1932, although presumably he had nothing whatever to do with it. What mattered here was establishing a principle of identification, or, in the language of the Nazis, "the mutual loyalty of the Leader and the people" on which "the Reich rests" (Hans Frank, *op. cit.*).

goats and gladly have them criticized in order to save himself from the wrath of the people, but he would always maintain an absolute distance from all his subordinates and all his subjects. The Leader, on the contrary, cannot tolerate criticism of his subordinates, since they act always in his name; if he wants to correct his own errors, he must liquidate those who carried them out; if he wants to blame his mistakes on others, he must kill them.[88] For within this organizational framework a mistake can only be a fraud: the impersonation of the Leader by an impostor.

This total responsibility for everything done by the movement and this total identification with every one of its functionaries have the very practical consequence that nobody ever experiences a situation in which he has to be responsible for his own actions or can explain the reasons for them. Since the Leader has monopolized the right and possibility of explanation, he appears to the outside world as the only person who knows what he is doing, *i.e.*, the only representative of the movement with whom one may still talk in nontotalitarian terms and who, if reproached or opposed, cannot say: Don't ask me, ask the Leader. Being in the center of the movement, the Leader can act as though he were above it. It is therefore perfectly understandable (and perfectly futile) for outsiders to set their hopes time and again on a personal talk with the Leader himself when they have to deal with totalitarian movements or governments. The real mystery of the totalitarian Leader resides in an organization which makes it possible for him to assume the total responsibility for all crimes committed by the elite formations of the movement *and* to claim at the same time, the honest, innocent respectability of its most naïve fellow-traveler.[89]

[88] "One of Stalin's distinctive characteristics . . . is systematically to throw his own misdeeds and crimes, as well as his political errors . . . on the shoulders of those whose discredit and ruin he is plotting" (Souvarine, *op. cit.*, p. 655). It is obvious that a totalitarian leader can choose freely whom he wants to impersonate his own errors since all acts committed by subleaders are supposed to be inspired by him, so that anybody can be forced into the role of an impostor.

[89] That it was Hitler himself—and not Himmler, or Bormann, or Goebbels—who always initiated the actually "radical" measures; that they were always more radical than the proposals made by his immediate environment; that even Himmler was appalled when he was entrusted with the "final solution" of the Jewish question—all this has now been proved by innumerable documents. And the fairy tale that Stalin was more moderate than the leftist factions of the Bolshevist Party is no longer believed, either. It is all the more important to remember that totalitarian leaders invariably try to appear more moderate to the outside world and that their real role—namely, to drive the movement forward at any price and if anything to step up its speed—remains carefully concealed. See, for instance, Admiral Erich Raeder's memo on "My Relationship to Adolf Hitler and to the Party" in *Nazi Conspiracy*, VIII, 707 ff. "When information or rumours arose about radical measures of the Party and the Gestapo, one could come to the conclusion by the conduct of the Fuehrer that such measures were not ordered by the Fuehrer himself. . . . In the course of future years, I gradually came to the conclusion that the Fuehrer himself always leaned toward the more radical solution without letting on outwardly."

The totalitarian movements have been called "secret societies established in broad daylight."[90] Indeed, little as we know of the sociological structure and the more recent history of secret societies, the structure of the movements, unprecedented if compared with parties and factions, reminds one of nothing so much as of certain outstanding traits of secret societies.[91] Secret societies also form hierarchies according to degrees of "initiation," regulate the life of their members according to a secret and fictitious assumption which makes everything look as though it were something else, adopt a strategy of consistent lying to deceive the noninitiated external masses, demand unquestioning obedience from their members who are held together by allegiance to a frequently unknown and always mysterious leader, who himself is surrounded, or supposed to be surrounded, by a small group of initiated who in turn are surrounded by the half-initiated who form a "buffer area" against the hostile profane world.[92] With secret societies, the totalitarian movements also share the dichotomous division of the world between "sworn blood brothers" and an indistinct inarticulate mass

In the intraparty struggle which preceded his rise to absolute power, Stalin was careful always to pose as "the man of the golden mean" (see Deutscher, *op. cit.*, pp. 295 ff); though certainly no "man of compromise," he never abandoned this role altogether. When, for instance, in 1936 a foreign journalist questioned him about the movement's aim of world revolution, he replied: "We have never had such plans and intentions. . . . This is the product of a misunderstanding . . . a comic one, or rather a tragicomic one" (Deutscher, *op. cit.*, p. 422).

[90] See Alexandre Koyré, "The Political Function of the Modern Lie," in *Contemporary Jewish Record*, June, 1945.

Hitler, *op. cit.*, Book II, chapter ix, discusses extensively the pros and cons of secret societies as models for totalitarian movements. His considerations actually led him to Koyré's conclusion, *i.e.*, to adopt the principles of secret societies without their secretiveness and to establish them in "broad daylight." There was, in the prepower stage of the movement, hardly anything which the Nazis consistently kept secret. It was only during the war, when the Nazi regime became fully totalitarianized and the party leadership found itself surrounded from all sides by the military hierarchy on which it depended for the conduct of the war, that the elite formations were instructed in no uncertain terms to keep everything connected with "final solutions"—*i.e.*, deportations and mass exterminations—absolutely secret. This was also the time when Hitler began to act like the chief of a band of conspirators, but not without personally announcing and circulating this fact explicitly. During a discussion with the General Staff in May, 1939, Hitler laid down the following rules, which sound as if they had been copied from a primer for a secret society: "1. No one who need not know must be informed. 2. No one must know any more than he needs to. 3. No one must know any earlier than he has to" (quoted from Heinz Holldack, *Was wirklich geschah*, 1949, p. 378).

[91] The following analysis follows closely Georg Simmel's "Sociology of Secrecy and of Secret Societies," in *The American Journal of Sociology*, Vol. XI, No. 4, January, 1906, which forms chapter v of his *Soziologie*, Leipzig, 1908, selections of which are translated by Kurt H. Wolff under the title *The Sociology of Georg Simmel*, 1950.

[92] "Precisely because the lower grades of the society constitute a mediating transition to the actual center of the secret, they bring about the gradual compression of the sphere of repulsion around the same, which affords more secure protection than the abruptness of a radical standing wholly without or wholly within could secure" (*ibid.*, p. 489).

of sworn enemies.[93] This distinction, based on absolute hostility to the surrounding world, is very different from the ordinary parties' tendency to divide people into those who belong and those who don't. Parties and open societies in general will consider only those who expressly oppose them to be their enemies, while it has always been the principle of secret societies that "whosoever is not expressly included is excluded."[94] This esoteric principle seems to be entirely inappropriate for mass organizations; yet the Nazis gave their members at least the psychological equivalent for the initiation ritual of secret societies when, instead of simply excluding Jews from membership, they demanded proof of non-Jewish descent from their members and set up a complicated machine to shed light on the dark ancestry of some 80 million Germans. It was of course a comedy, and even an expensive one, when 80 million Germans set out to look for Jewish grandfathers; yet everybody came out of the examination with the feeling that he belonged to a group of included which stood against an imaginary multitude of ineligibles. The same principle is confirmed in the Bolshevik movement through repeated party purges which inspire in everybody who is not excluded a reaffirmation of his inclusion.

Perhaps the most striking similarity between the secret societies and the totalitarian movements lies in the role of the ritual. The marches around the Red Square in Moscow are in this respect no less characteristic than the pompous formalities of the Nuremberg party days. In the center of the Nazi ritual was the so-called "blood banner," and in the center of the Bolshevik ritual stands the mummified corpse of Lenin, both of which introduce a strong element of idolatry into the ceremony. Such idolatry hardly is proof

[93] The terms "sworn brothers," "sworn comrades," "sworn community," etc., are repeated *ad nauseam* throughout Nazi literature, partly because of their appeal to juvenile romanticism which was widespread in the German youth movement. It was mainly Himmler who used these terms in a more definite sense, introduced them into the "central watchword" of the SS ("Thus we have fallen in line and march forward to a distant future following the unchangeable laws as a National Socialist order of Nordic men and as a sworn community of their tribes *[Sippen]*," see D'Alquen, *op. cit.*) and gave them their articulate meaning of "absolute hostility" against all others (see Simmel, *op. cit.*, p. 489): "Then when the mass of humanity of 1 to 1½ milliards *[sic!]* lines up against us, the Germanic people, . . ." See Himmler's speech at the meeting of the SS Major Generals at Posen, October 4, 1943, *Nazi Conspiracy*, IV, 558.

[94] Simmel, *op. cit.*, p. 490.—This, like so many other principles, was adopted by the Nazis after careful reflection on the implications of the "Protocols of the Elders of Zion." Hitler said as early as 1922: "[The gentlemen of the Right] have never yet understood that it is not necessary to be an enemy of the Jew to drag you one day . . . to the scaffold . . . it is quite enough . . . *not to be a Jew:* that will secure the scaffold for you" (*Hitler's Speeches*, p. 12). At that time, nobody could guess that this particular form of propaganda actually meant: One day, it will not be necessary to be an enemy of ours to be dragged to the scaffold; it will be quite enough to be a Jew, or, ultimately, a member of some other people, to be declared "racially unfit" by some Health Commission. Himmler believed and preached that the whole SS was based on the principle that "we must be honest, decent, loyal and comradely to members of our own blood and nobody else" (*op. cit., loc. cit.*).

—as is sometimes asserted—of pseudoreligious or heretical tendencies. The "idols" are mere organizational devices, familiar from the ritual of secret societies, which also used to frighten their members into secretiveness by means of frightful, awe-inspiring symbols. It is obvious that people are more securely held together through the common experience of a secret ritual than by the common sharing of the secret itself. That the secret of totalitarian movements is exposed in broad daylight does not necessarily change the nature of the experience.[95]

These similarities are not, of course, accidental; they cannot simply be explained by the fact that both Hitler and Stalin had been members of modern secret societies before they became totalitarian leaders—Hitler in the secret service of the Reichswehr and Stalin in the conspiracy section of the Bolshevik party. They are to some extent the natural outcome of the conspiracy fiction of totalitarianism whose organizations supposedly have been founded to counteract secret societies—the secret society of the Jews or the conspiratory society of the Trotskyites. What is remarkable in the totalitarian organizations is rather that they could adopt so many organizational devices of secret societies without ever trying to keep their own goal a secret. That the Nazis wanted to conquer the world, deport "racially alien" peoples and exterminate those of "inferior biological heritage," that the Bolsheviks work for the world revolution, was never a secret; these aims, on the contrary, were always part of their propaganda. In other words, the totalitarian movements imitate all the paraphernalia of the secret societies but empty them of the only thing that could excuse, or was supposed to excuse, their methods—the necessity to safeguard a secret.

In this, as in so many other respects, Nazism and Bolshevism arrived at the same organizational result from very different historical beginnings. The Nazis started with the fiction of a conspiracy and modeled themselves, more or less consciously, after the example of the secret society of the Elders of Zion, whereas the Bolsheviks came from a revolutionary party, whose aim was one-party dictatorship, passed through a stage in which the party was "entirely apart and above everything" to the moment when the Politburo of the party was "entirely apart from and above everything";[96] finally Stalin imposed upon this party structure the rigid totalitarian rules of its conspiratory sector and only then discovered the need for a central fiction to maintain the iron discipline of a secret society under the conditions of a mass organization. The Nazi development may be more logical, more consistent in itself, but the history of the Bolshevik party offers a better illustration of the essentially fictitious character of totalitarianism, precisely because the fictitious global conspiracies against and according to which the Bolshevik conspiracy is supposedly organized have not been ideologically fixed. They have changed—from the Trotskyites to the 300 families, then to various "imperialisms" and recently to "rootless cosmopolitanism"—and were adjusted to passing needs; yet at no moment and under none of the

[95] See Simmel, *op. cit.*, pp. 480-481.
[96] Souvarine, *op. cit.*, p. 319, follows a formulation of Bukharin.

most various circumstances has it been possible for Bolshevism to do without some such fiction.

The means by which Stalin changed the Russian one-party dictatorship into a totalitarian regime and the revolutionary Communist parties all over the world into totalitarian movements was the liquidation of factions, the abolition of inner-party democracy and the transformation of national Communist parties into Moscow-directed branches of the Comintern. Secret societies in general, and the conspiratory apparatus of revolutionary parties in particular, have always been characterized by absence of factions, suppression of dissident opinions, and absolute centralization of command. All these measures have the obvious utilitarian purpose of protecting the members against persecution and the society against treason; the total obedience asked of each member and the absolute power in the hands of the chief were only inevitable by-products of practical necessities. The trouble, however, is that conspirators have an understandable tendency to think that the most efficient methods in politics in general are those of conspiratory societies and that if one can apply them in broad daylight and support them with a whole nation's instruments of violence, the possibilities for power accumulation become absolutely limitless.[97] The conspiratory sector of a revolutionary party can, as long as the party itself is still intact, be likened to the role of the army within an intact political body: although its own rules of conduct differ radically from those of the civilian body, it serves, remains subject to, and is controlled by it. Just as the danger of a military dictatorship arises when the army no longer serves but wants to dominate the body politic, so the danger of totalitarianism arises when the conspiratory sector of a revolutionary party emancipates itself from the control of the party and aspires to leadership. This is what happened to the Communist parties under the Stalin regime. Stalin's methods were always typical of a man who came from the conspiratory sector of the party: his devotion to detail, his emphasis on the personal side of politics, his ruthlessness in the use and liquidation of comrades and friends. His chief support in the succession struggle after Lenin's death came from the secret police[98] which at that time had already become one of the most important and powerful sections of the party.[99] It was only natural that the Cheka's sympathies should be with the representative of the conspiratory section, with the man who already looked upon it

[97] Souvarine, *op. cit.*, p. 113, mentions that Stalin "was always impressed by men who brought off 'an affair.' He looked on politics as an 'affair' requiring dexterity."

[98] In the inner-party struggles during the twenties, "the collaborators of the GPU were almost without exception fanatic adversaries of the Right and adherents of Stalin. The various services of the GPU were at that time the bulwarks of the Stalinist section" (Ciliga, *op. cit.*, p. 48).—Souvarine, *op. cit.*, p. 289, reports that Stalin even before had "continued the police activity he had begun during the Civil War" and been the representative of the Politburo in the GPU.

[99] Immediately after the civil war in Russia, *Pravda* stated "that the formula 'All power to the Soviets' had been replaced by 'All power to the Chekas.' . . . The end of the armed hostilities reduced military control . . . but left a ramified Cheka which perfected itself by simplification of its operation" (Souvarine, *op. cit.*, p. 251).

as a kind of secret society and therefore was likely to preserve and to expand its privileges.

The seizure of the Communist parties by their conspiratory sector, however, was only the first step in their transformation into totalitarian movements. It was not enough that the secret police in Russia and its agents in the Communist parties abroad played the same role in the movement as the elite formations which the Nazis had constituted in the form of paramilitary troops. The parties themselves had to be transformed, if the rule of the secret police was to remain stable. Liquidation of factions and inner-party democracy, consequently, was accompanied in Russia by the admission of large, politically uneducated and "neutral" masses to membership, a policy which was quickly followed by the Communist parties abroad after the Popular Front policy had initiated it.

Nazi totalitarianism started with a mass organization which was only gradually dominated by elite formations, while the Bolsheviks started with elite formations and organized the masses accordingly. The result was the same in both cases. The Nazis, moreover, because of their militaristic tradition and prejudices, originally modeled their elite formations after the army, while the Bolsheviks from the beginning endowed the secret police with the exercise of supreme power. Yet after a few years this difference too disappeared: the chief of the SS became the chief of the secret police, and the SS formations were gradually incorporated into and replaced the former personnel of the Gestapo, even though this personnel already consisted of reliable Nazis.[100]

It is because of the essential affinity between the functioning of a secret society of conspirators and of the secret police organized to combat it that totalitarian regimes, based on a fiction of global conspiracy and aiming at global rule, eventually concentrate all power in the hands of the police. In the prepower stage, however, the "secret societies in broad daylight" offer other organizational advantages. The obvious contradiction between a mass organization and an exclusive society, which alone can be trusted to keep a secret, is of no importance compared with the fact that the very structure of secret and conspiratory societies could translate the totalitarian ideological dichotomy—the blind hostility of the masses against the existing world regardless of its divergences and differences—into an organizational principle. From the viewpoint of an organization which functions according to the principle that whoever is not included is excluded, whoever is not with me is against me, the world at large loses all the nuances, differentiations, and pluralistic aspects which had in any event become confusing and un-

[100] The Gestapo was set up by Göring in 1933; Himmler was appointed chief of the Gestapo in 1934 and began at once to replace its personnel with his SS-men; at the end of the war, 75 per cent of all Gestapo agents were SS-men. It must also be considered that the SS units were particularly qualified for this job as Himmler had organized them, even in the prepower stage, for espionage duty among party members (Heiden, *op. cit.*, p. 308). For the history of the Gestapo, see Giles, *op. cit.*, and also *Nazi Conspiracy*, Vol. II, chapter xii.

bearable to the masses who had lost their place and their orientation in it.[101] What inspired them with the unwavering loyalty of members of secret societies was not so much the secret as the dichotomy between Us and all others. This could be kept intact by imitating the secret societies' organizational structure and emptying it of its rational purpose of safeguarding a secret. Nor did it matter if a conspiracy ideology was the origin of this development, as in the case of the Nazis, or a parasitic growth of the conspiratory sector of a revolutionary party, as in the case of the Bolsheviks. The claim inherent in totalitarian organization is that everything outside the movement is "dying," a claim which is drastically realized under the murderous conditions of totalitarian rule, but which even in the prepower stage appears plausible to the masses who escape from disintegration and disorientation into the fictitious home of the movement.

Totalitarian movements have proved time and again that they can command the same total loyalty in life and death which had been the prerogative of secret and conspiratory societies.[102] The complete absence of resistance in a thoroughly trained and armed troop like the SA in the face of the murder of a beloved leader (Röhm) and hundreds of close comrades was a curious spectacle. At that moment probably Röhm, and not Hitler, had the power of the Reichswehr behind him. But these incidents in the Nazi movement have by now been overshadowed by the ever-repeated spectacle of self-confessed "criminals" in the Bolshevik parties. Trials based on absurd confessions have become part of an internally all-important and externally incomprehensible ritual. But, no matter how the victims are being prepared today, this ritual owes its existence to the probably unfabricated confessions of the old Bolshevik guard in 1936. Long before the time of the Moscow Trials men condemned to death would receive their sentences with great calm, an attitude "particularly prevalent among members of the Cheka."[103] So long as the movement exists, its peculiar form of organization makes sure that at least the elite formations can no longer conceive of a life outside the closely knit band of men who, even if they are condemned, still feel superior to the rest of the uninitiated world. And since this organization's exclusive aim has always been to deceive and fight and ultimately conquer

[101] It was probably one of the decisive ideological errors of Rosenberg, who fell from the Fuehrer's favor and lost his influence in the movement to men like Himmler, Bormann, and even Streicher, that his *Myth of the Twentieth Century* admits a racial pluralism from which only the Jews were excluded. He thereby violated the principle that whoever is not included ("the Germanic people") is excluded ("the mass of humanity"). Cf. note 87.

[102] Simmel, *op. cit.*, p. 492, enumerates secret criminal societies in which the members voluntarily set up one commander whom they obey from then on without criticism and without limitation.

[103] Ciliga, *op. cit.*, pp. 96-97. He also describes how in the twenties even ordinary prisoners in the GPU prison of Leningrad who had been condemned to death allowed themselves to be taken to execution "without a word, without a cry of revolt against the Government that put them to death" (p. 183).

the outside world, its members are satisfied to pay with their lives if only this helps again to fool the world.[104]

The chief value, however, of the secret or conspiratory societies' organizational structure and moral standards for purposes of mass organization does not even lie in the inherent guarantees of unconditional belonging and loyalty, and organizational manifestation of unquestioned hostility to the outside world, but in their unsurpassed capacity to establish and safeguard the fictitious world through consistent lying. The whole hierarchical structure of totalitarian movements, from naïve fellow-travelers to party members, elite formations, the intimate circle around the Leader, and the Leader himself, could be described in terms of a curiously varying mixture of gullibility and cynicism with which each member, depending upon his rank and standing in the movement, is expected to react to the changing lying statements of the leaders and the central unchanging ideological fiction of the movement.

A mixture of gullibility and cynicism had been an outstanding characteristic of mob mentality before it became an everyday phenomenon of masses. In an ever-changing, incomprehensible world the masses had reached the point where they would, at the same time, believe everything and nothing, think that everything was possible and that nothing was true. The mixture in itself was remarkable enough, because it spelled the end of the illusion that gullibility was a weakness of unsuspecting primitive souls and cynicism the vice of superior and refined minds. Mass propaganda discovered that its audience was ready at all times to believe the worst, no matter how absurd, and did not particularly object to being deceived because it held every statement to be a lie anyhow. The totalitarian mass leaders based their propaganda on the correct psychological assumption that, under such conditions, one could make people believe the most fantastic statements one day, and trust that if the next day they were given irrefutable proof of their falsehood, they would take refuge in cynicism; instead of deserting the leaders who had lied to them, they would protest that they had known all along that the statement was a lie and would admire the leaders for their superior tactical cleverness.

What had been a demonstrable reaction of mass audiences became an important hierarchical principle for mass organizations. A mixture of gullibility and cynicism is prevalent in all ranks of totalitarian movements, and the higher the rank the more cynicism weighs down gullibility. The essential conviction shared by all ranks, from fellow-traveler to leader, is that politics is a game of cheating and that the "first commandment" of the movement: "The Fuehrer is always right," is as necessary for the purposes of world politics, *i.e.*, world-wide cheating, as the rules of military discipline are for the purposes of war.[105].

---

[104] Ciliga reports how the condemned party members "thought that if these executions saved the bureaucratic dictatorship as a whole, if they calmed the rebellious peasantry (or rather if they misled them into error), the sacrifice of their lives would not have been in vain" (*op. cit.*, pp. 96-97).

[105] Goebbels' notion of the role of diplomacy in politics is characteristic: "There is

The machine that generates, organizes, and spreads the monstrous falsehoods of totalitarian movements depends again upon the position of the Leader. To the propaganda assertion that all happenings are scientifically predictable according to the laws of nature or economics, totalitarian organization adds the position of one man who has monopolized this knowledge and whose principal quality is that he "was always right and will always be right."[106] To a member of a totalitarian movement this knowledge has nothing to do with truth and this being right nothing to do with the objective truthfulness of the Leader's statements which cannot be disproved by facts, but only by future success or failure. The Leader is always right in his actions and since these are planned for centuries to come, the ultimate test of what he does has been removed beyond the experience of his contemporaries.[107]

The only group supposed to believe loyally and textually in the Leader's words are the sympathizers whose confidence surrounds the movement with an atmosphere of honesty and simple-mindedness, and helps the Leader to fulfill half his task, that is, to inspire confidence in the movement. The party members never believe public statements and are not supposed to, but are complimented by totalitarian propaganda on that superior intelligence which supposedly distinguishes them from the nontotalitarian outside world, which, in turn, they know only from the abnormal gullibility of sympathizers. Only Nazi sympathizers believed Hitler when he swore his famous legality oath before the supreme court of the Weimar Republic; members of the movement knew very well that he lied, and trusted him more than ever because he apparently was able to fool public opinion and the authorities. When in later years Hitler repeated the performance for the whole world, when he swore to his good intentions and at the same time most openly prepared his crimes, the admiration of the Nazi membership naturally was boundless. Similarly, only Bolshevik fellow-travelers believed in the dissolution of the Comintern, and only the nonorganized masses of the Russian people and the fellow-travelers abroad were meant to take at face value Stalin's prodemocratic statements during the war. Bolshevik party members were explicitly warned not to be fooled by tactical maneuvers and were asked to admire their Leader's shrewdness in betraying his allies.[108]

Without the organizational division of the movement into elite formations, membership, and sympathizers, the lies of the Leader would not work.

no doubt that one does best if one keeps the diplomats uninformed about the background of politics. . . . Genuineness in playing an appeasement role is sometimes the most convincing argument for their political trustworthiness" (*op. cit.*, p. 87).

[106] Rudolf Hess in a broadcast in 1934. *Nazi Conspiracy*, I, 193.

[107] Werner Best *op. cit.*, explained: "Whether the will of the government lays down the 'right' rules . . . is no longer a question of law, but a question of fate. For actual misuses . . . will be punished more surely before history by fate itself with misfortune and overthrow and ruin, because of the violation of the 'laws of life,' than by a State Court of Justice." Translation quoted from *Nazi Conspiracy*, IV, 490.

[108] See Kravchenko, *op. cit.*, p. 422. "No properly indoctrinated Communist felt that the Party was 'lying' in professing one set of policies in public and its very opposite in private."

The graduation of cynicism expressed in a hierarchy of contempt is at least as necessary in the face of constant refutation as plain gullibility. The point is that the sympathizers in front organizations despise their fellow-citizens' complete lack of initiation, the party members despise the fellow-travelers' gullibility and lack of radicalism, the elite formations despise for similar reasons the party membership, and within the elite formations a similar hierarchy of contempt accompanies every new foundation and development.[109] The result of this system is that the gullibility of sympathizers makes lies credible to the outside world, while at the same time the graduated cynicism of membership and elite formations eliminates the danger that the Leader will ever be forced by the weight of his own propaganda to make good his own statements and feigned respectability. It has been one of the chief handicaps of the outside world in dealing with totalitarian systems that it ignored this system and therefore trusted that, on one hand, the very enormity of totalitarian lies would be their undoing and that, on the other, it would be possible to take the Leader at his word and force him, regardless of his original intentions, to make it good. The totalitarian system, unfortunately, is foolproof against such normal consequences; its ingeniousness rests precisely on the elimination of that reality which either unmasks the liar or forces him to live up to his pretense.

While the membership does not believe statements made for public consumption, it believes all the more fervently the standard clichés of ideological explanation, the keys to past and future history which totalitarian movements took from nineteenth-century ideologies, and transformed, through organization, into a working reality. These ideological elements in which the masses had come to believe anyhow, albeit rather vaguely and abstractly, were turned into factual lies of an all-comprehensive nature (the domination of the world by the Jews instead of a general theory about races, the conspiracy of Wall Street instead of a general theory about classes) and integrated into a general scheme of action in which only the "dying"—the dying classes of capitalist countries or the decadent nations—are supposed to stand in the way of the movement. In contrast to the movements' tactical lies which change literally from day to day, these ideological lies are supposed to be believed like sacred untouchable truths. They are surrounded by a carefully elaborated system of "scientific" proofs which do not have to be convincing for the completely "uninitiated," but still appeal to some vulgarized thirst for knowledge by "demonstrating" the inferiority of the Jews or the misery of people living under a capitalist system.

The elite formations are distinguished from the ordinary party membership in that they do not need such demonstrations and are not even supposed to believe in the literal truth of ideological clichés. These are fabricated to answer a quest for truth among the masses which in its insistence on explanation and demonstration still has much in common with the normal

[109] "The National Socialist despises his fellow German, the SA man the other National Socialists, the SS man the SA man" (Heiden, *op. cit.*, p. 308).

world. The elite is not composed of ideologists; its members' whole education is aimed at abolishing their capacity for distinguishing between truth and falsehood, between reality and fiction. Their superiority consists in their ability immediately to dissolve every statement of fact into a declaration of purpose. In distinction to the mass membership which, for instance, needs some demonstration of the inferiority of the Jewish race before it can safely be asked to kill Jews, the elite formations understand that the statement, all Jews are inferior, means, all Jews should be killed; they know that when they are told that only Moscow has a subway, the real meaning of the statement is that all subways should be destroyed, and are not unduly surprised when they discover the subway in Paris. The tremendous shock of disillusion which the Red Army suffered on its conquering trip to Europe could be cured only by concentration camps and forced exile for a large part of the occupation troops; but the police formations which accompanied the Army were prepared for the shock, not by different and more correct information—there is no secret training school in Soviet Russia which gives out authentic facts about life abroad—but simply by a general training in supreme contempt for all facts and all reality.

This mentality of the elite is no mere mass phenomenon, no mere consequence of social rootlessness, economic disaster, and political anarchy; it needs careful preparation and cultivation and forms a more important, though less easily recognizable, part of the curriculum of totalitarian leadership schools, the Nazi *Ordensburgen* for the SS troops, and the Bolshevik training centers for Comintern agents, than race indoctrination or the techniques of civil war. Without the elite and its artificially induced inability to understand facts as facts, to distinguish between truth and falsehood, the movement could never move in the direction of realizing its fiction. The outstanding negative quality of the totalitarian elite is that it never stops to think about the world as it really is and never compares the lies with reality. Its most cherished virtue, correspondingly, is loyalty to the Leader, who, like a talisman, assures the ultimate victory of lie and fiction over truth and reality.

The topmost layer in the organization of totalitarian movements is the intimate circle around the Leader, which can be a formal institution, like the Bolshevik Politburo, or a changing clique of men who do not necessarily hold office, like the entourage of Hitler. To them ideological clichés are mere devices to organize the masses, and they feel no compunction about changing them according to the needs of circumstances if only the organizing principle is kept intact. In this connection, the chief merit of Himmler's reorganization of the SS was that he found a very simple method for "solving the problem of blood by action," that is, for selecting the members of the elite according to "good blood" and preparing them to "carry on a racial struggle without mercy" against everyone who could not trace his "Aryan" ancestry back to 1750, or was less than 5 feet 8 inches tall ("I know that people who have reached a certain height must possess the desired blood to some degree") or did not have blue eyes and blond hair.[110] The importance of this racism in action was that the organization became independent of almost all concrete teachings of no matter what racial "science," independent also of antisemitism insofar as it was a specific doctrine concerning the nature and role of the Jews, whose usefulness would have ended with their extermination.[111] Racism was safe and independent of the scientificality of propaganda once an elite had been selected by a "race commission" and placed under the authority of special "marriage laws,"[112] while at the opposite end and under the jurisdiction of this "racial elite," concentration camps existed for the sake of "better demonstration of the laws of inheritance and race."[113] On the strength of this "living organization," the Nazis could dispense with dogmatism and offer friendship to Semitic peoples, like the Arabs, or enter into alliances with the very representatives of the Yellow Peril, the Japanese. The reality of a race society, the formation of an elite selected from an allegedly racial viewpoint, would indeed have been a better safeguard for the doctrine of racism than the finest scientific or pseudo-scientific proof.

The policy-makers of Bolshevism show the same superiority to their own avowed dogmas. They are quite capable of interrupting every existing class struggle with a sudden alliance with capitalism without undermining the reliability of their cadres or committing treason against their belief in class struggle. The dichotomous principle of class struggle having become an organizational device, having, as it were, petrified into uncompromising hostility against the whole world through the secret police cadres in Russia

[110] Himmler originally selected the candidates of the SS from photographs. Later a Race Commission, before which the applicant had to appear in person, approved or disapproved of his racial appearance. See Himmler on "Organization and Obligation of the SS and the Police," *Nazi Conspiracy*, IV, 616 ff.

[111] Himmler was well aware of the fact that it was one of his "most important and lasting accomplishments" to have transformed the racial question from "a negative concept based on matter-of-course antisemitism" into "an organizational task for building up the SS" (*Der Reichsführer SS und Chef der deutschen Polizei*, "exclusively for use within the police"; undated). Thus, "for the first time, the racial question had been placed into, or, better still, had become the focal point, going far beyond the negative concept underlying the natural hatred of Jews. The revolutionary idea of the Fuehrer had been infused with warm lifeblood" (*Der Weg der SS. Der Reichsführer SS.* SS-Hauptamt-Schulungsamt. Dust jacket: "Not for publication," undated, p. 25).

[112] As soon as he was appointed chief of the SS in 1929, Himmler introduced the principle of racial selection and marriage laws and added: "The SS knows very well that this order is of great significance. Taunts, sneers or misunderstanding don't touch us; the future is ours." Quoted from d'Alquen, *op. cit.* And again, fourteen years later, in his speech at Kharkov (*Nazi Conspiracy*, IV, 572 ff.), Himmler reminds his SS leaders that "we were the first really to solve the problem of blood by action . . . and by problem of blood, we of course do not mean antisemitism. Antisemitism is exactly the same as delousing. Getting rid of lice is not a question of ideology. It is a matter of cleanliness. . . . But for us the question of blood was a reminder of our own worth, a reminder of what is actually the basis holding this German people together."

[113] Himmler, *op. cit., Nazi Conspiracy*, IV, 616 ff.

and the Comintern agents abroad, Bolshevik policy has become remarkably free of "prejudices."

It is this freedom from the content of their own ideologies which characterizes the highest rank of the totalitarian hierarchy. These men consider everything and everybody in terms of organization, and this includes the Leader who to them is neither an inspired talisman nor the one who is infallibly right, but the simple consequence of this type of organization; he is needed, not as a person, but as a function, and as such he is indispensable to the movement. In contrast, however, to other despotic forms of government, where frequently a clique rules and the despot plays only the representative role of a puppet ruler, totalitarian leaders are actually free to do whatever they please and can count on the loyalty of their entourage even if they choose to murder them.

The more technical reason for this suicidal loyalty is that succession to the supreme office is not regulated by any inheritance or other laws. A successful palace revolt would have as disastrous results for the movement as a whole as a military defeat. It is in the nature of the movement that once the Leader has assumed his office, the whole organization is so absolutely identified with him that any admission of a mistake or removal from office would break the spell of infallibility which surrounds the office of the Leader and spell doom to all those connected with the movement. It is not the truthfulness of the Leader's words but the infallibility of his actions which is the basis for the structure. Without it and in the heat of a discussion which presumes fallibility, the whole fictitious world of totalitarianism goes to pieces, overwhelmed at once by the factuality of the real world which only the movement steered in an infallibly right direction by the Leader was able to ward off.

However, the loyalty of those who believe neither in ideological clichés nor in the infallibility of the Leader also has deeper, nontechnical reasons. What binds these men together is a firm and sincere belief in human omnipotence. Their moral cynicism, their belief that everything is permitted, rests on the solid conviction that everything is possible. It is true that these men, few in number, are not easily caught in their own specific lies and that they do not necessarily believe in racism or economics, in the conspiracy of the Jews or of Wall Street. Yet they too are deceived, deceived by their impudent conceited idea that everything can be done and their contemptuous conviction that everything that exists is merely a temporary obstacle that superior organization will certainly destroy. Confident that power of organization can destroy power of substance, as the violence of a well-organized gang might rob a rich man of ill-guarded wealth, they constantly underestimate the substantial power of stable communities and overestimate the driving force of a movement. Since, moreover, they do not actually believe in the factual existence of a world conspiracy against them, but use it only as an organizational device, they fail to understand that their own conspiracy may eventually provoke the whole world into uniting against them.

Yet no matter how the delusion of human omnipotence through organization is ultimately defeated, within the movement its practical consequence is that the entourage of the Leader, in case of disagreement with him, will never be very sure of their own opinions, since they believe sincerely that their disagreements do not really matter, that even the maddest device has a fair chance of success if properly organized. The point of their loyalty is not that they believe the Leader is infallible, but that they are convinced that everybody who commands the instruments of violence with the superior methods of totalitarian organization can become infallible. This delusion is greatly strengthened when totalitarian regimes hold the power to demonstrate the relativity of success and failure, and to show how a loss in substance can become a gain in organization. (The fantastic mismanagement of industrial enterprise in Soviet Russia led to the atomization of the working class, and the terrifying mistreatment of civilian prisoners in Eastern territories under Nazi occupation, though it caused a "deplorable loss of labor," "thinking in terms of generations, [was] not to be regretted."[114]) Moreover, the decision regarding success and failure under totalitarian circumstances is very largely a matter of organized and terrorized public opinion. In a totally fictitious world, failures need not be recorded, admitted, and remembered. Factuality itself depends for its continued existence upon the existence of the nontotalitarian world.

[114] Himmler in his speech at Posen, *Nazi Conspiracy*, IV, 558.

CHAPTER THREE:

Totalitarianism in Power

When a movement, international in organization, all-comprehensive in its ideological scope, and global in its political aspiration, seizes power in one country, it obviously puts itself in a paradoxical situation. The socialist movement was spared this crisis, first, because the national question—and that meant the strategical problem involved in the revolution—had been curiously neglected by Marx and Engels, and, secondly, because it faced governmental problems only after the first World War had divested the Second International of its authority over the national members, which everywhere had accepted the primacy of national sentiments over international solidarity as an unalterable fact. In other words, when the time came for the socialist movements to seize power in their respective countries, they had already been transformed into national parties.

This transformation never occurred in the totalitarian, the Bolshevik and the Nazi movements. At the time it seized power the danger to the movement lay in the fact that, on one hand, it might become "ossified" by taking over the state machine and frozen into a form of absolute government,[1] and that, on the other hand, its freedom of movement might be limited by the borders of the territory in which it came to power. To a totalitarian movement, both dangers are equally deadly: a development toward absolutism would put an end to the movement's interior drive, and a development toward nationalism would frustrate its exterior expansion, without which the movement cannot survive. The form of government the two movements developed, or, rather, which almost automatically developed from their double claim to total domination and global rule, is best characterized by Trotsky's slogan of "permanent revolution" although Trotsky's theory was no more than a socialist forecast of a series of revolutions, from the antifeudal bourgeois to the antibourgeois proletarian, which would spread from one country to the other.[2] Only the term itself suggests "per-

[1] The Nazis fully realized that the seizure of power might lead to the establishment of absolutism. "National Socialism, however, has not spearheaded the struggle against liberalism in order to bog down in absolutism and start the game all over again" (Werner Best, *Die deutsche Polizei*, p. 20). The warning expressed here, as in countless other places, is directed against the state's claim to be absolute.

[2] Trotsky's theory, first pronounced in 1905, did of course not differ from the revolutionary strategy of all Leninists in whose eyes "Russia herself was merely the first domain, the first rampart, of international revolution: her interests were to be subordinated to the supernational strategy of militant socialism. For the time being, however, the boundaries of both Russia and victorious socialism were the same" (Isaac Deutscher, *Stalin. A Political Biography*, New York and London, 1949, p. 243).

manency," with all its semi-anarchistic implications, and is, strictly speaking, a misnomer; yet even Lenin was more impressed by the term than by its theoretical content. In the Soviet Union, at any rate, revolutions, in the form of general purges, became a permanent institution of the Stalin regime after 1934.[3] Here, as in other instances, Stalin concentrated his attacks on Trotsky's half-forgotten slogan precisely because he had decided to use this technique.[4] In Nazi Germany, a similar tendency toward permanent revolution was clearly discernible though the Nazis did not have time to realize it to the same extent. Characteristically enough, their "permanent revolution" also started with the liquidation of the party faction which had dared to proclaim openly the "next stage of the revolution"[5]—

[3] The year 1934 is significant because of the new Party statute, announced at the Seventeenth Party Congress, which provided that "periodic . . . purges are to [be] carried out for the systematic cleansing of the Party." (Quoted from A. Avtorkhanov, "Social Differentiation and Contradictions in the Party," *Bulletin of the Institute for the Study of the USSR*, Munich, February, 1956.)—The party purges during the early years of the Russian Revolution have nothing in common with their later totalitarian perversion into an instrument of permanent instability. The first purges were conducted by local control commissions before an open forum to which party and non-party members had free access. They were planned as a democratic control organ against bureaucratic corruption in the party and "were to serve as a substitute for real elections" (Deutscher, *op. cit.*, pp. 233-34).—An excellent short survey of the development of the purges can be found in Avtorkhanov's recent article which also refutes the legend that the murder of Kirov gave rise to the new policy. The general purge had begun before Kirov's death which was no more than a "convenient pretext to give it added drive." In view of the many "inexplicable and mysterious" circumstances surrounding Kirov's murder, one suspects that the "convenient pretext" was carefully planned and executed by Stalin himself. See Khrushchev's "Speech on Stalin," New York *Times*, June 5, 1956.

[4] Deutscher, *op. cit.*, p. 282, describes the first attack on Trotsky's "permanent revolution" and Stalin's counterformulation of "socialism in one country" as an accident of political maneuvering. In 1924, Stalin's "immediate purpose was to descredit Trotsky. . . . Searching in Trotsky's past, the triumvirs came across the theory of 'permanent revolution,' which he had formulated in 1905. . . . It was in the course of that polemic that Stalin arrived at his formula of 'socialism in one country.'"

[5] The liquidation of the Röhm faction in June, 1934, was preceded by a short interval of stabilization. At the beginning of the year, Rudolf Diels, the chief of the political police in Berlin, could report that there were no more illegal ("revolutionary") arrests by the SA and that older arrests of this kind were being investigated. (*Nazi Conspiracy*. U. S. Government. Washington, 1946, V, 205.) In April, 1934, Reichsminister of the Interior Wilhelm Frick, an old member of the Nazi Party, issued a decree to place restrictions upon the exercise of "protective custody" (*ibid.*, III, 555) in consideration of the "stabilization of the national situation." (See *Das Archiv*, April, 1934, p. 31.) This decree, however, was never published (*Nazi Conspiracy*, VII, 1099; II, 259). The political police of Prussia had prepared a special report on the excesses of the SA for Hitler in the year 1933 and suggested the prosecution of the SA leaders named therein.

Hitler solved the situation by killing these SA leaders without legal proceedings *and* discharging all those police officers who had opposed the SA. (See the sworn affidavit of Rudolf Diels, *ibid.*, V, 224.) In this manner he had safeguarded himself completely against all legalization and stabilization. Among the numerous jurists who enthusiastically served the "National Socialist idea" only very few comprehended what was really at stake. In this group belongs primarily Theodor Maunz, whose essay

and precisely because "the Fuehrer and his old guard knew that the real struggle had just begun."[6] Here, instead of the Bolshevik concept of permanent revolution, we find the notion of a racial "selection which can never stand still" thus requiring a constant radicalization of the standards by which the selection, *i.e.*, the extermination of the unfit, is carried out.[7] The point is that both Hitler and Stalin held out promises of stability in order to hide their intention of creating a state of permanent instability.

There could have been no better solution for the perplexities inherent in the co-existence of a government and a movement, of both a totalitarian claim and limited power in a limited territory, of ostensible membership in a comity of nations in which each respects the other's sovereignty and claim to world rule, than this formula stripped of its original content. For the totalitarian ruler is confronted with a dual task which at first appears contradictory to the point of absurdity: he must establish the fictitious world of the movement as a tangible working reality of everyday life, and he must, on the other hand, prevent this new world from developing a new stability; for a stabilization of its laws and institutions would surely liquidate the movement itself and with it the hope for eventual world conquest. The totalitarian ruler must, at any price, prevent normalization from reaching the point where a new way of life could develop—one which might, after a time, lose its bastard qualities and take its place among the widely differing and profoundly contrasting ways of life of the nations of the earth. The moment the revolutionary institutions became a national way of life (that moment when Hitler's claim that Nazism is not an export commodity or Stalin's that socialism can be built in one country, would be more than an attempt to fool the nontotalitarian world), totalitarianism would lose its "total" quality and become subject to the law of the nations, according to which each possesses a specific territory, people, and historical tradition which relates it to other nations—a plurality which *ipso facto* refutes every contention that any specific form of government is absolutely valid.

Practically speaking, the paradox of totalitarianism in power is that the possession of all instruments of governmental power and violence in one country is not an unmixed blessing for a totalitarian movement. Its disregard

Gestalt und Recht der Polizei (Hamburg, 1943) is quoted with approval even by those authors, who, like Paul Werner, belonged to the higher Fuehrer Corps of the SS.

[6] Robert Ley, *Der Weg zur Ordensburg* (undated, about 1936). "Special edition . . . for the Fuehrer Corps of the Party . . . Not for free sale."

[7] Heinrich Himmler, "Die Schutzstaffel," in *Grundlagen, Aufbau und Wirtschaftsordnung des nationalsozialistischen Staates, Nr. 7b*. This constant radicalization of the principle of racial selection can be found in all phases of Nazi policy. Thus, the first to be exterminated were the full Jews, to be followed by those who were half-Jewish and one-quarter Jewish; or first the insane, to be followed by the incurably sick and, eventually, by all families in which there were any "incurably sick." The "selection which can never stand still" did not stop before the SS itself, either. A Fuehrer decree dated May 19, 1943, ordered that all men who were bound to foreigners by family ties, marriage or friendship were to be eliminated from state, party, Wehrmacht and economy; this affected 1,200 SS leaders (see Hoover Library Archives, Himmler File, Folder 330).

for facts, its strict adherence to the rules of a fictitious world, becomes steadily more difficult to maintain, yet remains as essential as it was before. Power means a direct confrontation with reality, and totalitarianism in power is constantly concerned with overcoming this challenge. Propaganda and organization no longer suffice to assert that the impossible is possible, that the incredible is true, that an insane consistency rules the world; the chief psychological support of totalitarian fiction—the active resentment of the status quo, which the masses refused to accept as the only possible world—is no longer there; every bit of factual information that leaks through the iron curtain, set up against the ever-threatening flood of reality from the other, nontotalitarian side, is a greater menace to totalitarian domination than counterpropaganda has been to totalitarian movements.

The struggle for total domination of the total population of the earth, the elimination of every competing nontotalitarian reality, is inherent in the totalitarian regimes themselves; if they do not pursue global rule as their ultimate goal, they are only too likely to lose whatever power they have already seized. Even a single individual can be absolutely and reliably dominated only under global totalitarian conditions. Ascendancy to power therefore means primarily the establishment of official and officially recognized headquarters (or branches in the case of satellite countries) for the movement and the acquisition of a kind of laboratory in which to carry out the experiment with or rather against reality, the experiment in organizing a people for ultimate purposes which disregard individuality as well as nationality, under conditions which are admittedly not perfect but are sufficient for important partial results. Totalitarianism in power uses the state administration for its long-range goal of world conquest and for the direction of the branches of the movement; it establishes the secret police as the executors and guardians of its domestic experiment in constantly transforming reality into fiction; and it finally erects concentration camps as special laboratories to carry through its experiment in total domination.

I: *The So-called Totalitarian State*

HISTORY TEACHES THAT rise to power and responsibility affects deeply the nature of revolutionary parties. Experience and common sense were perfectly justified in expecting that totalitarianism in power would gradually lose its revolutionary momentum and utopian character, that the everyday business of government and the possession of real power would moderate the pre-power claims of the movements and gradually destroy the fictitious world of their organizations. It seems, after all, to be in the very nature of things, personal or public, that extreme demands and goals are checked by objective conditions; and reality, taken as a whole, is only to a very small extent determined by the inclination toward fiction of a mass society of atomized individuals.

Many of the errors of the nontotalitarian world in its diplomatic dealings with totalitarian governments (the most conspicuous ones being confidence in the Munich pact with Hitler and the Yalta agreements with Stalin) can clearly be traced to an experience and a common sense which suddenly proved to have lost its grasp on reality. Contrary to all expectations, important concessions and greatly heightened international prestige did not help to reintegrate the totalitarian countries into the comity of nations or induce them to abandon their lying complaint that the whole world had solidly lined up against them. And far from preventing this, diplomatic victories clearly precipitated their recourse to the instruments of violence and resulted in all instances in increased hostility against the powers that had shown themselves willing to compromise.

These disappointments suffered by statesmen and diplomats find their parallel in the earlier disillusionment of benevolent observers and sympathizers with the new revolutionary governments. What they had looked forward to was the establishment of new institutions and the creation of a new code of law which, no matter how revolutionary in content, would lead to a stabilization of conditions and thus check the momentum of the totalitarian movements at least in the countries where they had seized power. What happened instead was that terror increased both in Soviet Russia and Nazi Germany in inverse ratio to the existence of internal political opposition, so that it looked as though political opposition had not been the pretext of terror (as liberal accusers of the regime were wont to assert) but the last impediment to its full fury.[8]

Even more disturbing was the handling of the constitutional question by the totalitarian regimes. In the early years of their power the Nazis let loose an avalanche of laws and decrees, but they never bothered to abolish offi-

[8] It is common knowledge that in Russia "the repression of socialists and anarchists had grown in severity in the same ratio as the country became pacified" (Anton Ciliga, *The Russian Enigma*, London, 1940, p. 244). Deutscher, *op. cit.*, p. 218, thinks that the reason for the vanishing of the "libertarian spirit of the revolution" at the moment of victory could be found in a changed attitude of the peasants: they turned against Bolshevism "the more resolutely the more they became confident that the power of the landlords and the White generals had been broken." This explanation seems rather weak in view of the dimensions which terror was to assume after 1930. It also fails to take into account that full terror did not break loose in the twenties but in the thirties, when the opposition of the peasant classes was no longer an active factor in the situation.—Khrushchev, too (*op. cit.*), notes that "extreme repressive measures were not used" against the opposition during the fight against the Trotskyites and the Bukharinites, but that "the repression against them began" much later after they had long been defeated.

Terror by the Nazi regime reached its peak during the war, when the German nation was actually "united." Its preparation goes back to 1936 when all organized interior resistance had vanished and Himmler proposed an expansion of the concentration camps. Characteristic of this spirit of oppression regardless of resistance is Himmler's speech at Kharkov before the SS leaders in 1943: "We have only one task, . . . to carry on the racial struggle without mercy. . . . We will never let that excellent weapon, the dread and terrible reputation which preceded us in the battles for Kharkov, fade, but will constantly add new meaning to it" (*Nazi Conspiracy*, IV, 572 ff.).

cially the Weimar constitution; they even left the civil services more or less intact—a fact which induced many native and foreign observers to hope for restraint of the party and for rapid normalization of the new regime. But when with the issuance of the Nuremberg Laws this development had come to an end, it turned out that the Nazis themselves showed no concern whatsoever about their own legislation. Rather, there was "only the constant going ahead on the road toward ever-new fields," so that finally the "purpose and scope of the secret state police" as well as of all other state or party institutions created by the Nazis could "in no manner be covered by the laws and regulations issued for them."[9] In practice, this permanent state of lawlessness found expression in the fact that "a number of valid regulations [were] no longer made public."[10] Theoretically, it corresponded to Hitler's dictum that "the total state must not know any difference between law and ethics";[11] because if it assumed that the valid law is identical with the ethics common to all and springing from their consciences, then there is indeed no further necessity for public decrees. The Soviet Union, where the prerevolutionary civil services had been exterminated in the revolution and the regime had paid scant attention to constitutional questions during the period of revolutionary change, even went to the trouble of issuing an entirely new and very elaborate constitution in 1936 ("a veil of liberal phrases and premises over the guillotine in the background"[12]), an event which was hailed in Russia and abroad as the conclusion of the revolutionary period. Yet the publication of the constitution turned out to be the beginning of the gigantic superpurge which in nearly two years liquidated the existing administration and erased all traces of normal life and economic recovery which had developed in the four years after the liquidation of kulaks and

[9] See Theodor Maunz, *op. cit.*, pp. 5 and 49.—How little the Nazis thought of the laws and regulations they themselves had issued, and which were regularly published by W. Hoche under the title of *Die Gesetzgebung des Kabinetts Hitler* (Berlin, 1933 ff.), may be gathered from a random remark made by one of their constitutional jurists. He felt that in spite of the absence of a comprehensive new legal order there nevertheless had occurred a "comprehensive reform" (see Ernst R. Huber, "Die deutsche Polizei," in *Zeitschrift für die gesamte Staatswissenschaft*, Band 101, 1940/1, p. 273 ff.).

[10] Maunz, *op. cit.*, p. 49. To my knowledge, Maunz is the only one among Nazi authors who has mentioned this circumstance and sufficiently emphasized it. Only by going through the five volumes of *Verfügungen, Anordnungen, Bekanntgaben*, which were collected and printed during the war by the party chancellery on instructions of Martin Bormann, is it possible to obtain an insight into this secret legislation by which Germany in fact was governed. According to the preface, the volumes were "meant solely for internal party work and to be treated as confidential." Four of these evidently very rare volumes, compared to which the Hoche collection of the legislation of Hitler's cabinet is merely a façade, are in the Hoover Library.

[11] This was the Fuehrer's "warning" to the jurists in 1933, quoted by Hans Frank, *Nationalsozialistische Leitsätze für ein neues deutsches Strafrecht*, Zweiter Teil, 1936, p. 8.

[12] Deutscher, *op. cit.*, p. 381.—There were earlier attempts at establishing a constitution, in 1918 and 1924. The constitutional reform in 1944 under which some of the Soviet Republics were to have their own foreign representatives and their own armies, was a tactical maneuver designed to assure the Soviet Union of some additional votes in the United Nations.

enforced collectivization of the rural population.[13] From then on, the constitution of 1936 played exactly the same role the Weimar constitution played under the Nazi regime: it was completely disregarded but never abolished; the only difference was that Stalin could afford one more absurdity—with the exception of Vishinsky, all those who had drafted the never-repudiated constitution were executed as traitors.

What strikes the observer of the totalitarian state is certainly not its monolithic structure. On the contrary, all serious students of the subject agree at least on the co-existence (or the conflict) of a dual authority, the party and the state. Many, moreover, have stressed the peculiar "shapelessness" of the totalitarian government.[14] Thomas Masaryk saw early that "the so-called Bolshevik system has never been anything but a complete absence of system";[15] and it is perfectly true that "even an expert would be driven mad if he tried to unravel the relationships between Party and State" in the Third Reich.[16] It has also been frequently observed that the relationship between the two sources of authority, between state and party, is one of ostensible and real authority, so that the government machine is usually pictured as the powerless façade which hides and protects the real power of the party.[17]

[13] See Deutscher, *op. cit.*, p. 375.—Upon close reading of Stalin's speech concerning the constitution (his report to the Extraordinary Eighth Soviet Congress of November 25, 1936) it becomes evident that it was never meant to be definitive. Stalin stated explicitly: "This is the framework of our constitution at the given historical moment. Thus the draft of the new constitution represents the sum total of the road already traveled, the sum total of achievements already existing." In other words, the constitution was already dated the moment it was announced, and was merely of historical interest. That this is not just an arbitrary interpretation is proved by Molotov, who in his speech about the constitution picks up Stalin's theme and underlines the provisional nature of the whole matter: "We have realized only the first, the lower phase, of Communism. Even this first phase of Communism, Socialism, is by no means completed; only its skeletal structure has been erected" (see *Die Verfassung des Sozialistischen Staates der Arbeiter und Bauern*, Editions Prométhée, Strasbourg, 1937, pp. 42 and 84).

[14] "German constitutional life is thus characterized by its utter shapelessness, in contrast to Italy" (Franz Neumann, *Behemoth*, 1942, Appendix, p. 521).

[15] Quoted from Boris Souvarine, *Stalin: A Critical Survey of Bolshevism*, New York 1939, p. 695.

[16] Stephen H. Roberts, *The House that Hitler Built*, London, 1939, p. 72.

[17] Justice Robert H. Jackson, in his opening speech at the Nuremberg Trials, based his description of the political structure of Nazi Germany consistently on the co-existence of "two governments in Germany—the real and the ostensible. The forms of the German Republic were maintained for a time and it was the outward and visible government. But the real authority in the State was outside of and above the law and rested in the Leadership Corps of the Nazi Party" (*Nazi Conspiracy*, I, 125). See also the distinction of Roberts, *op. cit.*, p. 101, between the party and a shadow state: "Hitler obviously leans toward increasing the duplication of functions."

Students of Nazi Germany seem agreed that the state had only ostensible authority. For the only exception, see Ernst Fraenkel, *The Dual State*, New York and London, 1941, who claims the co-existence of a "normative and a prerogative state" living in constant friction as "competitive and not complementary parts of the German Reich." According to Fraenkel, the normative state was maintained by the Nazis for the protection of the capitalist order and private property and had full authority in all economic matters, while the prerogative state of the party ruled supreme in all political matters.

All levels of the administrative machine in the Third Reich were subject to a curious duplication of offices. With a fantastic thoroughness, the Nazis made sure that every function of the state administration would be duplicated by some party organ:[18] the Weimar division of Germany into states and provinces was duplicated by the Nazi division into *Gaue* whose borderlines, however, did not coincide, so that every given locality belonged, even geographically, to two altogether different administrative units.[19] Nor was the duplication of functions abandoned when, after 1933, outstanding Nazis occupied the official ministries of the state; when Frick, for instance, became Minister of the Interior or Guerthner Minister of Justice. These old and trusted party members, once they had embarked upon official nonparty careers, lost their power and became as uninfluential as other civil servants. Both came under the factual authority of Himmler, the rising chief of the police, who normally would have been subordinate to the Minister of the Interior.[20] Better known abroad has been the fate of the old German Foreign Affairs Office in the Wilhelmstrasse. The Nazis left its personnel nearly untouched and of course never abolished it; yet at the same time they maintained the prepower Foreign Affairs Bureau of the Party, headed by Rosenberg;[21] and since this office had specialized in maintaining contacts with Fascist organizations in Eastern Europe and the Balkans, they set up another

[18] "For those positions of state power which the National Socialists could not occupy with their own people, they created corresponding 'shadow offices' in their own party organization, in this way setting up a second state beside the state . . ." (Konrad Heiden, *Der Fuehrer: Hitler's Rise to Power*, Boston, 1944, p. 616).

[19] O. C. Giles, *The Gestapo*, Oxford Pamphlets on World Affairs, No. 36, 1940, describes the constant overlapping of party and state departments.

[20] Characteristic is a memo of Minister of the Interior Frick, who resented the fact that Himmler, the leader of the SS, should have superior power. See *Nazi Conspiracy*, III, 547.—Noteworthy in this respect also are Rosenberg's notes about a discussion with Hitler in 1942: Rosenberg had never before the war held a state position but belonged to the intimate circle around Hitler. Now that he had become Reichsminister for the Eastern Occupied Territories, he was constantly confronted with "direct actions" of other plenipotentiaries (chiefly SS-men) who overlooked him because he now belonged to the ostensible apparatus of the state. See *ibid.*, IV, 65 ff. The same happened to Hans Frank, Governor General of Poland. There were only two cases in which the attainment of ministerial rank did not entail any loss of power and prestige: that of Minister of Propaganda Goebbels, and of Minister of the Interior Himmler. As regards Himmler, we possess a memorandum, presumably from the year 1935, which illustrates the systematic singlemindedness of the Nazis in regulating the relations between party and state. This memorandum, which apparently originated in Hitler's immediate entourage and was found among the correspondence of the *Reichsadjudantur* of the Fuehrer and the Gestapo, contains a warning against making Himmler state secretary of the Ministry of the Interior because in that case he could "no longer be a political leader" and "would be alienated from the party." Here, too, we find mention of the technical principle regulating the relations between party and state: "A *Reichsleiter* [a high party functionary] must not be subordinated to a *Reichsminister* [a high state functionary]." (The undated, unsigned memorandum, entitled *Die geheime Staatspolizei*, can be found in the archives of the Hoover Library, File P. Wiedemann.)

[21] See the "Brief Report on Activities of Rosenberg's Foreign Affairs Bureau of the Party from 1933 to 1943," *ibid.*, III, 27 ff.

organ to compete with the office in the Wilhelmstrasse, the so-called Ribbentrop Bureau, which handled foreign affairs in the West, and survived the departure of its chief as Ambassador to England, that is, his incorporation into the official apparatus of the Wilhelmstrasse. Finally, in addition to these party institutions, the Foreign Office received another duplication in the form of an SS Office, which was responsible "for negotiations with all racially Germanic groups in Denmark, Norway, Belgium and the Netherlands."[22] These examples prove that for the Nazis the duplication of offices was a matter of principle and not just an expedient for providing jobs for party members.

The same division between a real and an ostensible government developed from very different beginnings in Soviet Russia.[23] The ostensible government originally sprang from the All-Russian Soviet Congress, which during the civil war lost its influence and power to the Bolshevik party. This process started when the Red Army was made autonomous and the secret political police re-established as an organ of the party, and not of the Soviet Congress;[24] it was completed in 1923, during the first year of Stalin's General Secretaryship.[25] From then on, the Soviets became the shadow government in whose midst, through cells formed by Bolshevik party members, functioned the representatives of real power who were appointed and responsible to the Central Committee in Moscow. The crucial point in the later development was not the conquest of the Soviets by the party, but the fact that "although it would have presented no difficulties, the Bolsheviks did not abolish the Soviets and used them as the decorative outward symbol of their authority."[26]

The co-existence of an ostensible and a real government therefore was partly the outcome of the revolution itself and preceded Stalin's totalitarian dictatorship. Yet while the Nazis simply retained the existing administration and deprived it of all power, Stalin had to revive his shadow government, which in the early thirties had lost all its functions and was half forgotten

[22] Based on a Fuehrer decree of August 12, 1942. See *Verfügungen, Anordnungen, Bekanntgaben, op. cit.*, Nr. A 54/42.

[23] "Behind the ostensible government was a real government," which Victor Kravchenko (*I Chose Freedom: The Personal Life of a Soviet Official*, New York, 1946, p. 111) saw in the "secret police system."

[24] See Arthur Rosenberg, *A History of Bolshevism*, London, 1934, chapter vi. "There are in reality two political edifices in Russia that rise parallel to one another: the shadow government of the Soviets and the *de facto* government of the Bolshevik Party."

[25] Deutscher, *op. cit.*, pp. 255-256, sums up Stalin's report to the Twelfth Party Congress about the work of the personnel department during his first year in the General Secretariat: "The year before only 27 per cent of the regional leaders of the trade unions were members of the party. At present 57 per cent of them were Communists. The percentage of Communists in the management of co-operatives had risen from 5 to 50 per cent; and in the commanding staffs of the armed forces from 16 to 24. The same happened in all other institutions which Stalin described as the 'transmission belts' connecting the party with the people."

[26] Arthur Rosenberg, *op. cit., loc. cit.*

in Russia; he introduced the Soviet constitution as the symbol of the existence as well as the powerlessness of the Soviets. (None of its paragraphs ever had the slightest practical significance for life and jurisdiction in Russia.) The ostensible Russian government, utterly lacking the glamour of tradition so necessary for a façade, apparently needed the sacred halo of written law. The totalitarian defiance of law and legality (which "in spite of the greatest changes . . . still [remain] the expression of a permanently desired order")[27] found in the written Soviet constitution, as in the never-repudiated Weimar constitution, a permanent background for its own lawlessness, the permanent challenge to the nontotalitarian world and its standards whose helplessness and impotence could be demonstrated daily.[28]

Duplication of offices and division of authority, the co-existence of real and ostensible power, are sufficient to create confusion but not to explain the "shapelessness" of the whole structure. One should not forget that only a building can have a structure, but that a movement—if the word is to be taken as seriously and as literally as the Nazis meant it—can have only a direction, and that any form of legal or governmental structure can be only a handicap to a movement which is being propelled with increasing speed in a certain direction. Even in the prepower stage the totalitarian movements represented those masses that were no longer willing to live in any kind of structure, regardless of its nature; masses that had started to move in order to flood the legal and geographical borders securely determined by the government. Therefore, judged by our conceptions of government and state structure, these movements, so long as they find themselves physically still limited to a specific territory, necessarily must try to destroy all structure, and for this willful destruction a mere duplication of all offices into party and state institutions would not be sufficient. Since duplication involves a relationship between the façade of the state and the inner core of the party, it, too, would eventually result in some kind of structure, where the relationship between party and state would automatically end in a legal regulation which restricts and stabilizes their respective authority.[29]

[27] Maunz, *op. cit.*, p. 12.

[28] The jurist and Obersturmbannfuehrer, Professor R. Hoehn, has expressed this in the following words: "And there was still another thing which foreigners, but Germans, too, had to get used to: namely, that the task of the secret state police . . . was taken over by a community of persons who originated within the movement, and continue to be rooted in it. That the term state police actually makes no allowance for this fact shall be mentioned here only in passing" (*Grundfragen der deutschen Polizei*, Report on the Constitutive Session of the Committee on Police Law of the Academy for German Law, October 11, 1936. Hamburg, 1937, with contributions by Frank, Himmler and Hoehn).

[29] For example, such an attempt to circumscribe the separate responsibilities and to counter the "anarchy of authority" was made by Hans Frank in *Recht und Verwaltung*, 1939, and again in an address titled *Technik des Staates*, in 1941. He expressed the opinion that "legal guarantees" were not the "prerogative of liberal systems of government" and that the administration should continue to be governed, as before, by the laws of the Reich, which now were inspired and guided by the program of the National Socialist party. It was precisely because he wanted to prevent such a new legal order at any price that Hitler never acknowledged the program of the Nazi

As a matter of fact, duplication of offices, seemingly the result of the party-state problem in all one-party dictatorships, is only the most conspicuous sign of a more complicated phenomenon that is better defined as multiplication of offices than duplication. The Nazis were not content to establish *Gaue* in addition to the old provinces, but also introduced a great many other geographical divisions in accordance with the different party organizations: the territorial units of the SA were neither co-extensive with the *Gaue* nor with the provinces; they differed, moreover, from those of the SS and none of them corresponded to the zones dividing the Hitler Youth.[30] To this geographical confusion must be added the fact that the original relationship between real and ostensible power repeated itself throughout, albeit in an ever-changing way. The inhabitant of Hitler's Third Reich lived not only under the simultaneous and often conflicting authorities of competing powers, such as the civil services, the party, the SA, and the SS; he could never be sure and was never explicitly told whose authority he was supposed to place above all others. He had to develop a kind of sixth sense to know at a given moment whom to obey and whom to disregard.

Those, on the other hand, who had to execute the orders which the leadership, in the interest of the movement, regarded as genuinely necessary—in contradistinction to governmental measures, such orders were of course entrusted only to the party's elite formations—were not much better off. Mostly such orders were "intentionally vague, and given in the expectation that their recipient would recognize the intent of the order giver, and act accordingly";[31] for the elite formations were by no means merely obli-

party. Of party members who made such proposals he was wont to speak with contempt, describing them as "eternally tied to the past," as persons "who are unable to leap across their own shadow" (Felix Kersten, *Totenkopf und Treue*, Hamburg).

[30] "The 32 *Gaue* . . . do not coincide with the administrative or military regions, or even the 21 divisions of the SA, or the 10 regions of the SS, or the 23 zones of the Hitler Youth. . . . Such discrepancies are the more remarkable because there is no reason for them" (Roberts, *op. cit.*, p. 98).

[31] Nuremberg Documents, PS 3063 in the Centre de Documentation Juive in Paris. The document is a report of the supreme party court about "events and party court proceedings connected with the antisemitic demonstrations of November 9, 1938." On the basis of investigations by the police and the office of the Attorney General the supreme court came to the conclusion that "the verbal instructions of the Reichspropagandaleiter must have been understood by all party leaders to mean that, to the outside, the party did not wish to appear as the instigator of the demonstration, but in reality was to organize and carry it through. . . . The re-examination of the command echelons has shown . . . that the active National Socialist molded in the prepower struggle [*Kampfzeit*] takes it for granted that actions in which the party does not wish to appear in the role of organizer are not ordered with unequivocal clarity and down to the last detail. Hence he is accustomed to understand that an order may mean more than its verbal content, just as it has more or less become routine with the order giver, in the interests of the party . . . not to say everything and only to intimate what he wants to achieve by the order. . . . Thus, the . . . orders—for instance, not the Jew Grünspan but all Jewry must be blamed for the death of Party Comrade vom Rath, . . . pistols should be brought along, . . . every SA-man now ought to know what he had to do—were understood by a number of subleaders to mean that Jewish blood would now have to be shed for the blood of

gated to obey the orders of the Fuehrer (this was mandatory for all existing organizations anyway), but "to execute the *will* of the leadership."[32] And, as can be gathered from the lengthy proceedings concerning "excesses" before the party courts, this was by no means one and the same thing. The only difference was that the elite formations, thanks to their special indoctrination for such purposes, had been trained to understand that certain "hints meant more than their mere verbal contents."[33]

Technically speaking, the movement within the apparatus of totalitarian domination derives its mobility from the fact that the leadership constantly shifts the actual center of power, often to other organizations, but without dissolving or even publicly exposing the groups that have thus been deprived of their power. In the early period of the Nazi regime, immediately after the Reichstag fire, the SA was the real authority and the party the ostensible one; power then shifted from the SA to the SS and finally from the SS to the Security Service.[34] The point is that none of the organs of power was ever deprived of its right to pretend that it embodied the will of the Leader.[35] But not only was the will of the Leader so unstable that compared with it the whims of Oriental despots are a shining example of steadfastness; the consistent and ever-changing division between real secret authority and ostensible open representation made the actual seat of power a mystery by definition, and this to such an extent that the members of the ruling clique themselves could never be absolutely sure of their own position in the secret power hierarchy. Alfred Rosenberg, for instance, despite his long career in the party and his impressive accumulation of ostensible power and offices in the party hierarchy, still talked about the creation of a series of Eastern European States

Party Comrade vom Rath. . . ." Particularly significant is the end of the report, in which the supreme party court quite openly takes exception to these methods: "It is another question whether, in the interest of discipline, the order that is intentionally vague, and given in the expectation that its recipient will recognize the intent of the order giver and act accordingly, must not be relegated to the past." Here, too, there were persons who, in Hitler's words, "were unable to leap across their own shadow" and insisted upon legislative measures, because they did not understand that not the order but the *will* of the Fuehrer was the supreme law. Here, the difference between the mentality of the elite formations and the party agencies is particularly clear.

[32] Best (*op. cit.*) puts it this way: "So long as the police execute this will of the leadership, they are acting within the law; if the will of the leadership is transgressed, then not the police, but a member of the police, has committed a violation."

[33] See footnote 31.

[34] In 1933, after the Reichstag fire, "SA leaders were more powerful than Gauleiter. They also refused obedience to Göring." See Rudolf Diels's sworn affidavit in *Nazi Conspiracy*, V, 224; Diels was chief of the political police under Göring.

[35] The SA obviously resented its loss of rank and power in the Nazi hierarchy and tried desperately to keep up appearances. In their magazines—*Der SA-Mann, Das Archiv, etc.*—many indications, veiled and unveiled, of this impotent rivalry with the SS can be found. More interesting is that Hitler still in 1936, when the SA had already lost its power, would assure them in a speech: "All that you are, you are through me; and all that I am, I am through you alone." See Ernst Bayer, *Die SA*, Berlin, 1938. Translation quoted from *Nazi Conspiracy*, IV, 782.

as a security wall against Moscow at a time when those invested with real power had already decided that no state structure would succeed the defeat of the Soviet Union and that the population of the Eastern occupied territories had become definitely stateless and could therefore be exterminated.[36] In other words, since knowledge of whom to obey and a comparatively permanent settlement of hierarchy would introduce an element of stability which is essentially absent from totalitarian rule, the Nazis constantly disavowed real authority whenever it had come into the open and created new instances of government compared with which the former became a shadow government—a game which obviously could go indefinitely. One of the most important technical differences between the Soviet and the National Socialist system is that Stalin, whenever he shifted the power emphasis within his own movement from one apparatus to another, had the tendency to liquidate the apparatus together with its staff, while Hitler, in spite of his contemptuous comments on people who "are unable to leap across their own shadows,"[37] was perfectly willing to continue using these shadows even though in another function.

The multiplication of offices was extremely useful for the constant shifting of power; the longer, moreover, a totalitarian regime stays in power, the greater becomes the number of offices and the possibility of jobs exclusively dependent upon the movement, since no office is abolished when its authority is liquidated. The Nazi regime started this multiplication with an initial co-ordination of all existing associations, societies, and institutions. The interesting thing in this nation-wide manipulation was that co-ordination did not signify incorporation into the already existing respective party organizations. The result was that up to the end of the regime, there were not one, but two National Socialist student organizations, two Nazi women's organizations, two Nazi organizations for university professors, lawyers, physicians, and so forth.[38] It was by no means sure, however, that in all cases the original party organization would be more powerful than its co-

[36] Compare Rosenberg's speech of June, 1941: "I believe that our political task will consist of . . . organizing these peoples in certain types of political bodies . . . and building them up against Moscow" with the "Undated Memorandum for the Administration in the Occupied Eastern Territories": "With the dissolution of the USSR after her defeat, no body politic is left in the Eastern territories and therefore . . . no citizenship for their population" (*Trial of the Major War Criminals*, Nuremberg, 1947, XXVI, p. 616 and 604, respectively).

[37] *Hitlers Tischgespräche*, Bonn, 1951, p. 213. Usually, Hitler meant some high-ranking Nazi functionaries who had their reservations about murdering all those without compunctions, whom he described as "human junk [*Gesox*]" (see p. 248 ff. and *passim*).

[38] For the variety of overlapping party organizations, see *Rang-und Organisationsliste der NSDAP*, Stuttgart, 1947, and *Nazi Conspiracy*, I, 178, which distinguishes four main categories: 1. *Gliederungen der NSDAP*, which had existed before its rise to power; 2. *Angeschlossene Verbände der NSDAP*, which comprise those societies which had been co-ordinated; 3. *Betreute Organisationen der NSDAP;* and 4. *Weitere nationalsozialistische Organisationen*. In nearly every category, one finds a different students', women's, teachers', and workers' organization.

ordinated counterpart.[39] Nor could anybody predict with any assurance which party organ would rise in the ranks of the internal party hierarchy.[40]

A classical instance of this planned shapelessness occurred in the organization of scientific antisemitism. In 1933, an institute for study of the Jewish question (Institut zur Erforschung der Judenfrage) was founded in Munich which, since the Jewish question presumably had determined the whole of German history, quickly enlarged into a research institute for modern German history. Headed by the well-known historian Walter Frank, it transformed the traditional universities into seats of ostensible learning or façades. In 1940, another institute for the study of the Jewish question was founded in Frankfurt, headed by Alfred Rosenberg, whose standing as a party member was considerably higher. The Munich institute consequently was relegated to a shadowy existence; the Frankfurt, not the Munich institution was supposed to receive the treasures from looted European Jewish collections and become the seat of a comprehensive library on Judaism. Yet, when these collections actually arrived in Germany a few years later, their most precious parts went not to Frankfurt, but to Berlin, where they were received by Himmler's special Gestapo department for the liquidation (not merely the study) of the Jewish question, which was headed by Eichmann. None of the older institutions was ever abolished, so that in 1944 the situation was this: behind the façade of the universities' history departments stood threateningly the more real power of the Munich institute, behind which rose Rosenberg's institute in Frankfurt, and only behind these three façades, hidden and protected by them, lay the real center of authority, the *Reichssicherheitshauptamt*, a special division of the Gestapo.

The façade of the Soviet government, despite its written constitution, is even less impressive, erected even more exclusively for foreign observation than the state administration which the Nazis inherited and retained from the Weimar Republic. Lacking the Nazis' original accumulation of offices in the period of co-ordination, the Soviet regime relies even more on constant creation of new offices to put the former centers of power in the shadow. The gigantic increase of the bureaucratic apparatus, inherent in this method, is checked by repeated liquidation through purges. Nevertheless, in Russia, too, we can distinguish at least three strictly separate organizations: the Soviet or state apparatus, the party apparatus, and the NKVD apparatus, each of which has its own independent department of economy, a political

[39] The gigantic organization for public works, headed by Todt and later led by Albert Speer, was created by Hitler outside of all party hierarchies and affiliations. This organization might have been used against the authority of party or even police organizations. It is noteworthy that Speer could risk pointing out to Hitler (during a conference in 1942) the impossibility of organizing production under Himmler's regime, and even demand jurisdiction over slave labor and concentration camps. See *Nazi Conspiracy*, I, 916-917.

[40] Such an innocuous and unimportant society, for instance, as the NSKK (the National Socialist corps of automobilists founded in 1930) was suddenly elevated, in 1933, to the status of an elite formation, sharing with the SA and the SS the privilege of an independent affiliated unit of the party. Nothing followed this rise in the ranks of the Nazi hierarchy; retrospectively, it looks like an idle threat to the SA and SS.

department, a ministry of education and culture, a military department, etc.[41]

In Russia, the ostensible power of the party bureaucracy as against the real power of the secret police corresponds to the original duplication of party and state as known in Nazi Germany, and the multiplication becomes evident only in the secret police itself, with its extremely complicated, widely ramified network of agents, in which one department is always assigned to supervising and spying on another. Every enterprise in the Soviet Union has its special department of the secret police, which spies on party members and ordinary personnel alike. Co-existent with this department is another police division of the party itself, which again watches everybody, including the agents of the NKVD, and whose members are not known to the rival body. Added to these two espionage organizations must be the unions in the factories, which must see to it that the workers fulfill their prescribed quotas. Far more important than these apparatuses, however, is "the special department" of the NKVD which represents "an NKVD within the NKVD," *i.e.*, a secret police within the secret police.[42] All reports of these competing police agencies ultimately end up in the Moscow Central Committee and the Politburo. Here it is decided which of the reports is decisive and which of the police divisions shall be entitled to carry out the respective police measures. Neither the average inhabitant of the country nor any one of the police departments knows, of course, what decision will be made; today it may be the special division of the NKVD, tomorrow the party's network of agents; the day after, it may be the local committees or one of the regional bodies. Among all these departments there exists no legally rooted hierarchy of power or authority; the only certainty is that eventually one of them will be chosen to embody "the will of the leadership."

The only rule of which everybody in a totalitarian state may be sure is that the more visible government agencies are, the less power they carry, and the less is known of the existence of an institution, the more powerful it will ultimately turn out to be. According to this rule, the Soviets, recognized by a written constitution as the highest authority of the state, have less power than the Bolshevik party; the Bolshevik party, which recruits its members openly and is recognized as the ruling class, has less power than the secret police. Real power begins where secrecy begins. In this respect the Nazi and the Bolshevik states were very much alike; their difference lay chiefly in the monopolization and centralization of secret police services in Himmler on one hand, and the maze of apparently unrelated and unconnected police activities in Russia on the other.

[41] F. Beck and W. Godin, *Russian Purge and the Extraction of Confession*, 1951, p. 153.

[42] *Ibid.*, p. 159 ff.—According to other reports, there are different examples of the staggering multiplication of the Soviet police apparatus, primarily the local and regional associations of the NKVD, which work independently of one another and which have their counterparts in the local and regional networks of party agents. It is in the nature of things that we know considerably less about Russian conditions than we do about those in Nazi Germany, especially as far as organizational details are concerned.

If we consider the totalitarian state solely as an instrument of power and leave aside questions of administrative efficiency, industrial capacity, and economic productivity, then its shapelessness turns out to be an ideally suited instrument for the realization of the so-called Leader principle. A continuous competition between offices, whose functions not only overlap but which are charged with identical tasks,[43] gives opposition or sabotage almost no chance to become effective; a swift change of emphasis which relegates one office to the shadow and elevates another to authority can solve all problems without anybody's becoming aware of the change or of the fact that opposition had existed, the additional advantage of the system being that the opposing office is likely never to learn of its defeat, since it is either not abolished at all (as in the case of the Nazi regime) or it is liquidated much later and without any apparent connection with the specific matter. This can be done all the more easily since nobody, except those few initiated, knows the exact relationship between the authorities. Only once in a while does the nontotalitarian world catch a glimpse of these conditions, as when a high official abroad confesses that an obscure clerk in the Embassy had been his immediate superior. In retrospect it is often possible to determine why such a sudden loss of power occurred, or, rather, that it occurred at all. For instance, it is not hard to understand today why at the outbreak of war people like Alfred Rosenberg or Hans Frank were removed to state positions and thus eliminated from the real center of power, namely, the Fuehrer's inner circle.[44] The important thing is that they not only did not know the reasons for these moves, but presumably did not even suspect that such apparently exalted positions as Governor General of Poland or Reichsminister for all Eastern territories did not signify the climax but the end of their National Socialist careers.

The Leader principle does not establish a hierarchy in the totalitarian state any more than it does in the totalitarian movement; authority is not filtered down from the top through all intervening layers to the bottom of the body politic as is the case in authoritarian regimes. The factual reason is that there is no hierarchy without authority and that, in spite of the numerous misunderstandings concerning the so-called "authoritarian personality," the principle of authority is in all important respects diametrically opposed to that of totalitarian domination. Quite apart from its origin

[43] According to the testimony of one of his former employees (*Nazi Conspiracy*, VI, 461), it was "a specialty of Himmler to give one task to two different people."

[44] In the aforementioned address (see footnote 29) Hans Frank showed that at some point he wanted to stabilize the movement, and his numerous complaints as Governor General of Poland testify to a total lack of understanding of the deliberately anti-utilitarian tendencies of Nazi policy. He cannot understand why the subjected peoples are not exploited but exterminated. Rosenberg, in the eyes of Hitler, was racially unreliable because he meant to establish satellite states in the conquered Eastern territories and did not understand that Hitler's population policy aimed at depopulating these territories.

in Roman history, authority, no matter in what form, always is meant to restrict or limit freedom, but never to abolish it. Totalitarian domination, however, aims at abolishing freedom, even at eliminating human spontaneity in general, and by no means at a restriction of freedom no matter how tyrannical. Technically, this absence of any authority or hierarchy in the totalitarian system is shown by the fact that between the supreme power (the Fuehrer) and the ruled there are no reliable intervening levels, each of which would receive its due share of authority and obedience. The will of the Fuehrer can be embodied everywhere and at all times, and he himself is not tied to any hierarchy, not even the one he might have established himself. Therefore, it is not accurate to say that the movement, after its seizure of power, founds a multiplicity of principalities in whose realm each little leader is free to do as he pleases and to imitate the big leader at the top.[45] The Nazi claim that "the party is the order of fuehrers"[46] was an ordinary lie. Just as the infinite multiplication of offices and confusion of authority leads to a state of affairs in which every citizen feels himself directly confronted with the will of the Leader, who arbitrarily chooses the executing organ of his decisions, so the one and a half million "fuehrers" throughout the Third Reich[47] knew very well that their authority derived directly from Hitler without the intervening levels of a functioning hierarchy.[48] The direct dependence was real and the intervening hierarchy, certainly of social importance, was an ostensible, spurious imitation of an authoritarian state.

The Leader's absolute monopoly of power and authority is most conspicuous in the relationship between him and his chief of police, who in a totalitarian country occupies the most powerful public position. Yet despite the enormous material and organizational power at his disposal as the head of a veritable police army and of the elite formations, the chief of police apparently is in no position ever to seize power and himself become the ruler of the country. Thus prior to Hitler's fall, Himmler never dreamed of touching Hitler's claim to leadership[49] and was never proposed

[45] The notion of a division into "little principalities" which formed "a pyramid of power outside the law with the Fuehrer at its apex" is Robert H. Jackson's. See chapter xii of *Nazi Conspiracy*, II, 1 ff. In order to avoid the establishment of such an authoritarian state, Hitler, as early as 1934, issued the following party decree: "The form of address 'Mein Fuehrer' is reserved for the Fuehrer alone. I herewith forbid all subleaders of the NSDAP to allow themselves to be addressed as 'Mein Reichsleiter,' etc., either in words or in writing. Rather, the form of address has to be Pg. [Party Comrade] . . . or Gauleiter, etc." See *Verfügungen, Anordnungen, Bekanntgaben*, *op. cit.*, decree of August 20, 1934.

[46] See the *Organisationsbuch der NSDAP*.

[47] See Chart 14 in Vol. VIII of *Nazi Conspiracy*.

[48] All oaths in the party as well as the elite formations were taken on the person of Adolf Hitler.

[49] The first step of Himmler in this direction occurred in the fall of 1944, when he ordered on his own initiative that the gas installations in the extermination camps

as Hitler's successor. Even more interesting in this context is Beria's ill-fated attempt at seizing power after Stalin's death. Although Stalin had never permitted any of his police chiefs to enjoy a position comparable to that of Himmler during the last years of Nazi rule, Beria, too, disposed of enough troops to challenge the rule of the party after Stalin's death simply by occupying the whole of Moscow and all accesses to the Kremlin; nobody except the Red Army might have disrupted his claim to power and this would have led to a bloody civil war whose outcome would by no means have been assured. The point is that Beria voluntarily abandoned all his positions only a few days later even though he must have known that he would forfeit his life because for a matter of days he had dared to play off the power of the police against the power of the party.[50]

This lack of absolute power of course does not prevent the chief of police from organizing his enormous apparatus in accordance with totalitarian power principles. Thus it is most remarkable to see how Himmler after his appointment began the reorganization of the German police by introducing into the hitherto centralized apparatus of the secret police the multiplication of offices—*i.e.*, he apparently did what all experts of power who preceded the totalitarian regimes would have feared as decentralization leading to a diminution of power. To the service of the Gestapo Himmler first added the Security Service, originally a division of the SS and founded as an inner-party police body. While the main offices of the Gestapo and the Security Service were eventually centralized in Berlin, the regional branches of these two huge secret services retained their separate identities and each reported directly to Himmler's own office in Berlin.[51] In the course of the war, Himmler added two more intelligence services: one consisted of so-called inspectors who were supposed to control and co-ordinate the Security Service with the police and who were subject to the jurisdiction of the SS; the second was a specifically military intelligence bureau which acted independently of the Reich's military forces and finally succeeded in absorbing the army's own military intelligence.[52]

The complete absence of successful or unsuccessful palace revolutions is one of the most remarkable characteristics of totalitarian dictatorships.

---

be dismantled and the mass slaughter be stopped. This was his way of initiating peace negotiations with the Western powers. Interestingly enough, Hitler apparently was never informed of these preparations; it seems that no one dared tell him that one of his most important war aims had already been given up. See Léon Poliakov, *Brévaire de la Haine*, 1951, p. 232.

[50] For the events following Stalin's death, see Harrison E. Salisbury, ***American in Russia***, New York, 1955.

[51] See the excellent analysis of the structure of the Nazi police in ***Nazi Conspiracy***, II, 250 ff., esp. p. 256.

[52] *Ibid.*, p. 252.

(With one exception no dissatisfied Nazis took part in the military conspiracy against Hitler of July, 1944.) On the surface, the Leader principle seems to invite bloody changes of personal power without a change of regime. This is but one of many indications that the totalitarian form of government has very little to do with lust for power or even the desire for a power-generating machine, with the game of power for power's sake which has been characteristic of the last stages of imperialist rule. Technically speaking, however, it is one of the most important indications that totalitarian government, all appearances notwithstanding, is not rule by a clique or a gang.[53] The evidence of Hitler's as well as Stalin's dictatorship points clearly to the fact that isolation of atomized individuals provides not only the mass basis for totalitarian rule, but is carried through to the very top of the whole structure. Stalin has shot almost everybody who could claim to belong to the ruling clique and has moved the members of the Politburo back and forth whenever a clique was on the point of consolidating itself. Hitler destroyed cliques in Nazi Germany with less drastic means—the only bloody purge having been directed against the Röhm clique which indeed was firmly kept together through the homosexuality of its leading members; he prevented their formation by constant shifts in power and authority, and frequent changes of intimates in his immediate surroundings, so that all former solidarity between those who had come into power with him quickly evaporated. It seems obvious, moreover, that the monstrous unfaithfulness which is reported in almost identical terms as the outstanding trait in both Hitler's and Stalin's characters did not allow them to preside over anything so lasting and durable as a clique. However that may be, the point is that there exists no interrelationship between those holding office; they are not bound together by equal status in a political hierarchy or the relationship between superiors and inferiors, or even the uncertain loyalties of gangsters. In Soviet Russia, everybody knows that the top manager of a big industrial concern can as well as the Minister of Foreign Affairs be demoted any day to the lowest social and political status, and that a complete unknown may step into his place. The gangster complicity, on the other hand, which played some role in the early stages of the Nazi dictatorship, loses all cohesive force, for totalitarianism uses its power precisely

[53] Franz Neumann, *op. cit.*, pp. 521 ff., is doubtful "whether Germany can be called a State. It is far more a gang where the leaders are perpetually compelled to agree after disagreements." Konrad Heiden's works on Nazi Germany are representative for the theory of government by a clique.—As regards the formation of cliques around Hitler, *The Bormann Letters*, published by Trevor-Roper, are quite enlightening. In the trial of the doctors (the United States *vs.* Karl Brandt *et al.*, hearing of May 13, 1947), Victor Brack testified that as early as 1933 Bormann, acting no doubt on Hitler's orders, had begun to organize a group of persons who stood above state and party.

to spread this complicity through the population until it has organized the guilt of the whole people under its domination.[54]

The absence of a ruling clique has made the question of a successor to the totalitarian dictator especially baffling and troublesome. It is true that this issue has plagued all usurpers, and it is quite characteristic that none of the totalitarian dictators ever tried the old method of establishing a dynasty and appointing their sons. Against Hitler's numerous and therefore self-defeating appointments stands Stalin's method, which made the succession one of the most dangerous honors in the Soviet Union. Under totalitarian conditions, knowledge of the labyrinth of transmission belts equals supreme power, and every appointed successor who actually comes to know what is going on is automatically removed after a certain time. A valid and comparatively permanent appointment would indeed presuppose the existence of a clique whose members would share the Leader's monopoly of knowledge of what is going on, which the Leader must avoid by all means. Hitler once explained this in his own terms to the supreme commanders of the Wehrmacht, who in the midst of the turmoil of war were presumably racking their brains over this problem: "As the ultimate factor I must, in all modesty, name my own person: irreplaceable. . . . The destiny of the Reich depends on me alone."[55] There is no need to look for any irony in the word modesty; the totalitarian leader, in marked contrast to all former usurpers, despots and tyrants, seems to believe that the question of his succession is not overly important, that no special qualities or training are needed for the job, that the country will eventually obey anybody who happens to hold the appointment at the moment of his death, and that no power-thirsty rivals will dispute his legitimacy.[56]

As techniques of government, the totalitarian devices appear simple and

[54] Compare the author's contribution to the discussion of the problem of German guilt: "Organized Guilt," in *Jewish Frontier*, January, 1945.

[55] In a speech of November 23, 1939, quoted from *Trial of Major War Criminals*, Vol. 26, p. 332. That this pronouncement was more than a hysterical aberration dictated by chance is apparent from Himmler's speech (the stenographic transcript can be found in the archives of the Hoover Library, Himmler File, Folder 332) at the conference of mayors at Posen in March, 1944. It says: "What values can we place onto the scales of history? The value of our own people. . . . The second, I would almost say, even greater value is the unique person of our Fuehrer Adolf Hitler, . . . who for the first time after two thousand years . . . was sent to the Germanic race as a great leader. . . ."

[56] See Hitler's statements on this question in *Hitlers Tischgespräche*, pp. 253 f. and 222 f.: The new Fuehrer would have to be elected by a "senate"; the guiding principle for the Fuehrer's election must be that any discussion among the personalities participating in the election should cease for the duration of the proceedings. Within three hours Wehrmacht, party and all civil servants will have to be newly sworn in. "He had no illusions about the fact that in this election of the supreme head of the state there might not always be an outstanding Fuehrer personality at the helm of the Reich." But this entailed no dangers, "so long as the over-all machinery functions properly."

ingeniously effective. They assure not only an absolute power monopoly, but unparalleled certainty that all commands will always be carried out; the multiplicity of the transmission belts, the confusion of the hierarchy, secure the dictator's complete independence of all his inferiors and make possible the swift and surprising changes in policy for which totalitarianism has become famous. The body politic of the country is shock-proof because of its shapelessness.

The reasons why such extraordinary efficiency was never tried before are as simple as the device itself. The multiplication of offices destroys all sense of responsibility and competence; it is not merely a tremendously burdensome and unproductive increase of administration, but actually hinders productivity because conflicting orders constantly delay real work until the order of the Leader has decided the matter. The fanaticism of the elite cadres, absolutely essential for the functioning of the movement, abolishes systematically all genuine interest in specific jobs and produces a mentality which sees every conceivable action as an instrument for something entirely different.[57] And this mentality is not confined to the elite but gradually pervades the entire population, the most intimate details of whose life and death depend upon political decisions—that is, upon causes and ulterior motives which have nothing to do with performance. Constant removal, demotion, and promotion make reliable teamwork impossible and prevent the development of experience. Economically speaking, slave labor is a luxury which Russia should not be able to afford; in a time of acute shortage of technical skill, the camps were filled with "highly qualified engineers [who] compete for the right to do plumbing jobs, repair clocks, electric lighting and telephone."[58] But then, from a purely utilitarian point of view, Russia should not have been able to afford the purges in the thirties that interrupted a long-awaited economic recovery, or the physical destruction of the Red Army general staff, which led almost to a defeat in the Russian-Finnish war.

Conditions in Germany were different in degree. In the beginning, the Nazis showed a certain tendency to retain technical and administrative skill, to allow profits in business, and to dominate economically without too much interference. At the outbreak of the war Germany was not yet completely totalitarianized, and if one accepts preparation for war as a rational motive, it must be conceded that until roughly 1942 her economy was allowed to

[57] One of the guiding principles for the SS formulated by Himmler himself reads: "No task exists for its own sake." See Gunter d'Alquen, *Die SS. Geschichte, Aufgabe und Organisation der Schutzstaffeln der NSDAP*, 1939, in Schriften der Hochschule für Politik.

[58] See David J. Dallin and Boris I. Nicolaevsky, *Forced Labor in Russia*, 1947, who also report that during the war when mobilization had created an acute problem of manpower, the death rate in the labor camps was about 40 per cent during one year. In general, they estimate that the output of a worker in the camps is below 50 per cent of that of a free laborer.

function more or less rationally. The preparation for war in itself is not anti-utilitarian, despite its prohibitive costs,[59] for it may indeed be much "cheaper to seize the wealth and resources of other nations by conquest than to buy them from foreign countries or produce them at home."[60] Economic laws of investment and production, of stabilizing gains and profits, and of exhaustion do not apply if one intends in any event to replenish the depleted home economy with loot from other countries; it is quite true, and the sympathizing German people were perfectly aware of it, that the famous Nazi slogan of "guns or butter" actually meant "butter through guns."[61] It was not until 1942 that the rules of totalitarian domination began to outweigh all other considerations.

The radicalization began immediately at the outbreak of war; one may even surmise that one of Hitler's reasons for provoking this war was that it enabled him to accelerate the development in a manner that would have been unthinkable in peacetime.[62] The remarkable thing about this process, however, is that it was by no means checked by such a shattering defeat as Stalingrad, and that the danger of losing the war altogether was only another incitement to throw overboard all utilitarian considerations and make an all-out attempt to realize through ruthless total organization the goals of totalitarian racial ideology, no matter for how short a time.[63] After Stalingrad, the elite formations which had been strictly separated from the people were greatly

[59] Thomas Reveille, *The Spoil of Europe*, 1941, estimates that Germany during the first year of war was able to cover her entire preparatory war expenses of the years 1933 to 1939.

[60] William Ebenstein, *The Nazi State*, p. 257.

[61] *Ibid.*, p. 270.

[62] This is supported by the fact that the decree to murder all incurably sick was issued on the day the war broke out, but even more so by Hitler's statements during the war, quoted by Goebbels (*The Goebbels Diaries*, ed. Louis P. Lochner, 1948) to the effect that "the war had made possible for us the solution of a whole series of problems that could never have been solved in normal times," and that, no matter how the war turned out, "the Jews will certainly be the losers" (p. 314).

[63] The Wehrmacht of course tried time and again to explain to the various party organs the dangers of a war conduct in which commands were issued with utter disregard for all military, civilian and economic necessities (see, for instance, Poliakov, *op. cit.*, p. 321). But even many high Nazi functionaries had difficulty understanding this neglect of all objective economic and military factors in the situation. They had to be told time and again that "economic considerations should fundamentally remain unconsidered in the settlement of the [Jewish] problem" (*Nazi Conspiracy*, VI, 402), but still would complain that the interruption of a big building program in Poland "would not have happened if the many thousands of Jews working at it had not been deported. Now the order is given that the Jews will have to be removed from the armament projects. I hope that this . . . order will soon be cancelled, for then the situation will be still worse." This hope of Hans Frank, Governor General of Poland, was as little fulfilled as his later expectations of a militarily more sensible policy toward Poles and Ukrainians. His complaints are interesting (see his Diary in *Nazi Conspiracy*, IV, 902 ff.) because he is frightened exclusively by the anti-utilitarian aspect of Nazi policies during the war. "Once we have won the war, then for all I care, mince-meat can be made of the Poles and the Ukrainians and all the others who run around here. . . ."

expanded; the ban on party membership for those in the armed forces was lifted and the military command was subordinated to SS commanders. The jealously guarded crime monopoly of the SS was abandoned and soldiers were assigned at will to duties of mass murder.[64] Neither military, nor economic, nor political considerations were allowed to interfere with the costly and troublesome program of mass exterminations and deportations.

If one considers these last years of Nazi rule and their version of a "five-year plan," which they had no time to carry out but which aimed at the extermination of the Polish and Ukrainian people, of 170 million Russians (as mentioned in one plan), the intelligentsia of Western Europe such as the Dutch and the people of Alsace and Lorraine, as well as of all those Germans who would be disqualified under the prospective Reich health bill or the planned "community alien law," the analogy to the Bolshevik five-year plan of 1929, the first year of clear-cut totalitarian dictatorship in Russia, is almost inescapable. Vulgar eugenic slogans in one case, high-sounding economic phrases in the other, were the prelude to "a piece of prodigious insanity, in which all rules of logic and principles of economics were turned upside down."[65]

To be sure, totalitarian dictators do not consciously embark upon the road to insanity. The point is rather that our bewilderment about the anti-utilitarian character of the totalitarian state structure springs from the mistaken notion that we are dealing with a normal state after all—a bureaucracy, a tyranny, a dictatorship—from our overlooking the emphatic assertions by totalitarian rulers that they consider the country where they happened to seize power only the temporary headquarters of the international movement on the road to world conquest, that they reckon victories and defeats in terms of centuries or millennia, and that the global interests always overrule the local interests of their own territory.[66] The famous "Right is what is

[64] Originally, only special units of the SS—the Death Head formations—were employed in the concentration camps. Later replacements came from the Armed SS divisions. From 1944 on, units of the regular armed forces were also employed but usually incorporated in the Armed SS. (See the Affidavit of a former SS official of the concentration camp of Neuengamme in *Nazi Conspiracy*, VII, 211.) How the active presence of the Wehrmacht made itself felt in the concentration camps has been described in Odd Nansen's concentration camp diary *Day After Day*, London, 1949. Unfortunately, it shows that these regular army troops were at least as brutal as the SS.

[65] Deutscher, *op. cit.*, p. 326. This quotation carries weight because it comes from the most benevolent of Stalin's non-Communist biographers.

[66] The Nazis were especially fond of reckoning in terms of millennia. Himmler's pronouncements that SS-men were solely interested in "ideological questions whose importance counted in terms of decades and centuries" and that they "served a cause which in two thousand years occurred only once" are repeated, with slight variations, throughout the entire indoctrination material issued by the SS-Hauptamt-Schulungsamt (*Wesen und Aufgabe der SS und der Polizei*, p. 160).—As for the Bolshevik version, the best reference is the program of the Communist International as formulated by Stalin as early as 1928 at the Party Congress in Moscow. Particularly interesting is the evaluation of the Soviet Union as "the basis for the world movement, the center of international revolution, the greatest factor in world history. In the USSR, the world proletariat for the first time acquires a country . . ." (quoted from

good for the German people" was meant only for mass propaganda; Nazis were told that "Right is what is good for the movement,"[67] and these two interests did by no means always coincide. The Nazis did not think that the Germans were a master race, to whom the world belonged, but that they should be led by a master race, as should all other nations, and that this race was only on the point of being born.[68] Not the Germans were the dawn of the master race, but the SS.[69] The "Germanic world empire," as Himmler said, or the "Aryan" world empire, as Hitler would have put it, was in any event still centuries off.[70] For the "movement" it was more important to demonstrate that it was possible to fabricate a race by annihilating other "races" than to win a war with limited aims. What strikes the outside observer as a "piece of prodigious insanity" is nothing but the consequence of the absolute primacy of the movement not only over the state, but also over the nation, the people and the positions of power held by the rulers themselves. The reason why the ingenious devices of totalitarian rule, with their absolute and unsurpassed concentration of power in the hands of a single man, were never tried out before, is that no ordinary tyrant was ever mad enough to discard all limited and local interests—economic, national, human, military—in favor of a purely fictitious reality in some indefinite distant future.

Since totalitarianism in power remains faithful to the original tenets of the movement, the striking similarities between the organizational devices of the movement and the so-called totalitarian state are hardly surprising. The division between party members and fellow-travelers organized in front

---

W. H. Chamberlin, *Blueprint for World Conquest*, 1946, where the programs of the Third International are reprinted verbatim).

[67] This change of the official motto can be found in the *Organisationsbuch der NSDAP*, p. 7.

[68] See Heiden, *op. cit.*, p. 722.—Hitler stated in a speech of November 23, 1937, before the future political leaders at the Ordensburg Sonthofen: Not "ridiculously small tribes, tiny countries, states or dynasties . . . but only races [can] function as world conquerors. A race, however—at least in the conscious sense—we still have to become" (see *Hitlers Tischgespräche*, p. 445).—In complete harmony with this by no means accidental phrasing is a decree of August 9, 1941, in which Hitler prohibited the further use of the term "German race" because it would lead to the "sacrifice of the racial idea as such in favor of a mere nationality principle, and to the destruction of important conceptual preconditions of our whole racial and folk policy" (*Verfügungen, Anordnungen, Bekanntgaben*). It is obvious that the concept of a German race would have constituted an impediment to the progressive "selection" and extermination of undesirable parts among the German population which in those very years was being planned for the future.

[69] Himmler consequently "very soon formed a Germanic SS in the various countries" whom he told: "We do not expect you to become German out of opportunism. But we do expect you to subordinate your national ideal to the greater racial and historical ideal, to the Germanic Reich" (Heiden, *op. cit.*). Its future task would be to form through "the most copious breeding" a "racial superstratum" which in another twenty to thirty years would "present the whole of Europe with its leading class" (Himmler's speech at the meeting of the SS Major Generals at Posen in 1943, in *Nazi Conspiracy*, IV, 558 ff.).

[70] Himmler, *ibid.*, p. 572.

organizations, far from disappearing, leads to the "co-ordination" of the whole population, who are now organized as sympathizers. The tremendous increase in sympathizers is checked by limiting party strength to a privileged "class" of a few millions and creating a superparty of several hundred thousand, the elite formations. Multiplication of offices, duplication of functions, and adaptation of the party-sympathizer relationship to the new conditions mean simply that the peculiar onion-like structure of the movement, in which every layer was the front of the next more militant formation, is retained. The state machine is transformed into a front organization of sympathizing bureaucrats whose function in domestic affairs is to spread confidence among the masses of merely co-ordinated citizens and whose foreign affairs consist in fooling the outside, nontotalitarian world. The Leader, in his dual capacity as chief of the state and leader of the movement, again combines in his person the acme of militant ruthlessness and confidence-inspiring normality.

One of the important differences between a totalitarian movement and a totalitarian state is that the totalitarian dictator can and must practice the totalitarian art of lying more consistently and on a larger scale than the leader of a movement. This is partly the automatic consequence of swelling the ranks of fellow-travelers, and is partly due to the fact that unpleasant statements by a statesman are not as easily revoked as those of a demagogic party leader. For this purpose, Hitler chose to fall back, without any detours, on the old-fashioned nationalism which he had denounced many times before his ascent to power; by posing as a violent nationalist, claiming that National Socialism was not an "export commodity," he appeased Germans and non-Germans alike and implied that Nazi ambitions would be satisfied when the traditional demands of a nationalist German foreign policy—return of territories ceded in the Versailles treaties, *Anschluss* of Austria, annexation of the German-speaking parts of Bohemia—were fulfilled. Stalin likewise reckoned with both Russian public opinion and the non-Russian world when he invented his theory of "socialism in one country" and threw the onus of world revolution on Trotsky.[71]

Systematic lying to the whole world can be safely carried out only under the conditions of totalitarian rule, where the fictitious quality of everyday reality makes propaganda largely superfluous. In their prepower stage the movements can never afford to hide their true goals to the same degree —after all, they are meant to inspire mass organizations. But, given the possibility to exterminate Jews like bedbugs, namely, by poison gas, it is no longer necessary to propagate that Jews are bedbugs;[72] given the power to teach a whole nation the history of the Russian Revolution without men-

[71] Deutscher, *op. cit.*, describes Stalin's remarkable "sensibility to all those psychological undercurrents . . . of which he set himself up as a mouthpiece" (p. 292). "The very name of Trotsky's theory, 'permanent revolution,' sounded like an ominous warning to a tired generation. . . . Stalin appealed directly to the horror of risk and uncertainty that had taken possession of many Bolsheviks" (p. 291).

[72] Thus Hitler could afford to use the favorite cliché "decent Jew" once he had begun to exterminate them, namely, in December, 1941, in the *Tischgespräche*, p. 346.

tioning the name of Trotsky, there is no further need for propaganda against Trotsky. But the use of the methods for carrying out the ideological goals can be "expected" only from those who are "ideologically utterly firm"—whether they have acquired such firmness in the Comintern schools or the special Nazi indoctrination centers—even if these goals continue to be publicized. On such occasions it invariably turns out that the mere sympathizers never realize what is happening.[73] This leads to the paradox that "the secret society in broad daylight" is never more conspiratory in character and methods than after it has been recognized as a full-fledged member of the comity of nations. It is only logical that Hitler, prior to his seizure of power, resisted all attempts to organize the party and even the elite formations on a conspiratory basis; yet after 1933 he was quite eager to help transform the SS into a kind of secret society.[74] Similarly, the Moscow-directed Communist parties, in marked contrast to their predecessors, show a curious tendency to prefer the conditions of conspiracy even where complete legality is possible.[75] The more conspicuous the power of totalitarianism the more secret become its true goals. To know the ultimate aims of Hitler's rule in Germany, it was much wiser to rely on his propaganda speeches and *Mein Kampf* than on the oratory of the Chancellor of the Third Reich; just as it would have been wiser to distrust Stalin's words about "socialism in one country," invented for the passing purpose of seizing power after Lenin's death, and to take more seriously his repeated hostility to democratic countries. The totalitarian dictators have proved that they knew only too well the danger inherent in their pose of normality; that is, the danger of a true nationalist policy or of actually building socialism in one country. This they try to overcome through a permanent and consistent discrepancy between reassuring words and the reality of

[73] Hitler, therefore, speaking to members of the General Staff (Blomberg, Fritsch, Raeder) and high-ranking civilians (Neurath, Göring) in November, 1937, could permit himself to state openly that he needed depopulated space and reject the idea of conquering alien peoples. That this would automatically result in a policy of exterminating such peoples was evidently not realized by any one of his listeners.

[74] This began with an order in July, 1934, by which the SS was elevated to the rank of an independent organization within the NSDAP, and completed by a top secret decree of August, 1938, which declared that the SS special formations, the Death Head Units and the Shock Troops (*Verfügungstruppen*) were neither part of the army nor of the police; the Death Head Units had "to clear up special tasks of police nature" and the Shock Troops were "a standing armed unit exclusively at my disposal" (*Nazi Conspiracy*, III, 459). Two subsequent decrees of October, 1939, and April, 1940, established special jurisdiction in general matters for all SS members (*ibid.*, II, 184). From then on all pamphlets issued by the SS indoctrination office carry such notations as "Solely for use of the police," "Not for publication," "Exclusively for leaders and those entrusted with ideological education." It would be worth while to compile a bibliography of the voluminous secret literature, which includes a great many legislative measures, that was printed during the Nazi era. Interestingly enough, there is not a single SA booklet among this type of literature, and this is probably the most conclusive proof that after 1934 the SA ceased to be an elite formation.

[75] Compare Franz Borkenau, "Die neue Komintern," in *Der Monat*, Berlin, 1949, Heft 4.

rule, by consciously developing a method of always doing the opposite of what they say.[76] Stalin has carried this art of balance, which demands more skill than the ordinary routine of diplomacy, to the point where a moderation in foreign policy or the political line of the Comintern is almost invariably accompanied by radical purges in the Russian party. It was certainly more than coincidence that the Popular Front policy and the drafting of the comparatively liberal Soviet constitution were accompanied by the Moscow Trials.

Evidence that totalitarian governments aspire to conquer the globe and bring all countries on earth under their domination can be found repeatedly in Nazi and Bolshevik literature. Yet these ideological programs, inherited from pretotalitarian movements (from the supranationalist antisemitic parties and the Pan-German dreams of empire in the case of the Nazis, from the international concept of revolutionary socialism in the case of the Bolsheviks) are not decisive. What is decisive is that totalitarian regimes really conduct their foreign policy on the consistent assumption that they will eventually achieve this ultimate goal, and never lose sight of it no matter how distant it may appear or how seriously its "ideal" demands may conflict with the necessities of the moment. They therefore consider no country as permanently foreign, but, on the contrary, every country as their potential territory. Rise to power, the fact that in one country the fictitious world of the movement has become a tangible reality, creates a relationship to other nations which is similar to the situation of the totalitarian party under nontotalitarian rule: the tangible reality of the fiction, backed by internationally recognized state power, can be exported the same way contempt for parliament could be imported into a nontotalitarian parliament. In this respect, the prewar "solution" of the Jewish question was the outstanding export commodity of Nazi Germany: expulsion of Jews carried an important portion of Nazism into other countries; by forcing Jews to leave the Reich passportless and penniless, the legend of the Wandering Jew was realized, and by forcing the Jews into uncompromising hostility against them, the Nazis had created the pretext for taking a passionate interest in all nations' domestic policies.[77]

How seriously the Nazis took their conspiratorial fiction, according to which they were the future rulers of the world, came to light in 1940 when—despite necessity, and in the face of all their all-too-real chances of winning over the occupied peoples of Europe—they started their depopulation policies in the Eastern territories, regardless of loss of manpower and serious military consequences, and introduced legislation which with retroactive

[76] Instances are too obvious and too numerous to be quoted. This tactic, however, should not be simply identified with the enormous lack of faithfulness and truthfulness which all biographers of Hitler and Stalin report as outstanding traits of their character.

[77] See the Circular Letter from the Ministry of Foreign Affairs to all German authorities abroad of January, 1939, in *Nazi Conspiracy*, VI, 87 ff.

force exported part of the Third Reich's penal code into the Western occupied countries.[78] There was hardly a more effective way of publicizing the Nazi claim to world rule than punishing as high treason every utterance or action against the Third Reich, no matter when, where, or by whom it had been made. Nazi law treated the whole world as falling potentially under its jurisdiction, so that the occupying army was no longer an instrument of conquest that carried with it the new law of the conqueror, but an executive organ which enforced a law which already supposedly existed for everyone.

The assumption that Nazi law was binding beyond the German border and the punishment of non-Germans were more than mere devices of oppression. Totalitarian regimes are not afraid of the logical implications of world conquest even if they work the other way around and are detrimental to their own peoples' interests. Logically, it is indisputable that a plan for world conquest involves the abolition of differences between the conquering mother country and the conquered territories, as well as the difference between foreign and domestic politics, upon which all existing nontotalitarian institutions and all international intercourse are based. If the totalitarian conqueror conducts himself everywhere as though he were at home, by the same token he must treat his own population as though he were a foreign conqueror.[79] And it is perfectly true that the totalitarian movement seizes power in much the same sense as a foreign conqueror may occupy a country which he governs not for its own sake but for the benefit of something or somebody else. The Nazis behaved like foreign conquerors in Germany when, against all national interests, they tried and half succeeded in converting their defeat into a final catastrophe for the whole German people; similarly in case of victory, they intended to extend their extermination politics into the ranks of "racially unfit" Germans.[80]

A similar attitude seems to have inspired Soviet foreign policy after the war. The cost of its aggressiveness to the Russian people themselves is

[78] In 1940, the Nazi government decreed that offenses ranging from high treason against the Reich to "malicious agitatorial utterances against leading persons of the State or the Nazi Party" should be punished with retroactive force in all German occupied territories, no matter whether they had been committed by Germans or by natives of these countries. See Giles, *op. cit.*—For the disastrous consequences of the Nazi *"Siedlungspolitik"* in Poland and the Ukraine, see *Trial, op. cit.*, Vols. XXVI and XXIX.

[79] The term is Kravchenko's, *op. cit.*, p. 303, who, describing conditions in Russia after the superpurge of 1936-1938, remarks: "Had a foreign conqueror taken over the machinery of Soviet life . . . the change could hardly have been more thorough or more cruel."

[80] Hitler contemplated during the war the introduction of a National Health Bill: "After national X-ray examination, the Fuehrer is to be given a list of sick persons, particularly those with lung and heart diseases. On the basis of the new Reich Health Law . . . these families will no longer be able to remain among the public and can no longer be allowed to produce children. What will happen to these families will be the subject of further orders of the Fuehrer." It does not need much imagination to guess what these further orders would have been. The number of people no longer allowed "to remain among the public" would have formed a considerable portion of the German population (*Nazi Conspiracy*, VI, 175).

prohibitive: it has foregone the great postwar loan from the United States which would have enabled Russia to reconstruct devastated areas and industrialize the country in a rational, productive way. The extension of Comintern governments throughout the Balkans and the occupation of large Eastern territories brought no tangible benefits, but on the contrary strained Russian resources still further. But this policy certainly served the interests of the Bolshevik movement, which has spread over almost half of the inhabited world.

Like a foreign conqueror, the totalitarian dictator regards the natural and industrial riches of each country, including his own, as a source of loot and a means of preparing the next step of aggressive expansion. Since this economy of systematic spoliation is carried out for the sake of the movement and not of the nation, no people and no territory, as the potential beneficiary, can possibly set a saturation point to the process. The totalitarian dictator is like a foreign conqueror who comes from nowhere, and his looting is likely to benefit nobody. Distribution of the spoils is calculated not to strengthen the economy of the home country but only as a temporary tactical maneuver. For economic purposes, the totalitarian regimes are as much at home in their countries as the proverbial swarms of locusts. The fact that the totalitarian dictator rules his own country like a foreign conqueror makes matters worse because it adds to ruthlessness an efficiency which is conspicuously lacking in tyrannies in alien surroundings. Stalin's war against the Ukraine in the early thirties was twice as effective as the terribly bloody German invasion and occupation.[81] This is the reason why totalitarianism prefers quisling governments to direct rule despite the obvious dangers of such regimes.

The trouble with totalitarian regimes is not that they play power politics in an especially ruthless way, but that behind their politics is hidden an entirely new and unprecedented concept of power, just as behind their *Realpolitik* lies an entirely new and unprecedented concept of reality. Supreme disregard for immediate consequences rather than ruthlessness; rootlessness and neglect of national interests rather than nationalism; contempt for utilitarian motives rather than unconsidered pursuit of self-interest; "idealism," *i.e.*, their unwavering faith in an ideological fictitious world, rather than lust

[81] The total number of Russian dead in four years of war is estimated at between 12 and 21 million. Stalin exterminated in a single year in the Ukraine alone about 8 million people (estimate). See *Communism in Action*. U. S. Government. Washington, 1946, House Document No. 754, pp. 140-141.—Unlike the Nazi regime which kept rather accurate accounts on the number of its victims, there are no reliable figures for the millions of people who were killed in the Russian system. Nevertheless the following estimate, quoted by Souvarine, *op. cit.*, p. 669, carries some weight insofar as it stems from Walter Krivitsky, who had direct access to the information contained in the GPU files. According to these figures the census of 1937 in the Soviet Union, which Soviet statisticians had expected to reach 171 million persons, showed that there were actually only 145 millions. This would point to a loss in population of 26 millions, a figure which does not include the losses quoted above.

for power—these have all introduced into international politics a new and more disturbing factor than mere aggressiveness would have been able to do.

Power, as conceived by totalitarianism, lies exclusively in the force produced through organization. Just as Stalin saw every institution, independent of its actual function, only as a "transmission belt connecting the party with the people"[82] and honestly believed that the most precious treasures of the Soviet Union were not the riches of its soil or the productive capacity of its huge manpower, but the "cadres" of the party[83] (*i.e.*, the police), so Hitler, as early as 1929, saw the "great thing" of the movement in the fact that sixty thousand men "have outwardly become almost a unit, that actually these members are uniform not only in ideas, but that even the facial expression is almost the same. Look at these laughing eyes, this fanatical enthusiasm and you will discover . . . how a hundred thousand men in a movement become a single type."[84] Whatever connection power had in the minds of Western man with earthly possessions, with wealth, treasures, and riches, has been dissolved into a kind of dematerialized mechanism whose every move generates power as friction or galvanic currents generate electricity. The totalitarian division of states into Have and Have-not countries is more than a demagogic device; those who make it are actually convinced that the power of material possessions is negligible and only stands in the way of the development of organizational power. To Stalin constant growth and development of police cadres were incomparably more important than the oil in Baku, the coal and ore in the Urals, the granaries in the Ukraine, or the potential treasures of Siberia—in short the development of Russia's full power arsenal. The same mentality led Hitler to sacrifice all Germany to the cadres of the SS; he did not consider the war lost when German cities lay in rubble and industrial capacity was destroyed, but only when he learned that the SS troops were no longer reliable.[85] To a man who believed in organizational omnipotence against all mere material factors, military or economic, and who, moreover, calculated the eventual victory of his enterprise in centuries, defeat was not military catastrophe or threatened starvation of the population, but only the destruction of the elite formations which were supposed to carry the conspiracy for world rule through a line of generations to its eventual end.

The structurelessness of the totalitarian state, its neglect of material

[82] Deutscher, *op. cit.*, p. 256.

[83] B. Souvarine, *op. cit.*, p. 605, quotes Stalin as saying at the height of terror in 1937: "You must reach the understanding that of all the precious assets existing in the world, the most precious and decisive are the cadres." All reports show that in Soviet Russia the secret police must be regarded as the real elite formation of the party. Characteristic for this nature of the police is that since the early twenties NKVD agents were "not recruited on a voluntary basis," but drawn from the ranks of the party. Furthermore, "the NKVD could not be chosen as a career" (see Beck and Godin, *op. cit.*, p. 160).

[84] Quoted from Heiden, *op. cit.*, p. 311.

[85] According to reports of the last meeting, Hitler decided to commit suicide after he had learned that the SS troops could no longer be trusted. See H. R. Trevor-Roper, *The Last Days of Hitler*, 1947, pp. 116 ff.

interests, its emancipation from the profit motive, and its nonutilitarian attitudes in general have more than anything else contributed to making contemporary politics well-nigh unpredictable. The inability of the nontotalitarian world to grasp a mentality which functions independently of all calculable action in terms of men and material, and is completely indifferent to national interest and the well-being of its people, shows itself in a curious dilemma of judgment: those who rightly understand the terrible efficiency of totalitarian organization and police are likely to overestimate the material force of totalitarian countries, while those who understand the wasteful incompetence of totalitarian economics are likely to underestimate the power potential which can be created in disregard of all material factors.

II: *The Secret Police*

UP TO NOW we know only two authentic forms of totalitarian domination: the dictatorship of National Socialism after 1938, and the dictatorship of Bolshevism since 1930. These forms of domination differ basically from other kinds of dictatorial, despotic or tyrannical rule; and even though they have developed, with a certain continuity, from party dictatorships, their essentially totalitarian features are new and cannot be derived from one-party systems. The goal of one-party systems is not only to seize the government administration but, by filling all offices with party members, to achieve a complete amalgamation of state and party, so that after the seizure of power the party becomes a kind of propaganda organization for the government. This system is "total" only in a negative sense, namely, in that the ruling party will tolerate no other parties, no opposition and no freedom of political opinion. Once a party dictatorship has come to power, it leaves the original power relationship between state and party intact; the government and the army exercise the same power as before, and the "revolution" consists only in the fact that all government positions are now occupied by party members. In all these cases the power of the party rests on a monopoly guaranteed by the state and the party no longer possesses its own power center.

The revolution initiated by the totalitarian movements after they have seized power is of a considerably more radical nature. From the start, they consciously strive to maintain the essential differences between state and movement and to prevent the "revolutionary" institutions of the movement from being absorbed by the government.[86] The problem of seizing the state

[86] Hitler frequently commented on the relationship between state and party, and always emphasized that not the state, but the race, or the "united folk community," was of primary importance (cf. the afore-quoted speech, reprinted as annex to the *Tischgespräche*). In his speech at the Nuremberg Parteitag of 1935, he gave this theory its most succinct expression: "It is not the state that commands us, but we who command the state." It is self-evident that, in practice, such powers of command are possible only if the institutions of the party remain independent from those of the state.

machine without amalgamating with it is solved by permitting only those party members whose importance for the movement is secondary to rise in the state hierarchy. All real power is vested in the institutions of the movement, and outside the state and military apparatuses. It is inside the movement, which remains the center of action of the country, that all decisions are made; the official civil services are often not even informed of what is going on, and party members with the ambition to rise to the rank of ministers have in all cases paid for such "bourgeois" wishes with the loss of their influence on the movement and of the confidence of its leaders.

Totalitarianism in power uses the state as its outward façade, to represent the country in the nontotalitarian world. As such, the totalitarian state is the logical heir of the totalitarian movement from which it borrows its organizational structure. Totalitarian rulers deal with nontotalitarian governments in the same way they dealt with parliamentary parties or intraparty factions before their rise to power and, though on an enlarged international scene, are again faced with the double problem of shielding the fictitious world of the movement (or the totalitarian country) from the impact of factuality and of presenting a semblance of normality and common sense to the normal outside world.

Above the state and behind the façades of ostensible power, in a maze of multiplied offices, underlying all shifts of authority and in a chaos of inefficiency, lies the power nucleus of the country, the superefficient and supercompetent services of the secret police.[86a] The emphasis on the police as the sole organ of power, and the corresponding neglect of the seemingly greater power arsenal of the army, which is characteristic of all totalitarian regimes, can still be partially explained by the totalitarian aspiration to world rule and its conscious abolition of the distinction between a foreign country and a home country, between foreign and domestic affairs. The military forces, trained to fight a foreign aggressor, have always been a dubious instrument for civil-war purposes; even under totalitarian conditions they find it difficult to regard their own people with the eyes of a foreign conqueror.[87] More important in this respect, however, is that their value becomes dubious even in time of war. Since the totalitarian ruler conducts his policies on the assumption of an eventual world government, he treats the victims of his aggression as though they were rebels, guilty of high treason, and consequently prefers to rule occupied territories with police, and not with military forces.

Even before the movement seizes power, it possesses a secret police and spy service with branches in various countries. Later its agents receive more money and authority than the regular military intelligence service and are

[86a] Otto Gauweiler, *Rechtseinrichtungen und Rechtsaufgaben der Bewegung,* 1939, notes expressly that Himmler's special position as Reichsfuehrer-SS and head of the German police rested on the fact that the police administration had achieved "a genuine unity of party and state" which was not even attempted anywhere else in the government.

[87] During the peasant revolts of the twenties in Russia, Voroshilov allegedly refused the support of the Red Army; this led to the introduction of special divisions of the GPU for punitive expeditions. See Ciliga, *op. cit.*, p. 95.

frequently the secret chiefs of embassies and consulates abroad.[88] Its main tasks consist in forming fifth columns, directing the branches of the movement, influencing the domestic policies of the respective countries, and generally preparing for the time when the totalitarian ruler—after overthrow of the government or military victory—can openly feel at home. In other words, the international branches of the secret police are the transmission belts which constantly transform the ostensibly foreign policy of the totalitarian state into the potentially domestic business of the totalitarian movement.

These functions, however, which the secret police fulfill in order to prepare the totalitarian utopia of world rule, are secondary to those required for the present realization of the totalitarian fiction in one country. The dominant role of the secret police in the domestic politics of totalitarian countries has naturally contributed much to the common misconception of totalitarianism. All despotisms rely heavily on secret services and feel more threatened by their own than by any foreign people. However, this analogy between totalitarianism and despotism holds only for the first stages of totalitarian rule, when there is still a political opposition. In this as in other respects totalitarianism takes advantage of, and gives conscious support to, nontotalitarian misconceptions, no matter how uncomplimentary they may be. Himmler, in his famous speech to the Reichswehr staff in 1937, assumed the role of an ordinary tyrant when he explained the constant expansion of the police forces by assuming the existence of a "fourth theater in case of war, internal Germany."[89] Similarly, Stalin at almost the same moment half succeeded in convincing the old Bolshevik guard, whose "confessions" he needed, of a war threat against the Soviet Union and, consequently, an emergency in which the country must remain united even behind a despot. The most striking aspect of these statements was that both were made after all political opposition had been extinguished, that the secret services were expanded when actually no opponents were left to be spied upon. When war came, Himmler neither needed nor used his SS troops in Germany itself, except for the running of concentration camps and policing of foreign slave labor; the bulk of the armed SS served at the Eastern front where they were used for "special assignments"—usually mass murder—and the enforcement of policy which frequently ran counter to the military as well as the Nazi civilian hierarchy. Like the secret police of the Soviet Union, the SS formations usually arrived after the military forces had pacified the conquered territory and had dealt with outright political opposition.

In the first stages of a totalitarian regime, however, the secret police and the party's elite formations still play a role similar to that in other forms of dictatorship and the well-known terror regimes of the past; and the excessive cruelty of their methods is unparalleled only in the history of modern

[88] In 1935, the Gestapo agents abroad received 20 million marks while the regular espionage service of the Reichswehr had to get along with a budget of 8 million. See Pierre Dehillotte, *Gestapo*, Paris, 1940, p. 11.

[89] See *Nazi Conspiracy*, IV, 616 ff.

Western countries. The first stage of ferreting out secret enemies and hunting down former opponents is usually combined with drafting the entire population into front organizations and re-educating old party members for voluntary espionage services, so that the rather dubious sympathies of the drafted sympathizers need not worry the specially trained cadres of the police. It is during this stage that a neighbor gradually becomes a more dangerous enemy to one who happens to harbor "dangerous thoughts" than are the officially appointed police agents. The end of the first stage comes with the liquidation of open and secret resistance in any organized form; it can be set at about 1935 in Germany and approximately 1930 in Soviet Russia.

Only after the extermination of real enemies has been completed and the hunt for "objective enemies" begun does terror become the actual content of totalitarian regimes. Under the pretext of building socialism in one country, or using a given territory as a laboratory for a revolutionary experiment, or realizing the *Volksgemeinschaft*, the second claim of totalitarianism, the claim to total domination, is carried out. And although theoretically total domination is possible only under the conditions of world rule, the totalitarian regimes have proved that this part of the totalitarian utopia can be realized almost to perfection, because it is temporarily independent of defeat or victory. Thus Hitler could rejoice even in the midst of military setbacks over the extermination of Jews and the establishment of death factories; no matter what the final outcome, without the war it would never have been possible "to burn the bridges" and to realize some of the goals of the totalitarian movement.[90]

The elite formations of the Nazi movement and the "cadres" of the Bolshevik movement serve the goal of total domination rather than the security of the regime in power. Just as the totalitarian claim to world rule is only in appearance the same as imperialist expansion, so the claim to total domination only *seems* familiar to the student of despotism. If the chief difference between totalitarian and imperialist expansion is that the former recognizes no difference between a home and a foreign country, then the chief difference between a despotic and a totalitarian secret police is that the latter does not hunt secret thoughts and does not use the old method of secret services, the method of provocation.[91]

Since the totalitarian secret police begins its career after the pacification of the country, it always appears entirely superfluous to all outside observers —or, on the contrary, misleads them into thinking that there is some secret

[90] See note 62.

[91] Maurice Laporte, *Histoire de l'Okhrana*, Paris, 1935, rightly called the method of provocation "the foundation stone" of the secret police (p. 19).

In Soviet Russia, provocation, far from being the secret weapon of the secret police, has been used as the widely propagandized public method of the regime to gauge the temper of public opinion. The reluctance of the population to avail itself of the periodically recurring invitations to criticize or react to "liberal" interludes in the terror regime shows that such gestures are understood as provocation on a mass scale. Provocation has indeed become the totalitarian version of public opinion polls.

resistance.[92] The superfluousness of secret services is nothing new; they have always been haunted by the need to prove their usefulness and keep their jobs after their original task had been completed. The methods used for this purpose have made the study of the history of revolutions a rather difficult enterprise. It appears, for example, that there was not a single anti-government action under the reign of Louis Napoleon which had not been inspired by the police itself.[93] Similarly, the role of secret agents in all revolutionary parties in Czarist Russia strongly suggests that without their "inspiring" provocative actions the course of the Russian revolutionary movement would have been far less successful.[94] Provocation, in other words, helped as much to maintain the continuity of tradition as it did to disrupt time and again the organization of the revolution.

This dubious role of provocation might have been one reason why the totalitarian rulers discarded it. Provocation, moreover, is clearly necessary only on the assumption that suspicion is not sufficient for arrest and punishment. None of the totalitarian rulers, of course, ever dreamed of conditions in which he would have to resort to provocation in order to trap somebody he thought to be an enemy. More important than these technical considerations is the fact that totalitarianism defined its enemies ideologically before it seized power, so that categories of the "suspects" were not established through police information. Thus the Jews in Nazi Germany or the descendants of the former ruling classes in Soviet Russia were not really suspected of any hostile action; they had been declared "objective" enemies of the regime in accordance with its ideology.

The chief difference between the despotic and the totalitarian secret police lies in the difference between the "suspect" and the "objective enemy." The latter is defined by the policy of the government and not by his own desire to overthrow it.[95] He is never an individual whose dangerous thoughts must be

[92] Interesting in this respect are the attempts made by Nazi civil servants in Germany to reduce the competence and the personnel of the Gestapo on the ground that Nazification of the country had been achieved, so that Himmler, who on the contrary wanted to expand the secret services at this moment (around 1934), had to exaggerate the danger coming from the "internal enemies." See *Nazi Conspiracy*, II, 259; V, 205; III, 547.

[93] See Gallier-Boissière, *Mysteries of the French Secret Police*, 1938, p. 234.

[94] It seems, after all, no accident that the foundation of the Okhrana in 1880 ushered in a period of unsurpassed revolutionary activities in Russia. In order to prove its usefulness, it had occasionally to organize murders, and its agents "served despite themselves the ideas of those whom they denounced. . . . If a pamphlet was distributed by a police agent or if the execution of a minister was organized by an Azev—the result was the same" (M. Laporte, *op. cit.*, p. 25). The more important executions moreover seem to have been police jobs—Stolypin and von Plehve. Decisive for the revolutionary tradition was the fact that in times of calm the police agents had to "stir up anew the energies and stimulate the zeal" of the revolutionaries (*ibid.*, p. 71).

See also Bertram D. Wolfe, *Three Who Made A Revolution. Lenin, Trotsky, Stalin*, 1948, who calls this phenomenon "Police Socialism."

[95] Hans Frank, who later became Governor General of Poland, made a typical differentiation between a person "dangerous to the State" and a person who is "hostile to the State." The former implies an objective quality which is independent of will

provoked or whose past justifies suspicion, but a "carrier of tendencies" like the carrier of a disease.[96] Practically speaking, the totalitarian ruler proceeds like a man who persistently insults another man until everybody knows that the latter is his enemy, so that he can, with some plausibility, go and kill him in self-defense. This certainly is a little crude, but it works—as everybody will know who ever watched how certain successful careerists eliminate competitors.

The introduction of the notion of "objective enemy" is much more decisive for the functioning of totalitarian regimes than the ideological definition of the respective categories. If it were only a matter of hating Jews or bourgeois, the totalitarian regimes could, after the commission of one gigantic crime, return, as it were, to the rules of normal life and government. As we know, the opposite is the case. The category of objective enemies outlives the first ideologically determined foes of the movement; new objective enemies are discovered according to changing circumstances: the Nazis, foreseeing the completion of Jewish extermination, had already taken the necessary preliminary steps for the liquidation of the Polish people, while Hitler even planned the decimation of certain categories of Germans;[97] the Bolsheviks, having started with descendants of the former ruling classes, directed their full terror against the kulaks (in the early thirties), who in turn were followed by Russians of Polish origin (between 1936 and 1938), the Tartars and the Volga Germans during the war, former prisoners of war and units of the occupational forces of the Red Army after the war, and Russian Jewry after the establishment of a Jewish state. The choice of such categories is never entirely arbitrary; since they are publicized and used for propaganda purposes of the movement abroad, they must appear plausible as possible enemies; the choice of a particular category may even be due

---

and behavior; the political police of the Nazis is concerned not just with actions hostile to the state but with "all attempts—no matter what their aim—which in their effects endanger the State." See *Deutsches Verwaltungsrecht*, pp. 420-430. Translation quoted from *Nazi Conspiracy*, IV, 881 ff.—In the words of Maunz, *op. cit.*, p. 44: "By eliminating dangerous persons, the security measure . . . means to ward off a state of danger to the national community, independently of any offense that may have been committed by these persons. [It is a question of] warding off an *objective* danger."

[96] R. Hoehn, a Nazi jurist and member of the SS, said in an obituary on Reinhard Heydrich, who prior to his rule of Czechoslovakia had been one of the closest collaborators with Himmler: He regarded his opponents "not as individuals but as carriers of tendencies endangering the state and therefore beyond the pale of the national community." In *Deutsche Allgemeine Zeitung* of June 6, 1942; quoted from E. Kohn-Bramstedt, *Dictatorship and Political Police*, London, 1945.

[97] As early as 1941, during a staff meeting in Hitler's headquarters, it was proposed to impose upon the Polish population those regulations by which the Jews had been prepared for the extermination camps: change of names if these were of German origin; death sentences for sexual intercourse between Germans and Poles (*Rassenschande*); obligation to wear a P-sign in Germany similar to the Yellow Star for Jews. See *Nazi Conspiracy*, VIII, 237 ff., and Hans Frank's diary in *Trial, op. cit.*, XXIX, 683. Naturally, the Poles themselves soon began to worry about what would happen to them when the Nazis had finished the extermination of the Jews (*Nazi Conspiracy*, IV, 916).—For Hitler's plans regarding the German people, see note 80.

to certain propaganda needs of the movement at large—as for instance the sudden entirely unprecedented emergence of governmental antisemitism in the Soviet Union, which may be calculated to win sympathies for the Soviet Union in the European satellite countries. The show trials which require subjective confessions of guilt from "objectively" identified enemies are meant for these purposes; they can best be staged with those who have received a totalitarian indoctrination that enables them "subjectively" to understand their own "objective" harmfulness and to confess "for the sake of the cause."[98] The concept of the "objective opponent," whose identity changes according to the prevailing circumstances—so that, as soon as one category is liquidated, war may be declared on another—corresponds exactly to the factual situation reiterated time and again by totalitarian rulers: namely, that their regime is not a government in any traditional sense, but a *movement,* whose advance constantly meets with new obstacles that have to be eliminated. So far as one may speak at all of any legal thinking within the totalitarian system, the "objective opponent" is its central idea.

Closely connected with this transformation of the suspect into the objective enemy is the change of position of the secret police in the totalitarian state. The secret services have rightly been called a state within the state, and this not only in despotisms but also under constitutional or semiconstitutional governments. The mere possession of secret information has always given this branch a decisive superiority over all other branches of the civil services and constituted an open threat to members of the government.[99] The totalitarian police, on the contrary, is totally subject to the will of the Leader, who alone can decide who the next potential enemy will be and who, as Stalin did, can also single out cadres of the secret police for liquidation. Since the police are no longer permitted to use provocation, they have been deprived of the only available means of perpetuating themselves independently of the government and have become entirely dependent on the higher authorities for the safeguarding of their jobs. Like the army in a nontotalitarian state, the police in totalitarian countries merely execute political policy and have lost all the prerogatives which they held under despotic bureaucracies.[100]

[98] Beck and Godin, *op. cit.*, p. 87, speak of the "objective characteristics" which invited arrest in the USSR; among them was membership in the NKVD (p. 153). Subjective insight into the objective necessity of arrest and confession could most easily be achieved with former members of the secret police. In the words of an ex-NKVD agent: "My superiors know me and my work well enough, and if the party and the NKVD now require me to confess to such things they must have good reasons for what they are doing. My duty as a loyal Soviet citizen is not to withhold the confession required of me" (*ibid.*, p. 231).

[99] Well known is the situation in France where ministers lived in constant fear of the secret "*dossiers*" of the police. For the situation in Czarist Russia, see Laporte, *op. cit.*, pp. 22-23: "Eventually the Okhrana will wield a power far superior to the power of the more regular authorities. . . . The Okhrana . . . will inform the Czar only of what it chooses to."

[100] "Unlike the Okhrana, which had been a state within a state, the GPU is a department of the Soviet government; . . . and its activities are much less independent" (Roger N. Baldwin, "Political Police," in *Encyclopedia of Social Sciences*).

The task of the totalitarian police is not to discover crimes, but to be on hand when the government decides to arrest a certain category of the population. Their chief political distinction is that they alone are in the confidence of the highest authority and know which political line will be enforced. This does not apply only to matters of high policy, such as the liquidation of a whole class or ethnic group (only the cadres of the GPU knew the actual goal of the Soviet government in the early thirties and only the SS formations knew that the Jews were to be exterminated in the early forties); the point about everyday life under totalitarian conditions is that only the agents of the NKVD in an industrial enterprise are informed of what Moscow wants when it orders, for instance, a speed-up in the fabrication of pipes—whether it simply wants more pipes, or to ruin the director of the factory, or to liquidate the whole management, or to abolish this particular factory, or, finally, to have this order repeated all over the nation so that a new purge can begin.

One of the reasons for the duplication of secret services whose agents are unknown to each other is that total domination needs the most extreme flexibility: to use our example, Moscow may not yet know, when it gives its order for pipes, whether it wants pipes—which are always needed—or a purge. Multiplication of secret services makes last-minute changes possible, so that one branch may be preparing to bestow the Order of Lenin on the director of the factory while another makes arrangements for his arrest. The efficiency of the police consists in the fact that such contradictory assignments can be prepared simultaneously.

Under totalitarian, as under other regimes, the secret police has a monopoly on certain vital information. But the kind of knowledge that can be possessed only by the police has undergone an important change: the police are no longer concerned with knowing what is going on in the heads of future victims (most of the time they ignore who these victims will be), and the police have become the trustees of the greatest state secrets. This automatically means a great improvement in prestige and position, even though it is accompanied by a definite loss of real power. The secret services no longer know anything that the Leader does not know better; in terms of power, they have sunk to the level of the executioner.

From a legal point of view, even more interesting than the change from the suspect to the objective enemy is the totalitarian replacement of the suspected offense by the possible crime. The possible crime is no more subjective than the objective enemy. While the suspect is arrested because he is thought to be capable of committing a crime that more or less fits his personality (or his suspected personality),[101] the totalitarian version of the

[101] Typical of the concept of the suspect is the following story related by C. Pobyedonostzev in *L'Autocratie Russe: Mémoires politiques, correspondance officiele et documents inédits . . . 1881-1894*, Paris, 1927: General Cherevin of the Okhrana is asked, because the opposing party has hired a Jewish lawyer, to intervene in favor of a lady who is about to lose a lawsuit. Says the General: "The same night I ordered the arrest of this cursed Jew and held him as a so-called politically suspect person. . . . After all, could I treat in the same manner friends and a dirty Jew who may be innocent today but who was guilty yesterday or will be guilty tomorrow?"

possible crime is based on the logical anticipation of objective developments. The Moscow Trials of the old Bolshevik guard and the chiefs of the Red Army were classic examples of punishment for possible crimes. Behind the fantastic, fabricated charges one can easily detect the following logical calculation: developments in the Soviet Union might lead to a crisis, a crisis might lead to the overthrow of Stalin's dictatorship, this might weaken the country's military force and possibly bring about a situation in which the new government would have to sign a truce or even conclude an alliance with Hitler. Whereupon Stalin proceeded to declare that a plot for the overthrow of the government and a conspiracy with Hitler existed.[102] Against these "objective," though entirely improbable, possibilities stood only "subjective" factors, such as the trustworthiness of the accused, their fatigue, their inability to understand what was going on, their firm conviction that without Stalin everything would be lost, their sincere hatred of Fascism—that is, a number of factual details which naturally lacked the consistency of the fictitious, logical, possible crime. Totalitarianism's central assumption that everything is possible thus leads through consistent elimination of all factual restraints to the absurd and terrible consequence that every crime the rulers can conceive of must be punished, regardless of whether or not it has been committed. The possible crime, like the objective enemy, is of course beyond the competence of the police, who can neither discover, invent, nor provoke it. Here again the secret services depend entirely upon the political authorities. Their independence as a state within the state is gone.

Only in one respect does the totalitarian secret police still resemble closely the secret services of nontotalitarian countries. The secret police has traditionally, *i.e.*, since Fouché, profited from its victims and has augmented the official state-authorized budget from certain unorthodox sources simply by assuming a position of partnership in activities it was supposed to suppress, such as gambling and prostitution.[103] These illegal methods of financing itself, ranging from friendly acceptance of bribes to outright blackmail, were a

[102] The charges in the Moscow Trials "were based . . . on a grotesquely brutalized and distorting anticipation of possible developments. [Stalin's] reasoning probably developed along the following lines: they may want to overthrow me in a crisis—I shall charge them with having made the attempt. . . . A change of government may weaken Russia's fighting capacity; and if they succeed, they may be compelled to sign a truce with Hitler, and perhaps even agree to a cession of territory. . . . I shall accuse them of having entered already into a treacherous alliance with Germany and ceded Soviet territory." This is I. Deutscher's brilliant explanation of the Moscow Trials, *op. cit.*, p. 377.

A good example of the Nazi version of the possible crime can be found in Hans Frank, *op. cit.:* "A complete catalogue of attempts 'dangerous to the State' can never be drawn up because it can never be foreseen what may endanger the leadership and the people some time in the future." (Translation quoted from *Nazi Conspiracy*, IV, 881.)

[103] The criminal methods of the secret police are of course no monopoly of the French tradition. In Austria, for example, the feared political police under Maria Theresa was organized by Kaunitz from the cadres of the so-called "chastity commissars" who used to live by blackmail. See Moritz Bermann, *Maria Theresia und Kaiser Joseph II*, Vienna-Leipzig, 1881. I owe this reference to Robert Pick.

prominent factor in freeing the secret services from the public authorities and strengthened their position as a state within the state. It is curious to see that the financing of police activities with income from its victims has survived all other changes. In Soviet Russia, the NKVD is almost entirely dependent upon the exploitation of slave labor which, indeed, seems to yield no other profit and to serve no other purpose but the financing of the huge secret apparatus.[104] Himmler first financed his SS troops, who were the cadres of the Nazi secret police, through the confiscation of Jewish property; he then concluded an agreement with Darré, the Minister of Agriculture, by which Himmler received the several hundred million marks which Darré earned annually by buying agricultural commodities cheaply abroad and selling them at fixed prices in Germany.[105] This source of regular income disappeared of course during the war; Albert Speer, the successor of Todt and the greatest employer of manpower in Germany after 1942, proposed a similar deal to Himmler in 1942; if Himmler agreed to release from SS authority the imported slave laborers whose work had been remarkably inefficient, the Speer organization would give him a certain percentage of the profits for the SS.[106] To such more or less regular sources of income, Himmler added the old blackmail methods of secret services in times of financial crisis: in their communities SS units formed groups of "Friends of the SS" who had to "volunteer" the necessary funds for the needs of the local SS men.[107] (It is noteworthy that in its various financial operations the Nazi secret police did not exploit its prisoners. Except in the last years of the war, when the use of human material in the concentration camps was no longer determined by Himmler alone, work in the camps "had no rational purpose except that of increasing the burden and torture of the unfortunate prisoners."[108])

However, these financial irregularities are the sole, and not very important, traces of the secret police tradition. They are possible because of

[104] That the huge police organization is paid with profits from slave labor is certain; surprising is that the police budget seems not even entirely covered by it; Kravchenko, *op. cit.*, mentions special taxes, imposed by the NKVD on convicted citizens who continue to live and work in freedom.

[105] See Fritz Thyssen, *I Paid Hitler*, London, 1941.

[106] See *Nazi Conspiracy*, I, 916-917.—The economic activity of the SS was consolidated in a central office for economic and administrative affairs. To the Treasury and Internal Revenue, the SS declared its financial assets as "party property earmarked for special purposes" (letter of May 5, 1943, quoted from M. Wolfson, *Uebersicht der Gliederung verbrecherischer Nazi-Organisationen. Omgus*, December, 1947).

[107] See Kohn-Bramstedt, *op. cit.*, p. 112.—The blackmail motive is clearly revealed if we consider that this kind of fund-raising was always organized by local SS units in the localities where they were stationed. See *Der Weg der SS*, issued by the *SS-Hauptamt-Schulungsamt* (undated), p. 14.

[108] *Ibid.*, p. 124.—Certain compromises in this respect were made for those requirements pertaining to the maintenance of the camps and the personal needs of the SS. See Wolfson, *op. cit.*, letter of September 19, 1941, from Oswald Pohl, head of the WVH (*Wirtschafts-und Verwaltungs-Hauptamt*) to the Reichskommissar for price control. It seems that all these economic activities in the concentration camps developed only during the war and under the pressure of acute labor shortage.

the general contempt of totalitarian regimes for economic and financial matters, so that methods which under normal conditions would be illegal, and would distinguish the secret police from other more respectable departments of the administration, no longer indicate that we are dealing here with a department which enjoys independence, is not controlled by other authorities, lives in an atmosphere of irregularity, nonrespectability, and insecurity. The position of the totalitarian secret police, on the contrary, has been completely stabilized, and its services are wholly integrated in the administration. Not only is the organization *not* beyond the pale of the law, but, rather, it is the embodiment of the law, and its respectability is above suspicion. It no longer organizes murders on its own initiative, no longer provokes offenses against state and society, and it sternly proceeds against all forms of bribery, blackmail and irregular financial gains. The moral lecture, coupled with very tangible threats, that Himmler could permit himself to deliver to his men in the middle of the war—"We had the moral right . . . to wipe out this [Jewish] people bent on wiping us out, but we do not have the right to enrich ourselves in any manner whatsoever, be it by a fur coat, a watch, a single mark, or a cigarette"[109]—strikes a note that one would look for in vain in the history of the secret police. If it still is concerned with "dangerous thoughts," they are hardly ones which the suspected persons know to be dangerous; the regimentation of all intellectual and artistic life demands a constant re-establishment and revision of standards which naturally is accompanied by repeated eliminations of intellectuals whose "dangerous thoughts" usually consist in certain ideas that were still entirely orthodox the day before. While, therefore, its police function in the accepted meaning of the word has become superfluous, the economic function of the secret police, sometimes thought to have replaced the first, is even more dubious. It is undeniable, to be sure, that the NKVD periodically rounds up a percentage of the Soviet population and sends them into camps which are known under the flattering misnomer of forced-labor camps;[110] yet although it is quite possible that this is the Soviet Union's

[109] Himmler's speech of October, 1943, at Posen, *International Military Trials*, Nuremberg, 1945-46, Vol. 29, p. 146.

[110] "Bek Bulat (the pen name of a former Soviet professor) has been able to study documents of the North Caucasian NKVD. From these documents it was obvious that in June, 1937, when the great purge was at its apex, the government prescribed the local NKVDs to have a certain percentage of the population arrested. . . . The percentage varied from one province to the other, reaching 5 per cent in the least loyal areas. The average for the whole of the Soviet Union was about 3 per cent." Reported by David J. Dallin in *The New Leader*, January 8, 1949.—Beck and Godin, *op. cit.*, p. 239, arrive at a slightly divergent and quite plausible assumption, according to which "arrests were planned as follows: The NKVD files covered practically the whole population, and everyone was classified in a category. Thus statistics were available in every town showing how many former Whites, members of opposing parties, etc., were living in them. All incriminating material collected . . . and gathered from prisoners' confessions was also entered in the files, and each person's card was marked to show how dangerous he was considered; this depending on the amount of suspicious or incriminating material appearing in his file. As the statistics were regu-

way of solving its unemployment problem, it is also generally known that the output in those camps is infinitely lower than that of ordinary Soviet labor and hardly suffices to pay the expenses of the police apparatus.

Neither dubious nor superfluous is the political function of the secret police, the "best organized and the most efficient" of all government departments,[111] in the power apparatus of the totalitarian regime. It constitutes the true executive branch of the government through which all orders are transmitted. Through the net of secret agents, the totalitarian ruler has created for himself a directly executive transmission belt which, in distinction to the onion-like structure of the ostensible hierarchy, is completely severed and isolated from all other institutions.[112] In this sense, the secret police agents are the only openly ruling class in totalitarian countries and their standards and scale of values permeate the entire texture of totalitarian society.

From this viewpoint, it may not be too surprising that certain peculiar qualities of the secret police are general qualities of totalitarian society rather than peculiarities of the totalitarian secret police. The category of the suspect thus embraces under totalitarian conditions the total population; every thought that deviates from the officially prescribed and permanently changing line is already suspect, no matter in which field of human activity it occurs. Simply because of their capacity to think, human beings are suspects by definition, and this suspicion cannot be diverted by exemplary behavior, for the human capacity to think is also a capacity to change one's mind. Since, moreover, it is impossible ever to know beyond doubt another man's heart—torture in this context is only the desperate and eternally futile attempt to achieve what cannot be achieved—suspicion can no longer be allayed if neither a community of values nor the predictabilities of self-interest exist as social (as distinguished from merely psychological) realities. Mutual suspicion, therefore, permeates all social relationships in totalitarian countries and creates an all-pervasive atmosphere even outside the special purview of the secret police.

In totalitarian regimes provocation, once only the specialty of the secret agent, becomes a method of dealing with his neighbor which everybody, willingly or unwillingly, is forced to follow. Everyone, in a way, is the *agent*

---

larly reported to higher authorities, it was possible to arrange a purge at any moment, with full knowledge of the exact number of persons in each category."

[111] Baldwin, *op. cit.*

[112] The Russian secret-police cadres were as much at the "personal disposal" of Stalin as the SS Shock Troops (*Verfügungstruppen*) were at the personal disposal of Hitler. Both, even if they are called to serve with the military forces in time of war, live under their own special jurisdiction. The special "marriage laws" which served to segregate the SS from the rest of the population, were the first and most fundamental regulations which Himmler introduced when he took over the reorganization of the SS. Even prior to Himmler's marriage laws, in 1927, the SS was instructed by official decree "never [to participate] in discussions at membership meetings" (*Der Weg der SS, op. cit.*). The same conduct is reported about the members of the NKVD, who kept deliberately to themselves and above all did not associate with other sections of the party aristocracy (Beck and Godin, *op. cit.*, p. 163).

provocateur of everyone else; for obviously everybody will call himself an *agent provocateur* if ever an ordinary friendly exchange of "dangerous thoughts" (or what in the meantime have become dangerous thoughts) should come to the attention of the authorities. Collaboration of the population in denouncing political opponents and volunteer service as stool pigeons are certainly not unprecedented, but in totalitarian countries they are so well organized that the work of specialists is almost superfluous. In a system of ubiquitous spying, where everybody may be a police agent and each individual feels himself under constant surveillance; under circumstances, moreover, where careers are extremely insecure and where the most spectacular ascents and falls have become everyday occurrences, every word becomes equivocal and subject to retrospective "interpretation."

The most striking illustration of the permeation of totalitarian society with secret police methods and standards can be found in the matter of careers. The double agent in nontotalitarian regimes served the cause he was supposed to combat almost as much as, and sometimes more than, the authorities. Frequently he harbored a sort of double ambition: he wanted to rise in the ranks of the revolutionary parties as well as in the ranks of the services. In order to win promotion in both fields, he had only to adopt certain methods which in a normal society belong to the secret daydreams of the small employee who depends on seniority for advancement: through his connections with the police, he could certainly eliminate his rivals and superiors in the party, and through his connections with the revolutionaries he had at least a chance to get rid of his chief in the police.[113] If we consider the career conditions in present Russian society, the similarity to such methods is striking. Not only do almost all higher officials owe their positions to purges that removed their predecessors, but promotions in all walks of life are accelerated in this way. About every ten years, a nation-wide purge makes room for the new generation, freshly graduated and hungry for jobs. The government has itself established those conditions for advancement which the police agent formerly had to create.

This regular violent turnover of the whole gigantic administrative machine, while it prevents the development of competence, has many advantages: it assures the relative youth of officials and prevents a stabilization of conditions which, at least in time of peace, are fraught with danger for totalitarian rule; by eliminating seniority and merit, it prevents the development of the loyalties that usually tie younger staff members to their elders, upon whose opinion and good will their advancement depends; it eliminates once and for all the dangers of unemployment and assures everyone of a job compatible with his education. Thus, in 1939, after the gigantic purge in the Soviet Union had come to an end, Stalin could note with great satisfaction that "the Party was able to promote to leading posts in State or Party affairs more than 500,000 young Bolsheviks."[114] The humiliation

[113] Typical is the splendid career of police agent Malinovsky, who ended as deputy of the Bolsheviks in parliament. See Bertram D. Wolfe, *op. cit.*, chapter xxxi.

[114] Quoted from Avtorkhanov, *op. cit.*

implicit in owing a job to the unjust elimination of one's predecessor has the same demoralizing effect that the elimination of the Jews had upon the German professions: it makes every jobholder a conscious accomplice in the crimes of the government, their beneficiary whether he likes it or not, with the result that the more sensitive the humiliated individual happens to be, the more ardently he will defend the regime. In other words, this system is the logical outgrowth of the Leader principle in its full implications and the best possible guarantee for loyalty, in that it makes every new generation depend for its livelihood on the current political line of the Leader which started the job-creating purge. It also realizes the identity of public and private interests, of which defenders of the Soviet Union used to be so proud (or, in the Nazi version, the abolition of the private sphere of life), insofar as every individual of any consequence owes his whole existence to the political interest of the regime; and when this factual identity of interest is broken and the next purge has swept him out of office, the regime makes sure that he disappears from the world of the living. In a not very different way, the double agent was identified with the cause of the revolution (without which he would lose his job), and not only with the secret police; in that sphere, too, a spectacular rise could end only in an anonymous death, since it was rather unlikely that the double game could be played forever. The totalitarian government, when it set such conditions for promotion in all careers as had previously prevailed only among social outcasts, has effected one of the most far-reaching changes in social psychology. The psychology of the double agent, who was willing to pay the price of a short life for the exalted existence of a few years at the peak, has necessarily become the philosophy in personal matters of the whole post-revolutionary generation in Russia, and to a lesser but still very dangerous extent, in postwar Germany.

This is the society, permeated by standards and living by methods which once had been the monopoly of the secret police, in which the totalitarian secret police functions. Only in the initial stages, when a struggle for power is still going on, are its victims those who can be suspected of opposition. It then embarks upon its totalitarian career with the persecution of the objective enemy, which may be the Jews or the Poles (as in the case of the Nazis) or so-called "counter-revolutionaries"—an accusation which "in Soviet Russia . . . is established . . . before any question as to [the] behavior [of the accused] has arisen at all"—who may be people who at any time owned a shop or a house or "had parents or grandparents who owned such things,"[115] or who happened to belong to one of the Red Army occupational forces, or were Russians of Polish origin. Only in its last and fully totalitarian stage are the concepts of the objective enemy and the logically possible crime abandoned, the victims chosen completely at random and, even without being accused, declared unfit to live. This new category of "undesirables" may consist, as in the case of the Nazis, of the mentally ill or persons with lung and heart disease, or in the Soviet Union, of

[115] *The Dark Side of the Moon*, New York, 1947.

people who happen to have been taken up in that percentage, varying from one province to another, which is ordered to be deported.

This consistent arbitrariness negates human freedom more efficiently than any tyranny ever could. One had at least to be an enemy of tyranny in order to be punished by it. Freedom of opinion was not abolished for those who were brave enough to risk their necks. Theoretically, the choice of opposition remains in totalitarian regimes too; but such freedom is almost invalidated if committing a voluntary act only assures a "punishment" that everyone else may have to bear anyway. Freedom in this system has not only dwindled down to its last and apparently still indestructible guarantee, the possibility of suicide, but has lost its distinctive mark because the consequences of its exercise are shared with completely innocent people. If Hitler had had the time to realize his dream of a General German Health Bill, the man suffering from a lung disease would have been subject to the same fate as a Communist in the early and a Jew in the later years of the Nazi regime. Similarly, the opponent of the regime in Russia, suffering the same fate as millions of people who are chosen for concentration camps to make up certain quotas, only relieves the police of the burden of arbitrary choice. The innocent and the guilty are equally undesirable.

The change in the concept of crime and criminals determines the new and terrible methods of the totalitarian secret police. Criminals are punished, undesirables disappear from the face of the earth; the only trace which they leave behind is the memory of those who knew and loved them, and one of the most difficult tasks of the secret police is to make sure that even such traces will disappear together with the condemned man.

The Okhrana, the Czarist predecessor of the GPU, is reported to have invented a filing system in which every suspect was noted on a large card in the center of which his name was surrounded by a red circle; his political friends were designated by smaller red circles and his nonpolitical acquaintances by green ones; brown circles indicated persons in contact with friends of the suspect but not known to him personally; cross-relationships between the suspect's friends, political and nonpolitical, and the friends of his friends were indicated by lines between the respective circles.[110] Obviously the limitations of this method are set only by the size of the filing cards, and, theoretically, a gigantic single sheet could show the relations and cross-relationships of the entire population. And this is the utopian goal of the totalitarian secret police. It has given up the traditional old police dream which the lie detector is still supposed to realize, and no longer tries to find out who is who, or who thinks what. (The lie detector is perhaps the most graphic example of the fascination that this dream apparently exerts over the mentality of all policemen; for obviously the complicated measuring equipment can hardly establish anything except the cold-blooded or nervous temperament of its victims. Actually, the feeble-minded reasoning underlying the use of this mechanism can only be explained by the irrational wish that some form of mind reading were possible after all.) This old dream

[110] See Laporte, *op. cit.*, p. 39.

was terrible enough and since time immemorial has invariably led to torture and the most abominable cruelties. There was only one thing in its favor: it asked for the impossible. The modern dream of the totalitarian police, with its modern techniques, is incomparably more terrible. Now the police dreams that one look at the gigantic map on the office wall should suffice at any given moment to establish who is related to whom and in what degree of intimacy; and, theoretically, this dream is not unrealizable although its technical execution is bound to be somewhat difficult. If this map really did exist, not even memory would stand in the way of the totalitarian claim to domination; such a map might make it possible to obliterate people without any traces, as if they had never existed at all.

If the reports of arrested NKVD agents can be trusted, the Russian secret police has come uncomfortably close to this ideal of totalitarian rule. The police has secret dossiers about each inhabitant of the vast country, carefully listing the many relationships that exist between people, from chance acquaintances to genuine friendship to family relations; for it is only to discover these relationships that the defendants, whose "crimes" have anyway been established "objectively" prior to their arrest, are questioned so closely. Finally, as for the gift of memory so dangerous to totalitarian rule, foreign observers feel that "if it is true that elephants never forget, Russians seem to us to be the very opposite of elephants. . . . Soviet Russian psychology seems to make forgetfulness really possible."[117]

How important to the total-domination apparatus this complete disappearance of its victims is can be seen in those instances where, for one reason or another, the regime was confronted with the memory of survivors. During the war, one SS commandant made the terrible mistake of informing a French woman of her husband's death in a German concentration camp; this slip caused a small avalanche of orders and instructions to all camp commandants, warning them that under no circumstances was information ever to be given to the outside world.[118] The point is that, as far as the French widow was concerned, her husband had supposedly ceased to live at the moment of his arrest, or rather had ceased ever to have lived. Similarly, the Soviet police officers, accustomed to this system since their birth, could only stare in amazement at those people in occupied Poland who tried desperately to find out what had happened to their friends and relatives under arrest.[119]

In totalitarian countries all places of detention ruled by the police are made to be veritable holes of oblivion into which people stumble by accident and without leaving behind them such ordinary traces of former existence as a body and a grave. Compared with this newest invention for doing away with people, the old-fashioned method of murder, political or criminal, is inefficient indeed. The murderer leaves behind him a corpse, and although he tries to efface the traces of his own identity, he has no power to erase the

[117] Beck and Godin, *op. cit.*, pp. 234 and 127.
[118] See *Nazi Conspiracy*, VII, 84 ff.
[119] *The Dark Side of the Moon.*

identity of his victim from the memory of the surviving world. The operation of the secret police, on the contrary, miraculously sees to it that the victim never existed at all.

The connection between secret police and secret societies is obvious. The establishment of the former always needed and used the argument of dangers arising from the existence of the latter. The totalitarian secret police is the first in history which neither needs nor uses these old-fashioned pretexts of all tyrants. The anonymity of its victims, who cannot be called enemies of the regime and whose identity is unknown to the persecutors until the arbitrary decision of the government eliminates them from the world of the living and exterminates their memory from the world of the dead, is beyond all secrecy, beyond the strictest silence, beyond the greatest mastery of double life that the discipline of conspiratory societies used to impose upon their members.

The totalitarian movements which, during their rise to power, imitate certain organizational features of secret societies and yet establish themselves in broad daylight, create a true secret society only after their ascendancy to rule. The secret society of totalitarian regimes is the secret police; the only strictly guarded secret in a totalitarian country, the only esoteric knowledge that exists, concerns the operations of the police and the conditions in the concentration camps.[120] Of course the population at large and the party members specifically know all the general facts—that concentration camps exist, that people disappear, that innocent persons are arrested; at the same time, every person in a totalitarian country knows also that it is the greatest crime ever to talk about these "secrets." Inasmuch as man depends for his knowledge upon the affirmation and comprehension of his fellow-men, this generally shared but individually guarded, this never-communicated information loses its quality of reality and assumes the nature of a mere nightmare. Only those who are in possession of the strictly esoteric knowledge concerning the eventual new categories of undesirables and the operational methods of the cadres are in a position to communicate with each other about what actually constitutes the reality for all. They alone are in a position to believe in what they know to be true. This is their secret, and in order to guard this secret they are established as a secret organization. They remain members even if this secret organization arrests them, forces them to make confessions, and finally liquidates them. So long as they guard the secret they belong to the elite, and as a rule they do not betray it even when they are in the prisons and concentration camps.[121]

We already have noted that one of the many paradoxes that offend the

[120] "There was little in the SS that was not secret. The greatest secret was the practices in the concentration camps. Not even members of the Gestapo were admitted . . . to the camps without a special permit" (Eugen Kogon, *Der SS-Staat,* Munich, 1946, p. 297).

[121] Beck and Godin, *op. cit.*, p. 169, report how the arrested NKVD officials "took the greatest care never to reveal any NKVD secrets."

common sense of the nontotalitarian world is the seemingly irrational use which totalitarianism makes of conspiratory methods. The totalitarian movements, apparently persecuted by the police, very sparingly use methods of conspiracy for the overthrow of the government in their struggle for power, whereas totalitarianism in power, after it has been recognized by all governments and seemingly outgrown its revolutionary stage, develops a true secret police as the nucleus of its government and power. It seems that official recognition is felt to be a greater menace to the conspiracy content of the totalitarian movement, a menace of interior disintegration, than the half-hearted police measures of nontotalitarian regimes.

The truth of the matter is that totalitarian leaders, though they are convinced that they must follow consistently the fiction and the rules of the fictitious world which were laid down during their struggle for power, discover only gradually the full implications of this fictitious world and its rules. Their faith in human omnipotence, their conviction that everything can be done through organization, carries them into experiments which human imaginations may have outlined but human activity certainly never realized. Their hideous discoveries in the realm of the possible are inspired by an ideological scientificality which has proved to be less controlled by reason and less willing to recognize factuality than the wildest fantasies of prescientific and prephilosophical speculation. They establish the secret society which now no longer operates in broad daylight, the society of the secret police or the political soldier or the ideologically trained fighter, in order to be able to carry out the indecent experimental inquiry into what is possible.

The totalitarian conspiracy against the nontotalitarian world, on the other hand, its claim to world domination, remains as open and unguarded under conditions of totalitarian rule as in the totalitarian movements. It is practically impressed upon the co-ordinated population of "sympathizers" in the form of a supposed conspiracy of the whole world against their own country. The totalitarian dichotomy is propagated by making it a duty for every national abroad to report home as though he were a secret agent, and by treating every foreigner as a spy for his home government.[122] It is for the practical realization of this dichotomy rather than because of specific secrets, military and other, that iron curtains separate the inhabitants of a totalitarian country from the rest of the world. Their real secret, the concentration camps, those laboratories in the experiment of total domination, is shielded by the totalitarian regimes from the eyes of their own people as well as from all others.

For a considerable length of time the normality of the normal world is the most efficient protection against disclosure of totalitarian mass crimes. "Normal men don't know that everything is possible,"[123] refuse to believe

[122] Typical is the following dialogue reported in *Dark Side of the Moon:* "To an admission that one had ever been outside Poland the next question invariably was: 'And for whom were you spying? . . . One man . . . asked: 'But you too have foreign visitors. Do you suppose they are all spies?' The answer was: 'What do you think? Do you imagine we are so naïve as not to be perfectly aware of it?' "

[123] David Rousset, *The Other Kingdom*, New York, 1947.

their eyes and ears in the face of the monstrous, just as the mass men did not trust theirs in the face of a normal reality in which no place was left for them.[124] The reason why the totalitarian regimes can get so far toward realizing a fictitious, topsy-turvy world is that the outside nontotalitarian world, which always comprises a great part of the population of the totalitarian country itself, indulges also in wishful thinking and shirks reality in the face of real insanity just as much as the masses do in the face of the normal world. This common-sense disinclination to believe the monstrous is constantly strengthened by the totalitarian ruler himself, who makes sure that no reliable statistics, no controllable facts and figures are ever published, so that there are only subjective, uncontrollable, and unreliable reports about the places of the living dead.

Because of this policy, the results of the totalitarian experiment are only partially known. Although we have enough reports from concentration camps to assess the possibilities of total domination and to catch a glimpse into the abyss of the "possible," we do not know the extent of character transformation under a totalitarian regime. We know even less how many of the normal people around us would be willing to accept the totalitarian way of life—that is, to pay the price of a considerably shorter life for the assured fulfillment of all their career dreams. It is easy to realize the extent to which totalitarian propaganda and even some totalitarian institutions answer the needs of the new homeless masses, but it is almost impossible to know how many of them, if they are further exposed to a constant threat of unemployment, will gladly acquiesce to a "population policy" that consists of regular elimination of surplus people, and how many, once they have fully grasped their growing incapacity to bear the burdens of modern life, will gladly conform to a system that, together with spontaneity, eliminates responsibility.

In other words, while we know the operation and the specific function of the totalitarian secret police, we do not know how well or to what an extent the "secret" of this secret society corresponds to the secret desires and the secret complicities of the masses in our time.

III: *Total Domination*

THE CONCENTRATION and extermination camps of totalitarian regimes serve as the laboratories in which the fundamental belief of totalitarianism that everything is possible is being verified. Compared with this, all other experiments are secondary in importance—including those in the field of

[124] The Nazis were well aware of the protective wall of incredulity which surrounded their enterprise. A secret report to Rosenberg about the massacre of 5,000 Jews in 1943 states explicitly: "Imagine only that these occurrences would become known to the other side and exploited by them. Most likely such propaganda would have no effect only because people who hear and read about it simply would not be ready to believe it" (*Nazi Conspiracy*, I, 1001).

medicine whose horrors are recorded in detail in the trials against the physicians of the Third Reich—although it is characteristic that these laboratories were used for experiments of every kind.

Total domination, which strives to organize the infinite plurality and differentiation of human beings as if all of humanity were just one individual, is possible only if each and every person can be reduced to a never-changing identity of reactions, so that each of these bundles of reactions can be exchanged at random for any other. The problem is to fabricate something that does not exist, namely, a kind of human species resembling other animal species whose only "freedom" would consist in "preserving the species."[125] Totalitarian domination attempts to achieve this goal both through ideological indoctrination of the elite formations and through absolute terror in the camps; and the atrocities for which the elite formations are ruthlessly used become, as it were, the practical application of the ideological indoctrination—the testing ground in which the latter must prove itself—while the appalling spectacle of the camps themselves is supposed to furnish the "theoretical" verification of the ideology.

The camps are meant not only to exterminate people and degrade human beings, but also serve the ghastly experiment of eliminating, under scientifically controlled conditions, spontaneity itself as an expression of human behavior and of transforming the human personality into a mere thing, into something that even animals are not; for Pavlov's dog, which, as we know, was trained to eat not when it was hungry but when a bell rang, was a perverted animal.

Under normal circumstances this can never be accomplished, because spontaneity can never be entirely eliminated insofar as it is connected not only with human freedom but with life itself, in the sense of simply keeping alive. It is only in the concentration camps that such an experiment is at all possible, and therefore they are not only *"la société la plus totalitaire encore réalisée"* (David Rousset) but the guiding social ideal of total domination in general. Just as the stability of the totalitarian regime depends on the isolation of the fictitious world of the movement from the outside world, so the experiment of total domination in the concentration camps depends on sealing off the latter against the world of all others, the world of the living in general, even against the outside world of a country under totalitarian rule. This isolation explains the peculiar unreality and lack of credibility that characterize all reports from the concentration camps and constitute one of the main difficulties for the true understanding of totalitarian domination, which stands or falls with the existence of these concentration and extermination camps; for, unlikely as it may sound, these camps are the true central institution of totalitarian organizational power.

[125] In the *Tischgespräche*, Hitler mentions several times that he "[strives] for a condition in which each individual knows that he lives and dies for the preservation of his species" (p. 349). See also p. 347: "A fly lays millions of eggs, all of which perish. But the flies remain."

There are numerous reports by survivors.[126] The more authentic they are, the less they attempt to communicate things that evade human understanding and human experience—sufferings, that is, that transform men into "uncomplaining animals."[127] None of these reports inspires those passions of outrage and sympathy through which men have always been mobilized for justice. On the contrary, anyone speaking or writing about concentration camps is still regarded as suspect; and if the speaker has resolutely returned to the world of the living, he himself is often assailed by doubts with regard to his own truthfulness, as though he had mistaken a nightmare for reality.[128]

This doubt of people concerning themselves and the reality of their own experience only reveals what the Nazis have always known: that men determined to commit crimes will find it expedient to organize them on the vastest, most improbable scale. Not only because this renders all punishments provided by the legal system inadequate and absurd; but because the very immensity of the crimes guarantees that the murderers who proclaim their innocence with all manner of lies will be more readily believed than the victims who tell the truth. The Nazis did not even consider it necessary to keep this discovery to themselves. Hitler circulated millions of copies of his book in which he stated that to be successful, a lie must be enormous—which did not prevent people from believing him as, similarly, the Nazis' proclamations, repeated *ad nauseam,* that the Jews would be exterminated like bedbugs (*i.e.,* with poison gas), prevented anybody from *not* believing them.

There is a great temptation to explain away the intrinsically incredible

[126] The best reports on Nazi concentration camps are David Rousset, *Les Jours de Notre Mort,* Paris, 1947; Eugen Kogon, *op. cit.;* Bruno Bettelheim, "On Dachau and Buchenwald" (from May, 1938, to April, 1939), in *Nazi Conspiracy,* VII, 824 ff. For Soviet concentration camps, see the excellent collection of reports by Polish survivors published under the title *The Dark Side of the Moon;* also David J. Dallin, *op. cit.,* though his reports are sometimes less convincing because they come from "prominent" personalities who are intent on drawing up manifestos and indictments.

[127] *The Dark Side of the Moon;* the introduction also stresses this peculiar lack of communication: "They record but do not communicate."

[128] See especially Bruno Bettelheim, *op. cit.* "It seemed as if I had become convinced that these horrible and degrading experiences somehow did not happen to 'me' as subject but to 'me' as an object. This experience was corroborated by the statements of other prisoners. . . . It was as if I watched things happening in which I only vaguely participated. . . . 'This cannot be true, such things just do not happen.' . . . The prisoners had to convince themselves that this was real, was really happening and not just a nightmare. They were never wholly successful."

See also Rousset, *op. cit.,* p. 213. ". . . Those who haven't seen it with their own eyes can't believe it. Did you yourself, before you came here, take the rumors about the gas chambers seriously?

"No, I said.

". . . You see? Well, they're all like you. The lot of them in Paris, London, New York, even at Birkenau, right outside the crematoriums . . . still incredulous, five minutes before they were sent down into the cellar of the crematorium. . . ."

by means of liberal rationalizations. In each one of us, there lurks such a liberal, wheedling us with the voice of common sense. The road to totalitarian domination leads through many intermediate stages for which we can find numerous analogies and precedents. The extraordinarily bloody terror during the initial stage of totalitarian rule serves indeed the exclusive purpose of defeating the opponent and rendering all further opposition impossible; but total terror is launched only after this initial stage has been overcome and the regime no longer has anything to fear from the opposition. In this context it has been frequently remarked that in such a case the means have become the end, but this is after all only an admission, in paradoxical disguise, that the category "the end justifies the means" no longer applies, that terror has lost its "purpose," that it is no longer the means to frighten people. Nor does the explanation suffice that the revolution, as in the case of the French Revolution, was devouring its own children, for the terror continues even after everybody who might be described as a child of the revolution in one capacity or another—the Russian factions, the power centers of party, the army, the bureaucracy—has long since been devoured. Many things that nowadays have become the specialty of totalitarian government are only too well known from the study of history. There have almost always been wars of aggression; the massacre of hostile populations after a victory went unchecked until the Romans mitigated it by introducing the *parcere subjectis;* through centuries the extermination of native peoples went hand in hand with the colonization of the Americas, Australia and Africa; slavery is one of the oldest institutions of mankind and all empires of antiquity were based on the labor of state-owned slaves who erected their public buildings. Not even concentration camps are an invention of totalitarian movements. They emerge for the first time during the Boer War, at the beginning of the century, and continued to be used in South Africa as well as India for "undesirable elements"; here, too, we first find the term "protective custody" which was later adopted by the Third Reich. These camps correspond in many respects to the concentration camps at the beginning of totalitarian rule; they were used for "suspects" whose offenses could not be proved and who could not be sentenced by ordinary process of law. All this clearly points to totalitarian methods of domination; all these are elements they utilize, develop and crystallize on the basis of the nihilistic principle that "everything is permitted," which they inherited and already take for granted. But wherever these new forms of domination assume their authentically totalitarian structure they transcend this principle, which is still tied to the utilitarian motives and self-interest of the rulers, and try their hand in a realm that up to now has been completely unknown to us: the realm where "everything is possible." And, characteristically enough, this is precisely the realm that cannot be limited by either utilitarian motives or self-interest, regardless of the latter's content.

What runs counter to common sense is not the nihilistic principle that "everything is permitted," which was already contained in the nineteenth-century utilitarian conception of common sense. What common sense and "normal people" refuse to believe is that everything is possible.[129] We attempt to understand elements in present or recollected experience that simply surpass our powers of understanding. We attempt to classify as criminal a thing which, as we all feel, no such category was ever intended to cover. What meaning has the concept of murder when we are confronted with the mass production of corpses? We attempt to understand the behavior of concentration-camp inmates and SS-men psychologically, when the very thing that must be realized is that the psyche *can* be destroyed even without the destruction of the physical man; that, indeed, psyche, character, and individuality seem under certain circumstances to express themselves only through the rapidity or slowness with which they disintegrate.[130] The end result in any case is inanimate men, *i.e.*, men who can no longer be psychologically understood, whose return to the psychologically or otherwise intelligibly human world closely resembles the resurrection of Lazarus. All statements of common sense, whether of a psychological or sociological nature, serve only to encourage those who think it "superficial" to "dwell on horrors."[131]

If it is true that the concentration camps are the most consequential institution of totalitarian rule, "dwelling on horrors" would seem to be indispensable for the understanding of totalitarianism. But recollection can no more do this than can the uncommunicative eyewitness report. In both these genres there is an inherent tendency to run away from the experience; instinctively or rationally, both types of writer are so much aware of the terrible abyss that separates the world of the living from that of the living dead, that they cannot supply anything more than a series of remembered occurrences that must seem just as incredible to those who relate them as to their audience. Only the fearful imagination of those who have been aroused by such reports but have not actually been smitten in their own flesh, of those who are consequently free from the bestial, desperate terror which, when confronted by real, present horror, inexorably paralyzes everything that is not mere reaction, can afford to keep thinking about horrors. Such thoughts are useful only for the perception of political contexts and the mobilization of political passions. A change of personality of any sort whatever can no more be induced by thinking about horrors than by the real experience of horror. The reduction of a man to a bundle of reactions separates him as radically as mental disease from everything within him that is personality or character. When, like Lazarus, he rises from the dead, he finds his personality or character unchanged, just as he had left it.

Just as the horror, or the dwelling on it, cannot affect a change of character in him, cannot make men better or worse, thus it cannot become the basis of a political community or party in a narrower sense. The attempts to build up a European elite with a program of intra-European understanding based on the common European experience of the concentration camps have

[129] The first to understand this was Rousset in his *Univers Concentrationnaire*, 1947.
[130] Rousset, *op. cit.*, p. 587.
[131] See Georges Bataille in *Critique*, January, 1948, p. 72.

foundered in much the same manner as the attempts following the first World War to draw political conclusions from the international experience of the front generation. In both cases it turned out that the experiences themselves can communicate no more than nihilistic banalities.[132] Political consequences such as postwar pacifism, for example, derived from the general fear of war, not from the experiences in war. Instead of producing a pacifism devoid of reality, the insight into the structure of modern wars, guided and mobilized by fear, might have led to the realization that the only standard for a necessary war is the fight against conditions under which people no longer wish to live—and our experiences with the tormenting hell of the totalitarian camps have enlightened us only too well about the possibility of such conditions.[133] Thus the fear of concentration camps and the resulting insight into the nature of total domination might serve to invalidate all obsolete political differentiations from right to left and to introduce beside and above them the politically most important yardstick for judging events in our time, namely: whether they serve totalitarian domination or not.

In any event, the fearful imagination has the great advantage to dissolve the sophistic-dialectical interpretations of politics which are all based on the superstition that something good might result from evil. Such dialectical acrobatics had at least a semblance of justification so long as the worst that man could inflict upon man was murder. But, as we know today, murder is only a limited evil. The murderer who kills a man—a man who has to die anyway—still moves within the realm of life and death familiar to us; both have indeed a necessary connection on which the dialectic is founded, even if it is not always conscious of it. The murderer leaves a corpse behind and does not pretend that his victim has never existed; if he wipes out any traces, they are those of his own identity, and not the memory and grief of the persons who loved his victim; he destroys a life, but he does not destroy the fact of existence itself.

The Nazis, with the precision peculiar to them, used to register their operations in the concentration camps under the heading "under cover of the night (*Nacht und Nebel*)." The radicalism of measures to treat people as if they had never existed and to make them disappear in the literal sense of the word is frequently not apparent at first glance, because both the German and the Russian system are not uniform but consist of a series of categories in which people are treated very differently. In the case of Germany, these different categories used to exist in the same camp, but without coming into contact with each other; frequently, the isolation between the categories was even stricter than the isolation from the outside world. Thus, out of racial considerations, Scandinavian nationals during the war were

[132] Rousset's book contains many such "insights" into human "nature," based chiefly on the observation that after a while the mentality of the inmates is scarcely distinguishable from that of the camp guards.

[133] In order to avoid misunderstandings it may be appropriate to add that with the invention of the hydrogen bomb the whole war question has undergone another decisive change. A discussion of this question is of course beyond the theme of this book.

quite differently treated by the Germans than the members of other peoples, although the former were outspoken enemies of the Nazis. The latter in turn were divided into those whose "extermination" was immediately on the agenda, as in the case of the Jews, or could be expected in the predictable future, as in the case of the Poles, Russians and Ukrainians, and into those who were not yet covered by instructions about such an over-all "final solution," as in the case of the French and Belgians. In Russia, on the other hand, we must distinguish three more or less independent systems. First, there are the authentic forced-labor groups that live in relative freedom and are sentenced for limited periods. Secondly, there are the concentration camps in which the human material is ruthlessly exploited and the mortality rate is extremely high, but which are essentially organized for labor purposes. And, thirdly, there are the annihilation camps in which the inmates are systematically wiped out through starvation and neglect.

The real horror of the concentration and extermination camps lies in the fact that the inmates, even if they happen to keep alive, are more effectively cut off from the world of the living than if they had died, because terror enforces oblivion. Here, murder is as impersonal as the squashing of a gnat. Someone may die as the result of systematic torture or starvation, or because the camp is overcrowded and superfluous human material must be liquidated. Conversely, it may happen that due to a shortage of new human shipments the danger arises that the camps become depopulated and that the order is now given to reduce the death rate at any price.[134] David Rousset called his report on the period in a German concentration camp *"Les Jours de Notre Mort,"* and it is indeed as if there were a possibility to give permanence to the process of dying itself and to enforce a condition in which both death and life are obstructed equally effectively.

It is the appearance of some radical evil, previously unknown to us, that puts an end to the notion of developments and transformations of qualities. Here, there are neither political nor historical nor simply moral standards but, at the most, the realization that something seems to be involved in modern politics that actually should never be involved in politics as we used to understand it, namely all or nothing—all, and that is an undetermined infinity of forms of human living-together, or nothing, for a victory of the concentration-camp system would mean the same inexorable doom for human beings as the use of the hydrogen bomb would mean the doom of the human race.

[134] This happened in Germany toward the end of 1942, whereupon Himmler served notice to all camp commandants "to reduce the death rate at all costs." For it had turned out that of the 136,000 new arrivals, 70,000 were already dead on reaching the camp or died immediately thereafter. See *Nazi Conspiracy*, IV, Annex II.—Later reports from Soviet Russian camps unanimously confirm that after 1949—that is, when Stalin was still alive—the death rate in the concentration camps, which previously had reached up to 60 per cent of the inmates, was systematically lowered, presumably due to a general and acute labor shortage in the Soviet Union. This improvement in living conditions should not be confused with the crisis of the regime after Stalin's death which, characteristically enough, first made itself felt in the concentration camps. Cf. Wilhelm Starlinger, *Grenzen der Sowjetmacht*, Würzburg, 1955.

There are no parallels to the life in the concentration camps. Its horror can never be fully embraced by the imagination for the very reason that it stands outside of life and death. It can never be fully reported for the very reason that the survivor returns to the world of the living, which makes it impossible for him to believe fully in his own past experiences. It is as though he had a story to tell of another planet, for the status of the inmates in the world of the living, where nobody is supposed to know if they are alive or dead, is such that it is as though they had never been born. Therefore all parallels create confusion and distract attention from what is essential. Forced labor in prisons and penal colonies, banishment, slavery, all seem for a moment to offer helpful comparisons, but on closer examination lead nowhere.

Forced labor as a punishment is limited as to time and intensity. The convict retains his rights over his body; he is not absolutely tortured and he is not absolutely dominated. Banishment banishes only from one part of the world to another part of the world, also inhabited by human beings; it does not exclude from the human world altogether. Throughout history slavery has been an institution within a social order; slaves were not, like concentration-camp inmates, withdrawn from the sight and hence the protection of their fellow-men; as instruments of labor they had a definite price and as property a definite value. The concentration-camp inmate has no price, because he can always be replaced; nobody knows to whom he belongs, because he is never seen. From the point of view of normal society he is absolutely superfluous, although in times of acute labor shortage, as in Russia and in Germany during the war, he is used for work.

The concentration camp as an institution was not established for the sake of any possible labor yield; the only permanent economic function of the camps has been the financing of their own supervisory apparatus; thus from the economic point of view the concentration camps exist mostly for their own sake. Any work that has been performed could have been done much better and more cheaply under different conditions.[135] Especially Russia, whose concentration camps are mostly described as forced-labor camps because Soviet bureaucracy has chosen to dignify them with this name, reveals most clearly that forced labor is not the primary issue; forced labor is the normal condition of all Russian workers, who have no freedom of movement and can be arbitrarily drafted for work to any place at any time.

[135] See Kogon, *op. cit.*, p. 58: "A large part of the work exacted in the concentration camps was useless, either it was superfluous or it was so miserably planned that it had to be done over two or three times." Also Bettelheim, *op. cit.*, pp. 831-32: "New prisoners particularly were forced to perform nonsensical tasks. . . . They felt debased . . . and preferred even harder work when it produced something useful. . . ." Even Dallin, who has built his whole book on the thesis that the purpose of Russian camps is to provide cheap labor, is forced to admit the inefficiency of camp labor, *op. cit.*, p. 105.—The current theories about the Russian camp system as an economic measure for providing a cheap labor supply would stand clearly refuted if recent reports on mass amnesties and the abolition of concentration camps should prove to be true. For if the camps had served an important economic purpose, the regime certainly could not have afforded their rapid liquidation without grave consequences for the whole economic system.

The incredibility of the horrors is closely bound up with their economic uselessness. The Nazis carried this uselessness to the point of open anti-utility when in the midst of the war, despite the shortage of building material and rolling stock, they set up enormous, costly extermination factories and transported millions of people back and forth.[136] In the eyes of a strictly utilitarian world the obvious contradiction between these acts and military expediency gave the whole enterprise an air of mad unreality.

This atmosphere of madness and unreality, created by an apparent lack of purpose, is the real iron curtain which hides all forms of concentration camps from the eyes of the world. Seen from outside, they and the things that happen in them can be described only in images drawn from a life after death, that is, a life removed from earthly purposes. Concentration camps can very aptly be divided into three types corresponding to three basic Western conceptions of a life after death: Hades, Purgatory, and Hell. To Hades correspond those relatively mild forms, once popular even in nontotalitarian countries, for getting undesirable elements of all sorts—refugees, stateless persons, the asocial and the unemployed—out of the way; as DP camps, which are nothing other than camps for persons who have become superfluous and bothersome, they have survived the war. Purgatory is represented by the Soviet Union's labor camps, where neglect is combined with chaotic forced labor. Hell in the most literal sense was embodied by those types of camp perfected by the Nazis, in which the whole of life was thoroughly and systematically organized with a view to the greatest possible torment.

All three types have one thing in common: the human masses sealed off in them are treated as if they no longer existed, as if what happened to them were no longer of any interest to anybody, as if they were already dead and some evil spirit gone mad were amusing himself by stopping them for a while between life and death before admitting them to eternal peace.

It is not so much the barbed wire as the skillfully manufactured unreality of those whom it fences in that provokes such enormous cruelties and ultimately makes extermination look like a perfectly normal measure. Everything that was done in the camps is known to us from the world of perverse, malignant fantasies. The difficult thing to understand is that, like such fantasies, these gruesome crimes took place in a phantom world, which, however, has materialized, as it were, into a world which is complete with all sensual data of reality but lacks that structure of consequence and responsibility without which reality remains for us a mass of incomprehensible data. The result is that a place has been established where men can be tortured and slaughtered, and yet neither the tormentors nor the tormented, and least of

[136] Apart from the millions of people whom the Nazis transported to the extermination camps, they constantly attempted new colonization plans—transported Germans from Germany or the occupied territories to the East for colonization purposes. This was of course a serious handicap for military actions and economic exploitation. For the numerous discussions on these subjects and the constant conflict between the Nazi civilian hierarchy in the Eastern occupied territories and the SS hierarchy see especially Vol. XXIX of *Trial of the Major War Criminals*, Nuremberg, 1947.

all the outsider, can be aware that what is happening is anything more than a cruel game or an absurd dream.[137]

The films which the Allies circulated in Germany and elsewhere after the war showed clearly that this atmosphere of insanity and unreality is not dispelled by pure reportage. To the unprejudiced observer these pictures are just about as convincing as snapshots of mysterious substances taken at spiritualist séances.[138] Common sense reacted to the horrors of Buchenwald and Auschwitz with the plausible argument: "What crime must these people have committed that such things were done to them!"; or, in Germany and Austria, in the midst of starvation, overpopulation, and general hatred: "Too bad that they've stopped gassing the Jews"; and everywhere with the skeptical shrug that greets ineffectual propaganda.

If the propaganda of truth fails to convince the average person because it is too monstrous, it is positively dangerous to those who know from their own imaginings what they themselves are capable of doing and who are therefore perfectly willing to believe in the reality of what they have seen. Suddenly it becomes evident that things which for thousands of years the human imagination had banished to a realm beyond human competence can be manufactured right here on earth, that Hell and Purgatory, and even a shadow of their perpetual duration, can be established by the most modern methods of destruction and therapy. To these people (and they are more numerous in any large city than we like to admit) the totalitarian hell proves only that the power of man is greater than they ever dared to think, and that man can realize hellish fantasies without making the sky fall or the earth open.

These analogies, repeated in many reports from the world of the dying,[139] seem to express more than a desperate attempt at saying what is outside the realm of human speech. Nothing perhaps distinguishes modern masses as radically from those of previous centuries as the loss of faith in a Last Judgment: the worst have lost their fear and the best have lost their hope. Unable as yet to live without fear and hope, these masses are attracted by every effort which seems to promise a man-made fabrication of the Paradise they had longed for and of the Hell they had feared. Just as the popularized features of Marx's classless society have a queer resemblance to the Messi-

[137] Bettelheim, *op. cit.*, notes that the guards in the camps embraced an attitude toward the atmosphere of unreality similar to that of the prisoners themselves.

[138] It is of some importance to realize that all pictures of concentration camps are misleading insofar as they show the camps in their last stages, at the moment the Allied troops marched in. There were no death camps in Germany proper, and at that point all extermination equipment had already been dismantled. On the other hand, what provoked the outrage of the Allies most and what gives the films their special horror—namely, the sight of the human skeletons—was not at all typical for the German concentration camps; extermination was handled systematically by gas, not by starvation. The condition of the camps was a result of the war events during the final months: Himmler had ordered the evacuation of all extermination camps in the East, the German camps were consequently vastly overcrowded, and he was no longer in a position to assure the food supply in Germany.

[139] That life in a concentration camp was simply a dragged-out process of dying is stressed by Rousset, *op. cit.*, *passim*.

anic Age, so the reality of concentration camps resembles nothing so much as medieval pictures of Hell.

The one thing that cannot be reproduced is what made the traditional conceptions of Hell tolerable to man: the Last Judgment, the idea of an absolute standard of justice combined with the infinite possibility of grace. For in the human estimation there is no crime and no sin commensurable with the everlasting torments of Hell. Hence the discomfiture of common sense, which asks: What crime must these people have committed in order to suffer so inhumanly? Hence also the absolute innocence of the victims: no man ever deserved this. Hence finally the grotesque haphazardness with which concentration-camp victims were chosen in the perfected terror state: such "punishment" can, with equal justice and injustice, be inflicted on anyone.

In comparison with the insane end-result—concentration-camp society—the process by which men are prepared for this end, and the methods by which individuals are adapted to these conditions, are transparent and logical. The insane mass manufacture of corpses is preceded by the historically and politically intelligible preparation of living corpses. The impetus and what is more important, the silent consent to such unprecedented conditions are the products of those events which in a period of political disintegration suddenly and unexpectedly made hundreds of thousands of human beings homeless, stateless, outlawed and unwanted, while millions of human beings were made economically superfluous and socially burdensome by unemployment. This in turn could only happen because the Rights of Man, which had never been philosophically established but merely formulated, which had never been politically secured but merely proclaimed, have, in their traditional form, lost all validity.

The first essential step on the road to total domination is to kill the juridical person in man. This was done, on the one hand, by putting certain categories of people outside the protection of the law and forcing at the same time, through the instrument of denationalization, the nontotalitarian world into recognition of lawlessness; it was done, on the other, by placing the concentration camp outside the normal penal system, and by selecting its inmates outside the normal judicial procedure in which a definite crime entails a predictable penalty. Thus criminals, who for other reasons are an essential element in concentration-camp society, are ordinarily sent to a camp only on completion of their prison sentence. Under all circumstances totalitarian domination sees to it that the categories gathered in the camps—Jews, carriers of diseases, representatives of dying classes—have already lost their capacity for both normal or criminal action. Propagandistically this means that the "protective custody" is handled as a "preventive police measure,"[140] that is, a measure that deprives people of the ability to act. Deviations from this rule in Russia must be attributed to the catastrophic shortage of prisons and to a desire, so far unrealized, to trans-

[140] Maunz, *op. cit.*, p. 50, insists that criminals should never be sent to the camps for the time of their regular sentences.

form the whole penal system into a system of concentration camps.[141]

The inclusion of criminals is necessary in order to make plausible the propagandistic claim of the movement that the institution exists for asocial elements.[142] Criminals do not properly belong in the concentration camps, if only because it is harder to kill the juridical person in a man who is guilty of some crime than in a totally innocent person. If they constitute a permanent category among the inmates, it is a concession of the totalitarian state to the prejudices of society, which can in this way most readily be accustomed to the existence of the camps. In order, on the other hand, to keep the camp system itself intact, it is essential as long as there is a penal system in the country that criminals should be sent to the camps only on completion of their sentence, that is when they are actually entitled to their freedom. Under no circumstances must the concentration camp become a calculable punishment for definite offenses.

The amalgamation of criminals with all other categories has moreover the advantage of making it shockingly evident to all other arrivals that they have landed on the lowest level of society. It soon turns out, to be sure, that they have every reason to envy the lowest thief and murderer; but meanwhile the lowest level is a good beginning. Moreover it is an effective means of camouflage: this happens only to criminals and nothing worse is happening than what deservedly happens to criminals.

The criminals everywhere constitute the aristocracy of the camps. (In Germany, during the war, they were replaced in the leadership by the Communists, because not even a minimum of rational work could be performed under the chaotic conditions created by a criminal administration. This was merely a temporary transformation of concentration camps into forced-labor camps, a thoroughly atypical phenomenon of limited duration.)[143] What places the criminals in the leadership is not so much the affinity between supervisory personnel and criminal elements—in the Soviet Union apparently the supervisors are not, like the SS, a special elite trained to commit crimes[144]—as the fact that only criminals have been sent to the camp in

[141] The shortage of prison space in Russia has been such that in the year 1925-26, only 36 per cent of all court sentences could be carried out. See Dallin, *op. cit.*, p. 158 ff.

[142] "Gestapo and SS have always attached great importance to mixing the categories of inmates in the camps. In no camp have the inmates belonged exclusively to one category" (Kogon, *op. cit.*, p. 19).

In Russia, it has also been customary from the beginning to mix political prisoners and criminals. During the first ten years of Soviet power, the Left political groups enjoyed certain privileges; only with the full development of the totalitarian character of the regime "after the end of the twenties, the politicals were even officially treated as inferior to the common criminals" (Dallin, *op. cit.*, p. 177 ff.).

[143] Rousset's book suffers from his overestimation of the influence of the German Communists, who dominated the internal administration of Buchenwald during the war.

[144] See for instance the testimony of Mrs. Buber-Neumann (former wife of the German Communist Heinz Neumann), who survived Soviet and German concentration camps: "The Russians never . . . evinced the sadistic streak of the Nazis. . . . Our Russian guards were decent men and not sadists, but they faithfully fulfilled the requirements of the inhuman system" (*Under Two Dictators*).

connection with some definite activity. They at least know why they are in a concentration camp and therefore have kept a remnant of their juridical person. For the politicals this is only subjectively true; their actions, insofar as they were actions and not mere opinions or someone else's vague suspicions, or accidental membership in a politically disapproved group, are as a rule not covered by the normal legal system of the country and not juridically defined.[145]

To the amalgam of politicals and criminals with which concentration camps in Russia and Germany started out, was added at an early date a third element which was soon to constitute the majority of all concentration-camp inmates. This largest group has consisted ever since of people who had done nothing whatsoever that, either in their own consciousness or the consciousness of their tormenters, had any rational connection with their arrest. In Germany, after 1938, this element was represented by masses of Jews, in Russia by any groups which, for any reason having nothing to do with their actions, had incurred the disfavor of the authorities. These groups, innocent in every sense, are the most suitable for thorough experimentation in disfranchisement and destruction of the juridical person, and therefore they are both qualitatively and quantitatively the most essential category of the camp population. This principle was most fully realized in the gas chambers which, if only because of their enormous capacity, could not be intended for individual cases but only for people in general. In this connection, the following dialogue sums up the situation of the individual: "For what purpose, may I ask, do the gas chambers exist?"—"For what purpose were you born?"[146] It is this third group of the totally innocent who in every case fare the worst in the camps. Criminals and politicals are assimilated to this category; thus deprived of the protective distinction that comes of their having done something, they are utterly exposed to the arbitrary. The ultimate goal, partly achieved in the Soviet Union and clearly indicated in the last phases of Nazi terror, is to have the whole camp population composed of this category of innocent people.

Contrasting with the complete haphazardness with which the inmates are selected are the categories, meaningless in themselves but useful from the standpoint of organization, into which they are usually divided on their arrival. In the German camps there were criminals, politicals, asocial elements, religious offenders, and Jews, all distinguished by insignia. When the French set up concentration camps after the Spanish Civil War, they immediately introduced the typical totalitarian amalgam of politicals with criminals and the innocent (in this case the stateless), and despite their inexperience proved remarkably inventive in creating meaningless categories of inmates.[147]

[145] Bruno Bettelheim, "Behavior in Extreme Situations," in *Journal of Abnormal and Social Psychology*, Vol. XXXVIII, No. 4, 1943, describes the self-esteem of the criminals and the political prisoners as compared with those who have not done anything. The latter "were least able to withstand the initial shock," the first to disintegrate. Bettelheim blames this on their middle-class origin.

[146] Rousset, *op. cit.*, p. 71.

[147] For conditions in French concentration camps, see Arthur Koestler, *Scum of the Earth*, 1941.

Originally devised in order to prevent any growth of solidarity among the inmates, this technique proved particularly valuable because no one could know whether his own category was better or worse than someone else's. In Germany this eternally shifting though pedantically organized edifice was given an appearance of solidity by the fact that under any and all circumstances the Jews were the lowest category. The gruesome and grotesque part of it was that the inmates identified themselves with these categories, as though they represented a last authentic remnant of their juridical person. Even if we disregard all other circumstances, it is no wonder that a Communist of 1933 should have come out of the camps more Communistic than he went in, a Jew more Jewish, and, in France, the wife of a Foreign Legionary more convinced of the value of the Foreign Legion; it would seem as though these categories promised some last shred of predictable treatment, as though they embodied some last and hence most fundamental juridical identity.

While the classification of inmates by categories is only a tactical, organizational measure, the arbitrary selection of victims indicates the essential principle of the institution. If the concentration camps had been dependent on the existence of political adversaries, they would scarcely have survived the first years of the totalitarian regimes. One only has to take a look at the number of inmates at Buchenwald in the years after 1936 in order to understand how absolutely necessary the element of the innocent was for the continued existence of the camps. "The camps would have died out if in making its arrests the Gestapo had considered only the principle of opposition,"[148] and toward the end of 1937 Buchenwald, with less than 1,000 inmates, was close to dying out until the November pogroms brought more than 20,000 new arrivals.[149] In Germany, this element of the innocent was furnished in vast numbers by the Jews after 1938; in Russia, it consisted of random groups of the population which for some reason entirely unconnected with their actions had fallen into disgrace.[150] But if in Germany the really totalitarian type of concentration camp with its enormous majority of completely "innocent" inmates was not established until 1938, in Russia it goes back to the early thirties, since up to 1930 the majority of the concentration-camp population still consisted of criminals, counterrevolutionaries and "politicals" (meaning, in this case, members of deviationist factions). Since then there have been so many innocent people in the camps that it is difficult to classify them—persons who had some sort of contact with a foreign country, Russians of Polish origin (particularly in the years 1936 to 1938), peasants whose villages for some economic reason were liquidated, deported nationalities, demobilized soldiers of the Red Army who happened to belong to regiments that stayed too long abroad as occupation forces or had become prisoners of war in Germany, etc. But the

[148] Kogon, *op. cit.*, p. 6.

[149] See *Nazi Conspiracy*, IV, 800 ff.

[150] Beck and Godin, *op. cit.*, state explicitly that "opponents constituted only a relatively small proportion of the [Russian] prison population" (p. 87), and that there was no connection whatever between "a man's imprisonment and any offense" (p. 95).

existence of a political opposition is for a concentration-camp system only a pretext, and the purpose of the system is not achieved even when, under the most monstrous terror, the population becomes more or less voluntarily co-ordinated, *i.e.*, relinquishes its political rights. The aim of an arbitrary system is to destroy the civil rights of the whole population, who ultimately become just as outlawed in their own country as the stateless and homeless. The destruction of a man's rights, the killing of the juridical person in him, is a prerequisite for dominating him entirely. And this applies not only to special categories such as criminals, political opponents, Jews, homosexuals, on whom the early experiments were made, but to every inhabitant of a totalitarian state. Free consent is as much an obstacle to total domination as free opposition.[151] The arbitrary arrest which chooses among innocent people destroys the validity of free consent, just as torture—as distinguished from death—destroys the possibility of opposition.

Any, even the most tyrannical, restriction of this arbitrary persecution to certain opinions of a religious or political nature, to certain modes of intellectual or erotic social behavior, to certain freshly invented "crimes," would render the camps superfluous, because in the long run no attitude and no opinion can withstand the threat of so much horror; and above all it would make for a new system of justice, which, given any stability at all, could not fail to produce a new juridical person in man, that would elude the totalitarian domination. The so-called "*Volksnutzen*" of the Nazis, constantly fluctuating (because what is useful today can be injurious tomorrow) and the eternally shifting party line of the Soviet Union which, being retroactive, almost daily makes new groups of people available for the concentration camps, are the only guaranty for the continued existence of the concentration camps, and hence for the continued total disfranchisement of man.

The next decisive step in the preparation of living corpses is the murder of the moral person in man. This is done in the main by making martyrdom, for the first time in history, impossible: "How many people here still believe that a protest has even historic importance? This skepticism is the real masterpiece of the SS. Their great accomplishment. They have corrupted all human solidarity. Here the night has fallen on the future. When no witnesses are left, there can be no testimony. To demonstrate when death can no longer be postponed is an attempt to give death a meaning, to act beyond one's own death. In order to be successful, a gesture must have social meaning. There are hundreds of thousands of us here, all living in absolute solitude. That is why we are subdued no matter what happens."[152]

[151] Bruno Bettelheim, "On Dachau and Buchenwald," when discussing the fact that most prisoners "made their peace with the values of the Gestapo," emphasizes that "this was not the result of propaganda . . . the Gestapo insisted that it would prevent them from expressing their feelings anyway" (pp. 834-35).

Himmler explicitly prohibited propaganda of any kind in the camps. "Education consists of discipline, never of any kind of instruction on an ideological basis." "On Organization and Obligation of the SS and the Police," in *National-politischer Lehrgang der Wehrmacht,* 1937. Quoted from *Nazi Conspiracy,* IV, 616 ff.

[152] Rousset, *op. cit.*, p. 464.

The camps and the murder of political adversaries are only part of organized oblivion that not only embraces carriers of public opinion such as the spoken and the written word, but extends even to the families and friends of the victim. Grief and remembrance are forbidden. In the Soviet Union a woman will sue for divorce immediately after her husband's arrest in order to save the lives of her children; if her husband chances to come back, she will indignantly turn him out of the house.[153] The Western world has hitherto, even in its darkest periods, granted the slain enemy the right to be remembered as a self-evident acknowledgment of the fact that we are all men (and *only* men). It is only because even Achilles set out for Hector's funeral, only because the most despotic governments honored the slain enemy, only because the Romans allowed the Christians to write their martyrologies, only because the Church kept its heretics alive in the memory of men, that all was not lost and never could be lost. The concentration camps, by making death itself anonymous (making it impossible to find out whether a prisoner is dead or alive) robbed death of its meaning as the end of a fulfilled life. In a sense they took away the individual's own death proving that henceforth nothing belonged to him and he belonged to no one. His death merely set a seal on the fact that he had never really existed.

This attack on the moral person might still have been opposed by man's conscience which tells him that it is better to die a victim than to live as a bureaucrat of murder. Totalitarian terror achieved its most terrible triumph when it succeeded in cutting the moral person off from the individualist escape and in making the decisions of conscience absolutely questionable and equivocal. When a man is faced with the alternative of betraying and thus murdering his friends or of sending his wife and children for whom he is in every sense responsible, to their death; when even suicide would mean the immediate murder of his own family—how is he to decide? The alternative is no longer between good and evil, but between murder and murder. Who could solve the moral dilemma of the Greek mother, who was allowed by the Nazis to choose which of her three children should be killed?[154]

Through the creation of conditions under which conscience ceases to be adequate and to do good becomes utterly impossible, the consciously organized complicity of all men in the crimes of totalitarian regimes is extended to the victims and thus made really total. The SS implicated concentration-camp inmates—criminals, politicals, Jews—in their crimes by making them responsible for a large part of the administration, thus confronting them with the hopeless dilemma whether to send their friends to their death, or to help murder other men who happened to be strangers, and forcing them, in any event, to behave like murderers.[155] The point is not only that hatred is diverted from those who are guilty (the *capos* were more hated than the

[153] See the report of Sergei Malakhov in Dallin, *op. cit.*, pp. 20 ff.

[154] See Albert Camus in *Twice A Year*, 1947.

[155] Rousset's book, *op. cit.*, consists largely of discussions of this dilemma by prisoners.

SS), but that the distinguishing line between persecutor and persecuted, between the murderer and his victim, is constantly blurred.[156]

Once the moral person has been killed, the one thing that still prevents men from being made into living corpses is the differentiation of the individual, his unique identity. In a sterile form such individuality can be preserved through a persistent stoicism, and it is certain that many men under totalitarian rule have taken and are each day still taking refuge in this absolute isolation of a personality without rights or conscience. There is no doubt that this part of the human person, precisely because it depends so essentially on nature and on forces that cannot be controlled by the will, is the hardest to destroy (and when destroyed is most easily repaired).[157]

The methods of dealing with this uniqueness of the human person are numerous and we shall not attempt to list them. They begin with the monstrous conditions in the transports to the camps, when hundreds of human beings are packed into a cattle-car stark naked, glued to each other, and shunted back and forth over the countryside for days on end; they continue upon arrival at the camp, the well-organized shock of the first hours, the shaving of the head, the grotesque camp clothing; and they end in the utterly unimaginable tortures so gauged as not to kill the body, at any event not quickly. The aim of all these methods, in any case, is to manipulate the human body—with its infinite possibilities of suffering—in such a way as to make it destroy the human person as inexorably as do certain mental diseases of organic origin.

It is here that the utter lunacy of the entire process becomes most apparent. Torture, to be sure, is an essential feature of the whole totalitarian police and judiciary apparatus; it is used every day to make people talk. This type of torture, since it pursues a definite, rational aim, has certain limitations: either the prisoner talks within a certain time, or he is killed. To this rationally conducted torture another, irrational, sadistic type was added in the first Nazi concentration camps and in the cellars of the Gestapo. Carried on for the most part by the SA, it pursued no aims and was not systematic, but depended on the initiative of largely abnormal elements. The mortality was so high that only a few concentration-camp inmates of 1933 survived these first years. This type of torture seemed to be not so much a calculated political institution as a concession of the regime to its criminal and abnormal elements, who were thus rewarded for services rendered. Behind the blind bestiality of the SA, there often lay a deep hatred and resentment against all those who were socially, intellectually, or physically better

[156] Bettelheim, *op. cit.*, describes the process by which the guards as well as the prisoners became "conditioned" to the life in the camp and were afraid of returning to the outer world.

Rousset, therefore, is right when he insists that the truth is that "victim and executioner are alike ignoble; the lesson of the camps is the brotherhood of abjection" (p. 588).

[157] Bettelheim, *op. cit.*, describes how "the main concern of the new prisoners seemed to be to remain intact as a personality" while the problem of the old prisoners was "how to live as well as possible within the camp."

off than themselves, and who now, as if in fulfillment of their wildest dreams, were in their power. This resentment, which never died out entirely in the camps, strikes us as a last remnant of humanly understandable feeling.[158]

The real horror began, however, when the SS took over the administration of the camps. The old spontaneous bestiality gave way to an absolutely cold and systematic destruction of human bodies, calculated to destroy human dignity; death was avoided or postponed indefinitely. The camps were no longer amusement parks for beasts in human form, that is, for men who really belonged in mental institutions and prisons; the reverse became true: they were turned into "drill grounds," on which perfectly normal men were trained to be full-fledged members of the SS.[159]

The killing of man's individuality, of the uniqueness shaped in equal parts by nature, will, and destiny, which has become so self-evident a premise for all human relations that even identical twins inspire a certain uneasiness, creates a horror that vastly overshadows the outrage of the juridical-political person and the despair of the moral person. It is this horror that gives rise

[158] Rousset, *op. cit.*, p. 390, reports an SS-man haranguing a professor as follows: "You used to be a professor. Well, you're no professor now. You're no big shot any more. You're nothing but a little runt now. Just as little as you can be. I'm the big fellow now."

[159] Kogon, *op. cit.*, p. 6, speaks of the possibility that the camps will be maintained as training and experimental grounds for the SS. He also gives a good report on the difference between the early camps administered by the SA and the later ones under the SS. "None of these first camps had more than a thousand inmates. . . . Life in them beggared all description. The accounts of the few old prisoners who survived those years agree that there was scarcely any form of sadistic perversion that was not practiced by the SA men. But they were all acts of individual bestiality, there was still no fully organized cold system, embracing masses of men. This was the accomplishment of the SS" (p. 7).

This new mechanized system eased the feeling of responsibility as much as was humanly possible. When, for instance, the order came to kill every day several hundred Russian prisoners, the slaughter was performed by shooting through a hole without seeing the victim. (See Ernest Feder, "Essai sur la Psychologie de la Terreur," in *Synthèses*, Brussels, 1946.) On the other hand, perversion was artificially produced in otherwise normal men. Rousset reports the following from a SS guard: "Usually I keep on hitting until I ejaculate. I have a wife and three children in Breslau. I used to be perfectly normal. That's what they've made of me. Now when they give me a pass out of here, I don't go home. I don't dare look my wife in the face" (p. 273). —The documents from the Hitler era contain numerous testimonials for the average normality of those entrusted with carrying out Hitler's program of extermination. A good collection is found in Léon Poliakov's "The Weapon of Antisemitism," published by UNESCO in *The Third Reich*, London, 1955. Most of the men in the units used for these purposes were not volunteers but had been drafted from the ordinary police for these special assignments. But even trained SS-men found this kind of duty worse than front-line fighting. In his report of a mass execution by the SS, an eyewitness gives high praise to this troop which had been so "idealistic" that it was able to bear "the entire extermination without the help of liquor."

That one wanted to eliminate all personal motives and passions during the "exterminations" and hence keep the cruelties to a minimum is revealed by the fact that a group of doctors and engineers entrusted with handling the gas installations were making constant improvements that were not only designed to raise the productive capacity of the corpse factories but also to accelerate and ease the agony of death.

to the nihilistic generalizations which maintain plausibly enough that essentially all men alike are beasts.[160] Actually the experience of the concentration camps does show that human beings can be transformed into specimens of the human animal, and that man's "nature" is only "human" insofar as it opens up to man the possibility of becoming something highly unnatural, that is, a man.

After murder of the moral person and annihilation of the juridical person, the destruction of the individuality is almost always successful. Conceivably some laws of mass psychology may be found to explain why millions of human beings allowed themselves to be marched unresistingly into the gas chambers, although these laws would explain nothing else but the destruction of individuality. It is more significant that those individually condemned to death very seldom attempted to take one of their executioners with them, that there were scarcely any serious revolts, and that even in the moment of liberation there were very few spontaneous massacres of SS men. For to destroy individuality is to destroy spontaneity, man's power to begin something new out of his own resources, something that cannot be explained on the basis of reactions to environment and events.[161] Nothing then remains but ghastly marionettes with human faces, which all behave like the dog in Pavlov's experiments, which all react with perfect reliability even when going to their own death, and which do nothing but react. This is the real triumph of the system: "The triumph of the SS demands that the tortured victim allow himself to be led to the noose without protesting, that he renounce and abandon himself to the point of ceasing to affirm his identity. And it is not for nothing. It is not gratuitously, out of sheer sadism, that the SS men desire his defeat. They know that the system which succeeds in destroying its victim before he mounts the scaffold . . . is incomparably the best for keeping a whole people in slavery. In submission. Nothing is more terrible than these processions of human beings going like dummies to their death. The man who sees this says to himself: 'For them to be thus reduced, what power must be concealed in the hands of the masters,' and he turns away, full of bitterness but defeated."[162]

If we take totalitarian aspirations seriously and refuse to be misled by the

[160] This is very prominent in Rousset's work. "The social conditions of life in the camps have transformed the great mass of inmates, both the Germans and the deportees, regardless of their previous social position and education . . . into a degenerate rabble, entirely submissive to the primitive reflexes of the animal instinct" (p. 183).

[161] In this context also belongs the astonishing rarety of suicides in the camps. Suicide occurred far more often before arrest and deportation than in the camp itself, which is of course partly explained by the fact that every attempt was made to prevent suicides which are, after all, spontaneous acts. From the statistical material for Buchenwald (*Nazi Conspiracy,* IV, 800 ff.) it is evident that scarcely more than one-half per cent of the deaths could be traced to suicide, that frequently there were only two suicides per year, although in the same year the total number of deaths reached 3,516. The reports from Russian camps mention the same phenomenon. Cf., for instance, Starlinger, *op. cit.*, p. 57.

[162] Rousset, *op. cit.*, p. 525.

common-sense assertion that they are utopian and unrealizable, it develops that the society of the dying established in the camps is the only form of society in which it is possible to dominate man entirely. Those who aspire to total domination must liquidate all spontaneity, such as the mere existence of individuality will always engender, and track it down in its most private forms, regardless of how unpolitical and harmless these may seem. Pavlov's dog, the human specimen reduced to the most elementary reactions, the bundle of reactions that can always be liquidated and replaced by other bundles of reactions that behave in exactly the same way, is the model "citizen" of a totalitarian state; and such a citizen can be produced only imperfectly outside of the camps.

The uselessness of the camps, their cynically admitted anti-utility, is only apparent. In reality they are more essential to the preservation of the regime's power than any of its other institutions. Without concentration camps, without the undefined fear they inspire and the very well-defined training they offer in totalitarian domination, which can nowhere else be fully tested with all of its most radical possibilities, a totalitarian state can neither inspire its nuclear troops with fanaticism nor maintain a whole people in complete apathy. The dominating and the dominated would only too quickly sink back into the "old bourgeois routine"; after early "excesses," they would succumb to everyday life with its human laws; in short, they would develop in the direction which all observers counseled by common sense were so prone to predict. The tragic fallacy of all these prophecies, originating in a world that was still safe, was to suppose that there was such a thing as one human nature established for all time, to identify this human nature with history, and thus to declare that the idea of total domination was not only inhuman but also unrealistic. Meanwhile we have learned that the power of man is so great that he really can be what he wishes to be.

It is in the very nature of totalitarian regimes to demand unlimited power. Such power can only be secured if literally all men, without a single exception, are reliably dominated in every aspect of their life. In the realm of foreign affairs new neutral territories must constantly be subjugated, while at home ever-new human groups must be mastered in expanding concentration camps, or, when circumstances require liquidated to make room for others. The question of opposition is unimportant both in foreign and domestic affairs. Any neutrality, indeed any spontaneously given friendship, is from the standpoint of totalitarian domination just as dangerous as open hostility, precisely because spontaneity as such, with its incalculability, is the greatest of all obstacles to total domination over man. The Communists of non-Communist countries, who fled or were called to Moscow, learned by bitter experience that they constituted a menace to the Soviet Union. Convinced Communists are in this sense, which alone has any reality today, just as ridiculous and just as menacing to the regime in Russia, as, for example, the convinced Nazis of the Röhm faction were to the Nazis.

What makes conviction and opinion of any sort so ridiculous and dangerous under totalitarian conditions is that totalitarian regimes take the greatest pride in having no need of them, or of any human help of any kind. Men insofar as they are more than animal reaction and fulfillment of functions are entirely superfluous to totalitarian regimes. Totalitarianism strives not toward despotic rule over men, but toward a system in which men are superfluous. Total power can be achieved and safeguarded only in a world of conditioned reflexes, of marionettes without the slightest trace of spontaneity. Precisely because man's resources are so great, he can be fully dominated only when he becomes a specimen of the animal-species man.

Therefore character is a threat and even the most unjust legal rules are an obstacle; but individuality, anything indeed that distinguishes one man from another, is intolerable. As long as all men have not been made equally superfluous—and this has been accomplished only in concentration camps—the ideal of totalitarian domination has not been achieved. Totalitarian states strive constantly, though never with complete success, to establish the superfluity of man—by the arbitrary selection of various groups for concentration camps, by constant purges of the ruling apparatus, by mass liquidations. Common sense protests desperately that the masses are submissive and that all this gigantic apparatus of terror is therefore superfluous; if they were capable of telling the truth, the totalitarian rulers would reply: The apparatus seems superfluous to you only because it serves to make men superfluous.

The totalitarian attempt to make men superfluous reflects the experience of modern masses of their superfluity on an overcrowded earth. The world of the dying, in which men are taught they are superfluous through a way of life in which punishment is meted out without connection with crime, in which exploitation is practiced without profit, and where work is performed without product, is a place where senselessness is daily produced anew. Yet, within the framework of the totalitarian ideology, nothing could be more sensible and logical; if the inmates are vermin, it is logical that they should be killed by poison gas; if they are degenerate, they should not be allowed to contaminate the population; if they have "slave-like souls" (Himmler), no one should waste his time trying to re-educate them. Seen through the eyes of the ideology, the trouble with the camps is almost that they make too much sense, that the execution of the doctrine is too consistent.

While the totalitarian regimes are thus resolutely and cynically emptying the world of the only thing that makes sense to the utilitarian expectations of common sense, they impose upon it at the same time a kind of supersense which the ideologies actually always meant when they pretended to have found the key to history or the solution to the riddles of the universe. Over and above the senselessness of totalitarian society is enthroned the ridiculous supersense of its ideological superstition. Ideologies are harmless, uncritical, and arbitrary opinions only as long as they are not believed in seriously. Once their claim to total validity is taken literally they become the nuclei of logical systems in which, as in the systems of paranoiacs, everything follows comprehensibly and even compulsorily once the first premise is accepted. The insanity of such systems lies not only in their first premise but in the very logicality with which they are constructed. The curious logicality of all isms, their simple-minded trust in the salvation value of stubborn devotion without regard for specific, varying factors, already harbors the first germs of totalitarian contempt for reality and factuality.

Common sense trained in utilitarian thinking is helpless against this ideological supersense, since totalitarian regimes establish a functioning world of no-sense. The ideological contempt for factuality still contained the proud assumption of human mastery over the world; it is, after all, contempt for reality which makes possible changing the world, the erection of the human artifice. What destroys the element of pride in the totalitarian contempt for reality (and thereby distinguishes it radically from revolutionary theories and attitudes) is the supersense which gives the contempt for reality its cogency, logicality, and consistency. What makes a truly totalitarian device out of the Bolshevik claim that the present Russian system is superior to all others is the fact that the totalitarian ruler draws from this claim the logically impeccable conclusion that without this system people never could have built such a wonderful thing as, let us say, a subway; from this, he again draws the logical conclusion that anyone who knows of the existence of the Paris subway is a suspect because he may cause people to doubt that one can do things only in the Bolshevik way. This leads to the final conclusion that in order to remain a loyal Bolshevik, you have to destroy the Paris subway. Nothing matters but consistency.

With these new structures, built on the strength of supersense and driven by the motor of logicality, we are indeed at the end of the bourgeois era of profits and power, as well as at the end of imperialism and expansion. The aggressiveness of totalitarianism springs not from lust for power, and if it feverishly seeks to expand, it does so neither for expansion's sake nor for profit, but only for ideological reasons: to make the world consistent, to prove that its respective supersense has been right.

It is chiefly for the sake of this supersense, for the sake of complete consistency, that it is necessary for totalitarianism to destroy every trace of what we commonly call human dignity. For respect for human dignity implies the recognition of my fellow-men or our fellow-nations as subjects, as builders of worlds or cobuilders of a common world. No ideology which aims at the explanation of all historical events of the past and at mapping out the course of all events of the future can bear the unpredictability which springs from the fact that men are creative, that they can bring forward something so new that nobody ever foresaw it.

What totalitarian ideologies therefore aim at is not the transformation of the outside world or the revolutionizing transmutation of society, but the transformation of human nature itself. The concentration camps are the laboratories where changes in human nature are tested, and their shamefulness therefore is not just the business of their inmates and those who run them according to strictly "scientific" standards; it is the concern of all men. Suffering, of which there has been always too much on earth, is not the issue, nor is the number of victims. Human nature as such is at stake, and even though it seems that these experiments succeed not in changing man but only in destroying him, by creating a society in which the nihilistic banality of *homo homini lupus* is consistently realized, one should bear in mind the necessary limitations to an experiment which requires global control in order to show conclusive results.

Until now the totalitarian belief that everything is possible seems to have proved only that everything can be destroyed. Yet, in their effort to prove that everything is possible, totalitarian regimes have discovered without knowing it that there are crimes which men can neither punish nor forgive. When the impossible was made possible it became the unpunishable, unforgivable absolute evil which could no longer be understood and explained by the evil motives of self-interest, greed, covetousness, resentment, lust for power, and cowardice; and which therefore anger could not revenge, love could not endure, friendship could not forgive. Just as the victims in the death factories or the holes of oblivion are no longer "human" in the eyes of their executioners, so this newest species of criminals is beyond the pale even of solidarity in human sinfulness.

It is inherent in our entire philosophical tradition that we cannot conceive of a "radical evil," and this is true both for Christian theology, which conceded even to the Devil himself a celestial origin, as well as for Kant, the only philosopher who, in the word he coined for it, at least must have suspected the existence of this evil even though he immediately rationalized it in the concept of a "perverted ill will" that could be explained by comprehensible motives. Therefore, we actually have nothing to fall back on in order to understand a phenomenon that nevertheless confronts us with its overpowering reality and breaks down all standards we know. There is only one thing that seems to be discernible: we may say that radical evil has emerged in connection with a system in which all men have become equally superfluous. The manipulators of this system believe in their own superfluousness as much as in that of all others, and the totalitarian murderers are all the more dangerous because they do not care if they themselves are alive or dead, if they ever lived or never were born. The danger of the corpse factories and holes of oblivion is that today, with populations and homelessness everywhere on the increase, masses of people are continuously rendered superfluous if we continue to think of our world in utilitarian terms. Political, social, and economic events everywhere are in a silent conspiracy with totalitarian instruments devised for making men superfluous. The implied temptation is well understood by the utilitarian common sense of the masses, who in most countries are too desperate to retain much fear of death. The Nazis and the Bolsheviks can be sure that their factories of annihilation which demonstrate the swiftest solution to the problem of overpopulation, of economically superfluous and socially rootless human masses, are as much of an attraction as a warning. Totalitarian solutions may well survive the fall of totalitarian regimes in the form of strong temptations which will come up whenever it seems impossible to alleviate political, social, or economic misery in a manner worthy of man.

CHAPTER FOUR:

Ideology and Terror: A Novel Form of Government

IN THE PRECEDING chapers we emphasized repeatedly that the means of total domination are not only more drastic but that totalitarianism differs essentially from other forms of political oppression known to us such as despotism, tyranny and dictatorship. Wherever it rose to power, it developed entirely new political institutions and destroyed all social, legal and political traditions of the country. No matter what the specifically national tradition or the particular spiritual source of its ideology, totalitarian government always transformed classes into masses, supplanted the party system, not by one-party dictatorships, but by a mass movement, shifted the center of power from the army to the police, and established a foreign policy openly directed toward world domination. Present totalitarian governments have developed from one-party systems; whenever these became truly totalitarian, they started to operate according to a system of values so radically different from all others, that none of our traditional legal, moral, or common sense utilitarian categories could any longer help us to come to terms with, or judge, or predict their course of action.

If it is true that the elements of totalitarianism can be found by retracing the history and analyzing the political implications of what we usually call the crisis of our century, then the conclusion is unavoidable that this crisis is no mere threat from the outside, no mere result of some aggressive foreign policy of either Germany or Russia, and that it will no more disappear with the death of Stalin than it disappeared with the fall of Nazi Germany. It may even be that the true predicaments of our time will assume their authentic form—though not necessarily the cruelest—only when totalitarianism has become a thing of the past.

It is in the line of such reflections to raise the question whether totalitarian government, born of this crisis and at the same time its clearest and only unequivocal symptom, is merely a makeshift arrangement, which borrows its methods of intimidation, its means of organization and its instruments of violence from the well-known political arsenal of tyranny, despotism and dictatorships, and owes its existence only to the deplorable, but perhaps accidental failure of the traditional political forces—liberal or conservative, national or socialist, republican or monarchist, authoritarian or democratic. Or whether, on the contrary, there is such a thing as the *nature* of totalitarian government, whether it has its own essence and can be compared with and defined like other forms of government such as Western thought has known and recognized since the times of ancient philosophy. If this is true, then the entirely new and unprecedented forms of totalitarian organization and course of action must rest on one of the few basic experiences which men can have whenever they live together, and are concerned with public affairs. If there is a basic experience which finds its political expression in totalitarian domination, then, in view of the novelty of the totalitarian form of government, this must be an experience which, for whatever reason, has never before served as the foundation of a body politic and whose general mood—although it may be familiar in every other respect—never before has pervaded, and directed the handling of, public affairs.

If we consider this in terms of the history of ideas, it seems extremely unlikely. For the forms of government under which men live have been very few; they were discovered early, classified by the Greeks and have proved extraordinarily long-lived. If we apply these findings, whose fundamental idea, despite many variations, did not change in the two and a half thousand years that separate Plato from Kant, we are tempted at once to interpret totalitarianism as some modern form of tyranny, that is a lawless government where power is wielded by one man. Arbitrary power, unrestricted by law, wielded in the interest of the ruler and hostile to the interests of the governed, on one hand, fear as the principle of action, namely fear of the people by the ruler and fear of the ruler by the people, on the other—these have been the hallmarks of tyranny throughout our tradition.

Instead of saying that totalitarian government is unprecedented, we could also say that it has exploded the very alternative on which all definitions of the essence of governments have been based in political philosophy, that is the alternative between lawful and lawless government, between arbitrary and legitimate power. That lawful government and legitimate power, on one side, lawlessness and arbitrary power on the other, belonged together and were inseparable has never been questioned. Yet, totalitarian rule confronts us with a totally different kind of government. It defies, it is true, all positive laws, even to the extreme of defying those which it has itself established (as in the case of the Soviet Constitution of 1936, to quote only the most outstanding example) or which it did not care to abolish (as in the case of the Weimar Constitution which the Nazi government never revoked). But it operates neither without guidance of law nor is it arbitrary, for it claims to obey strictly and unequivocally those laws of Nature or of History from which all positive laws always have been supposed to spring.

It is the monstrous, yet seemingly unanswerable claim of totalitarian rule that, far from being "lawless," it goes to the sources of authority from which positive laws received their ultimate legitimation, that far from being arbitrary it is more obedient to these suprahuman forces than any government ever was before, and that far from wielding its power in the interest of one man, it is quite prepared to sacrifice everybody's vital immediate interests to the execution of what it assumes to be the law of History or the law of

Nature. Its defiance of positive laws claims to be a higher form of legitimacy which, since it is inspired by the sources themselves, can do away with petty legality. Totalitarian lawfulness pretends to have found a way to establish the rule of justice on earth—something which the legality of positive law admittedly could never attain. The discrepancy between legality and justice could never be bridged because the standards of right and wrong into which positive law translates its own source of authority—"natural law" governing the whole universe, or divine law revealed in human history, or customs and traditions expressing the law common to the sentiments of all men—are necessarily general and must be valid for a countless and unpredictable number of cases, so that each concrete individual case with its unrepeatable set of circumstances somehow escapes it.

Totalitarian lawfulness, defying legality and pretending to establish the direct reign of justice on earth, executes the law of History or of Nature without translating it into standards of right and wrong for individual behavior. It applies the law directly to mankind without bothering with the behavior of men. The law of Nature or the law of History, if properly executed, is expected to produce mankind as its end product; and this expectation lies behind the claim to global rule of all totalitarian governments. Totalitarian policy claims to transform the human species into an active unfailing carrier of a law to which human beings otherwise would only passively and reluctantly be subjected. If it is true that the link between totalitarian countries and the civilized world was broken through the monstrous crimes of totalitarian regimes, it is also true that this criminality was not due to simple aggressiveness, ruthlessness, warfare and treachery, but to a conscious break of that *consensus iuris* which, according to Cicero, constitutes a "people," and which, as international law, in modern times has constituted the civilized world insofar as it remains the foundation-stone of international relations even under the conditions of war. Both moral judgment and legal punishment presuppose this basic consent; the criminal can be judged justly only because he takes part in the *consensus iuris*, and even the revealed law of God can function among men only when they listen and consent to it.

At this point the fundamental difference between the totalitarian and all other concepts of law comes to light. Totalitarian policy does not replace one set of laws with another, does not establish its own *consensus iuris,* does not create, by one revolution, a new form of legality. Its defiance of all, even its own positive laws implies that it believes it can do without any *consensus iuris* whatever, and still not resign itself to the tyrannical state of lawlessness, arbitrariness and fear. It can do without the *consensus iuris* because it promises to release the fulfillment of law from all action and will of man; and it promises justice on earth because it claims to make mankind itself the embodiment of the law.

This identification of man and law, which seems to cancel the discrepancy between legality and justice that has plagued legal thought since ancient times, has nothing in common with the *lumen naturale* or the voice of conscience, by which Nature or Divinity as the sources of authority for the *ius naturale* or the historically revealed commands of God, are supposed to announce their authority in man himself. This never made man a walking embodiment of the law, but on the contrary remained distinct from him as the authority which demanded consent and obedience. Nature or Divinity as the source of authority for positive laws were thought of as permanent and eternal; positive laws were changing and changeable according to circumstances, but they possessed a relative permanence as compared with the much more rapidly changing actions of men; and they derived this permanence from the eternal presence of their source of authority. Positive laws, therefore, are primarily designed to function as stabilizing factors for the ever changing movements of men.

In the interpretation of totalitarianism, all laws have become laws of movement. When the Nazis talked about the law of nature or when the Bolsheviks talk about the law of history, neither nature nor history is any longer the stabilizing source of authority for the actions of mortal men; they are movements in themselves. Underlying the Nazis' belief in race laws as the expression of the law of nature in man, is Darwin's idea of man as the product of a natural development which does not necessarily stop with the present species of human beings, just as under the Bolsheviks' belief in class-struggle as the expression of the law of history lies Marx's notion of society as the product of a gigantic historical movement which races according to its own law of motion to the end of historical times when it will abolish itself.

The difference between Marx's historical and Darwin's naturalistic approach has frequently been pointed out, usually and rightly in favor of Marx. This has led us to forget the great and positive interest Marx took in Darwin's theories; Engels could not think of a greater compliment to Marx's scholarly achievements than to call him the "Darwin of history."[1] If one considers, not the actual achievement, but the basic philosophies of both men, it turns out that ultimately the movement of history and the movement of nature are one and the same. Darwin's introduction of the concept of development into nature, his insistence that, at least in the field of biology, natural movement is not circular but unilinear, moving in an infinitely progressing direction, means in fact that nature is, as it were, being swept into history, that natural life is considered to be historical. The "natural" law of the survival of the fittest is just as much a historical law and could be used as such by racism as Marx's law of the survival of the most progressive class. Marx's class struggle, on the other hand, as the driving force of history is only the outward expression of the development

[1] In his funeral speech on Marx, Engels said: "Just as Darwin discovered the law of development of organic life, so Marx discovered the law of development of human history." A similar comment is found in Engels' introduction to the edition of the *Communist Manifesto* in 1890, and in his introduction to the *Ursprung der Familie*, he once more mentions "Darwin's theory of evolution" and "Marx's theory of surplus value" side by side.

of productive forces which in turn have their origin in the "labor-power" of men. Labor, according to Marx, is not a historical but a natural-biological force—released through man's "metabolism with nature" by which he conserves his individual life and reproduces the species.[2] Engels saw the affinity between the basic convictions of the two men very clearly because he understood the decisive role which the concept of development played in both theories. The tremendous intellectual change which took place in the middle of the last century consisted in the refusal to view or accept anything "as it is" and in the consistent interpretation of everything as being only a stage of some further development. Whether the driving force of this development was called nature or history is relatively secondary. In these ideologies, the term "law" itself changed its meaning: from expressing the framework of stability within which human actions and motions can take place, it became the expression of the motion itself.

Totalitarian politics which proceeded to follow the recipes of ideologies has unmasked the true nature of these movements insofar as it clearly showed that there could be no end to this process. If it is the law of nature to eliminate everything that is harmful and unfit to live, it would mean the end of nature itself if new categories of the harmful and unfit-to-live could not be found; if it is the law of history that in a class struggle certain classes "wither away," it would mean the end of human history itself if rudimentary new classes did not form, so that they in turn could "wither away" under the hands of totalitarian rulers. In other words, the law of killing by which totalitarian movements seize and exercise power would remain a law of the movement even if they ever succeeded in making all of humanity subject to their rule.

By lawful government we understand a body politic in which positive laws are needed to translate and realize the immutable *ius naturale* or the eternal commandments of God into standards of right and wrong. Only in these standards, in the body of positive laws of each country, do the *ius naturale* or the Commandments of God achieve their political reality. In the body politic of totalitarian government, this place of positive laws is taken by total terror, which is designed to translate into reality the law of movement of history or nature. Just as positive laws, though they define transgressions, are independent of them—the absence of crimes in any society does not render laws superfluous but, on the contrary, signifies their most perfect rule—so terror in totalitarian government has ceased to be a mere means for the suppression of opposition, though it is also used for such purposes. Terror becomes total when it becomes independent of all opposition; it rules supreme when nobody any longer stands in its way. If lawfulness is the essence of non-tyrannical government and lawlessness is the essence of tyranny, then terror is the essence of totalitarian domination.

[2] For Marx's labor concept as "an eternal nature-imposed necessity, without which there can be no metabolism between man and nature, and therefore no life," see *Capital*, Vol. I, Part I, ch. 1 and 5. The quoted passage is from ch. 1, section 2.

Terror is the realization of the law of movement; its chief aim is to make it possible for the force of nature or of history to race freely through mankind, unhindered by any spontaneous human action. As such, terror seeks to "stabilize" men in order to liberate the forces of nature or history. It is this movement which singles out the foes of mankind against whom terror is let loose, and no free action of either opposition or sympathy can be permitted to interfere with the elimination of the "objective enemy" of History or Nature, of the class or the race. Guilt and innocence become senseless notions; "guilty" is he who stands in the way of the natural or historical process which has passed judgment over "inferior races,". over individuals "unfit to live," over "dying classes and decadent peoples." Terror executes these judgments, and before its court, all concerned are subjectively innocent: the murdered because they did nothing against the system, and the murderers because they do not really murder but execute a death sentence pronounced by some higher tribunal. The rulers themselves do not claim to be just or wise, but only to execute historical or natural laws; they do not apply laws, but execute a movement in accordance with its inherent law. Terror is lawfulness, if law is the law of the movement of some suprahuman force, Nature or History.

Terror as the execution of a law of movement whose ultimate goal is not the welfare of men or the interest of one man but the fabrication of mankind, eliminates individuals for the sake of the species, sacrifices the "parts" for the sake of the "whole." The suprahuman force of Nature or History has its own beginning and its own end, so that it can be hindered only by the new beginning and the individual end which the life of each man actually is.

Positive laws in constitutional government are designed to erect boundaries and establish channels of communication between men whose community is continually endangered by the new men born into it. With each new birth, a new beginning is born into the world, a new world has potentially come into being. The stability of the laws corresponds to the constant motion of all human affairs, a motion which can never end as long as men are born and die. The laws hedge in each new beginning and at the same time assure its freedom of movement, the potentiality of something entirely new and unpredictable; the boundaries of positive laws are for the political existence of man what memory is for his historical existence: they guarantee the pre-existence of a common world, the reality of some continuity which transcends the individual life span of each generation, absorbs all new origins and is nourished by them.

Total terror is so easily mistaken for a symptom of tyrannical government because totalitarian government in its initial stages must behave like a tyranny and raze the boundaries of man-made law. But total terror leaves no arbitrary lawlessness behind it and does not rage for the sake of some arbitrary will or for the sake of despotic power of one man against all, least of all for the sake of a war of all against all. It substitutes for the boundaries and channels of communication between individual men a band of iron which holds them so tightly together that it is as though their plurality had disappeared into One Man of gigantic dimensions. To abolish the fences of laws between men—as tyranny does—means to take away man's liberties and destroy freedom as a living political reality; for the space between men as it is hedged in by laws, is the living space of freedom. Total terror uses this old instrument of tyranny but destroys at the same time also the lawless, fenceless wilderness of fear and suspicion which tyranny leaves behind. This desert, to be sure, is no longer a living space of freedom, but it still provides some room for the fear-guided movements and suspicion-ridden actions of its inhabitants.

By pressing men against each other, total terror destroys the space between them; compared to the condition within its iron band, even the desert of tyranny, insofar as it is still some kind of space, appears like a guarantee of freedom. Totalitarian government does not just curtail liberties or abolish essential freedoms; nor does it, at least to our limited knowledge, succeed in eradicating the love for freedom from the hearts of man. It destroys the one essential prerequisite of all freedom which is simply the capacity of motion which cannot exist without space.

Total terror, the essence of totalitarian government, exists neither for nor against men. It is supposed to provide the forces of nature or history with an incomparable instrument to accelerate their movement. This movement, proceeding according to its own law, cannot in the long run be hindered; eventually its force will always prove more powerful than the most powerful forces engendered by the actions and the will of men. But it can be slowed down and is slowed down almost inevitably by the freedom of man, which even totalitarian rulers cannot deny, for this freedom—irrelevant and arbitrary as they may deem it—is identical with the fact that men are being born and that therefore each of them *is* a new beginning, begins, in a sense, the world anew. From the totalitarian point of view, the fact that men are born and die can be only regarded as an annoying interference with higher forces. Terror, therefore, as the obedient servant of natural or historical movement has to eliminate from the process not only freedom in any specific sense, but the very source of freedom which is given with the fact of the birth of man and resides in his capacity to make a new beginning. In the iron band of terror, which destroys the plurality of men and makes out of many the One who unfailingly will act as though he himself were part of the course of history or nature, a device has been found not only to liberate the historical and natural forces, but to accelerate them to a speed they never would reach if left to themselves. Practically speaking, this means that terror executes on the spot the death sentences which Nature is supposed to have pronounced on races or individuals who are "unfit to live," or History on "dying classes," without waiting for the slower and less efficient processes of nature or history themselves.

In this concept, where the essence of government itself has become motion, a very old problem of political thought seems to have found a solution similar to the one already noted for the discrepancy between legality and justice. If the essence of government is defined as lawfulness, and if it is understood that laws are the stabilizing forces in the public affairs of men (as indeed it always has been since Plato invoked Zeus, the god of the boundaries, in his *Laws*), then the problem of movement of the body politic and the actions of its citizens arises. Lawfulness sets limitations to actions, but does not inspire them; the greatness, but also the perplexity of laws in free societies is that they only tell what one should not, but never what one should do. The necessary movement of a body politic can never be found in its essence if only because this essence—again since Plato—has always been defined with a view to its permanence. Duration seemed one of the surest yardsticks for the goodness of a government. It is still for Montesquieu the supreme proof for the badness of tyranny that only tyrannies are liable to be destroyed from within, to decline by themselves, whereas all other governments are destroyed through exterior circumstances. Therefore what the definition of governments always needed was what Montesquieu called a "principle of action" which, different in each form of government, would inspire government and citizens alike in their public activity and serve as a criterion, beyond the merely negative yardstick of lawfulness, for judging all action in public affairs. Such guiding principles and criteria of action are, according to Montesquieu, honor in a monarchy, virtue in a republic and fear in a tyranny.

In a perfect totalitarian government, where all men have become One Man, where all action aims at the acceleration of the movement of nature or history, where every single act is the execution of a death sentence which Nature or History has already pronounced, that is, under conditions where terror can be completely relied upon to keep the movement in constant motion, no principle of action separate from its essence would be needed at all. Yet as long as totalitarian rule has not conquered the earth and with the iron band of terror made each single man a part of one mankind, terror in its double function as essence of government and principle, not of action, but of motion, cannot be fully realized. Just as lawfulness in constitutional government is insufficient to inspire and guide men's actions, so terror in totalitarian government is not sufficient to inspire and guide human behavior.

While under present conditions totalitarian domination still shares with other forms of government the need for a guide for the behavior of its citizens in public affairs, it does not need and could not even use a principle of action strictly speaking, since it will eliminate precisely the capacity of man to act. Under conditions of total terror not even fear can any longer serve as an advisor of how to behave, because terror chooses its victims without reference to individual actions or thoughts, exclusively in accordance with the objective necessity of the natural or historical process. Under totalitarian conditions, fear probably is more widespread than ever before; but fear has lost its practical usefulness when actions guided by it can no longer help to avoid the dangers man fears. The same is true for sympathy or support of the regime; for total terror not only selects its victims according to objective standards; it chooses its executioners with as complete a disregard as possible for the candidate's conviction and sympathies. The consistent elimination of conviction as a motive for action has become a matter of record since the great purges in Soviet Russia and the satellite countries. The aim of totalitarian education has never been to instill convictions but to destroy the capacity to form any. The introduction of purely objective criteria into the selective system of the SS troops was Himmler's great organizational invention; he selected the candidates from photographs according to purely racial criteria. Nature itself decided, not only who was to be eliminated, but also who was to be trained as an executioner.

No guiding principle of behavior, taken itself from the realm of human action, such as virtue, honor, fear, is necessary or can be useful to set into motion a body politic which no longer uses terror as a means of intimidation, but whose essence *is* terror. In its stead, it has introduced an entirely new principle into public affairs that dispenses with human will to action altogether and appeals to the craving need for some insight into the law of movement according to which the terror functions and upon which, therefore, all private destinies depend.

The inhabitants of a totalitarian country are thrown into and caught in the process of nature or history for the sake of accelerating its movement; as such, they can only be executioners or victims of its inherent law. The process may decide that those who today eliminate races and individuals or the members of dying classes and decadent peoples are tomorrow those who must be sacrificed. What totalitarian rule needs to guide the behavior of its subjects is a preparation to fit each of them equally well for the role of executioner and the role of victim. This two-sided preparation, the substitute for a principle of action, is the ideology.

Ideologies—isms which to the satisfaction of their adherents can explain everything and every occurence by deducing it from a single premise—are a very recent phenomenon and, for many decades, played a negligible role in political life. Only with the wisdom of hindsight can we discover in them certain elements which have made them so disturbingly useful for totalitarian rule. Not before Hitler and Stalin were the great political potentialities of the ideologies discovered.

Ideologies are known for their scientific character: they combine the scientific approach with results of philosophical relevance and pretend to be scientific philosophy. The word "ideology" seems to imply that an idea can become the subject matter of a science just as animals are the subject matter of zoology, and that the suffix *-logy* in ideology, as in zoology, indicates nothing but the *logoi*, the scientific statements made on it. If this were true, an ideology would indeed be a pseudo-science and a pseudo-philosophy, transgressing at the same time the limitations of science and the limitations of philosophy. Deism, for example, would then be the ideology which treats the idea of God, with which philosophy is concerned, in the scientific manner of theology for which God is a revealed reality. (A theology which is not based on revelation as a given reality but treats God as an idea would be as mad as a zoology which is no longer sure of the physical, tangible existence of animals.) Yet we know that this is only part of the truth. Deism, though it denies divine revelation, does not simply make "scientific" statements on a God which is only an "idea," but uses the idea of God in order to explain the course of the world. The "ideas" of isms—race in racism, God in deism, etc.—never form the subject matter of the ideologies and the suffix *-logy* never indicates simply a body of "scientific" statements.

An ideology is quite literally what its name indicates: it is the logic of an idea. Its subject matter is history, to which the "idea" is applied; the result of this application is not a body of statements about something that *is,* but the unfolding of a process which is in constant change. The ideology treats the course of events as though it followed the same "law" as the logical exposition of its "idea." Ideologies pretend to know the mysteries of the whole historical process—the secrets of the past, the intricacies of the present, the uncertainties of the future—because of the logic inherent in their respective ideas.

Ideologies are never interested in the miracle of being. They are historical, concerned with becoming and perishing, with the rise and fall of cultures, even if they try to explain history by some "law of nature." The word "race" in racism does not signify any genuine curiosity about the human races as a field for scientific exploration, but is the "idea" by which the movement of history is explained as one consistent process.

The "idea" of an ideology is neither Plato's eternal essence grasped by the eyes of the mind nor Kant's regulative principle of reason but has become an instrument of explanation. To an ideology, history does not appear in the light of an idea (which would imply that history is seen *sub specie* of some ideal eternity which itself is beyond historical motion) but as something which can be calculated by it. What fits the "idea" into this new role is its own "logic," that is a movement which is the consequence of the "idea" itself and needs no outside factor to set it into motion. Racism is the belief that there is a motion inherent in the very idea of race, just as deism is the belief that a motion is inherent in the very notion of God.

The movement of history and the logical process of this notion are supposed to correspond to each other, so that whatever happens, happens according to the logic of one "idea." However, the only possible movement in the realm of logic is the process of deduction from a premise. Dialectical logic, with its process from thesis through antithesis to synthesis which in turn becomes the thesis of the next dialectical movement, is not different in principle, once an ideology gets hold of it; the first thesis becomes the premise and its advantage for ideological explanation is that this dialectical device can explain away factual contradictions as stages of one identical, consistent movement.

As soon as logic as a movement of thought—and not as a necessary control of thinking—is applied to an idea, this idea is transformed into a premise. Ideological world explanations performed this operation long before it became so eminently fruitful for totalitarian reasoning. The purely negative coercion of logic, the prohibition of contradictions, became "productive" so that a whole line of thought could be initiated, and forced upon the mind, by drawing conclusions in the manner of mere argumentation. This argumentative process could be interrupted neither by a new idea (which would have been another premise with a different set of consequences) nor by a new experience. Ideologies always assume that one idea is sufficient to explain everything in the development from the premise, and that no experience can teach anything because everything is comprehended in this consistent process of logical deduction. The danger in exchanging the necessary insecurity of philosophical thought for the total explanation of an ideology and its *Weltanschauung,* is not even so much the risk of falling for some usually vulgar, always uncritical assumption as of exchanging the freedom inherent in man's capacity to think for the strait jacket of logic with which man can force himself almost as violently as he is forced by some outside power.

The *Weltanschauungen* and ideologies of the nineteenth century are not in themselves totalitarian, and although racism and communism have become the decisive ideologies of the twentieth century they were not, in principle, any "more totalitarian" than the others; it happened because the elements of experience on which they were originally based—the struggle between the races for world domination, and the struggle between the classes for political power in the respective countries—turned out to be politically more important than those of other ideologies. In this sense the ideological victory of racism and communism over all other isms was decided before the totalitarian movements took hold of precisely these ideologies. On the other hand, all ideologies contain totalitarian elements, but these are fully developed only by totalitarian movements, and this creates the deceptive impression that only racism and communism are totalitarian in character. The truth is, rather, that the real nature of all ideologies was revealed only in the role that the ideology plays in the apparatus of totalitarian domination. Seen from this aspect, there appear three specifically totalitarian elements that are peculiar to all ideological thinking.

First, in their claim to total explanation, ideologies have the tendency to explain not what is, but what becomes, what is born and passes away. They are in all cases concerned solely with the element of motion, that is, with history in the customary sense of the word. Ideologies are always oriented toward history, even when, as in the case of racism, they seemingly proceed from the premise of nature; here, nature serves merely to explain historical matters and reduce them to matters of nature. The claim to total explanation promises to explain all historical happenings, the total explanation of the past, the total knowledge of the present, and the reliable prediction of the future. Secondly, in this capacity ideological thinking becomes independent of all experience from which it cannot learn anything new even if it is a question of something that has just come to pass. Hence ideological thinking becomes emancipated from the reality that we perceive with our five senses, and insists on a "truer" reality concealed behind all perceptible

things, dominating them from this place of concealment and requiring a sixth sense that enables us to become aware of it. The sixth sense is provided by precisely the ideology, that particular ideological indoctrination which is taught by the educational institutions, established exclusively for this purpose, to train the "political soldiers" in the *Ordensburgen* of the Nazis or the schools of the Comintern and the Cominform. The propaganda of the totalitarian movement also serves to emancipate thought from experience and reality; it always strives to inject a secret meaning into every public, tangible event and to suspect a secret intent behind every public political act. Once the movements have come to power, they proceed to change reality in accordance with their ideological claims. The concept of enmity is replaced by that of conspiracy, and this produces a mentality in which reality—real enmity or real friendship—is no longer experienced and understood in its own terms but is automatically assumed to signify something else.

Thirdly, since the ideologies have no power to transform reality, they achieve this emancipation of thought from experience through certain methods of demonstration. Ideological thinking orders facts into an absolutely logical procedure which starts from an axiomatically accepted premise, deducing everything else from it; that is, it proceeds with a consistency that exists nowhere in the realm of reality. The deducing may proceed logically or dialectically; in either case it involves a consistent process of argumentation which, because it thinks in terms of a process, is supposed to be able to comprehend the movement of the suprahuman, natural or historical processes. Comprehension is achieved by the mind's imitating, either logically or dialectically, the laws of "scientifically" established movements with which through the process of imitation it becomes integrated. Ideological argumentation, always a kind of logical deduction, corresponds to the two aforementioned elements of the ideologies—the element of movement and of emancipation from reality and experience—first, because its thought movement does not spring from experience but is self-generated, and, secondly, because it transforms the one and only point that is taken and accepted from experienced reality into an axiomatic premise, leaving from then on the subsequent argumentation process completely untouched from any further experience. Once it has established its premise, its point of departure, experiences no longer interfere with ideological thinking, nor can it be taught by reality.

The device both totalitarian rulers used to transform their respective ideologies into weapons with which each of their subjects could force himself into step with the terror movement was deceptively simple and inconspicuous: they took them dead seriously, took pride the one in his supreme gift for "ice cold reasoning" (Hitler) and the other in the "mercilessness of his dialectics," and proceeded to drive ideological implications into extremes of logical consistency which, to the onlooker, looked preposterously "primitive" and absurd: a "dying class" consisted of people condemned to death; races that are "unfit to live" were to be exterminated. Whoever agreed that there are such things as "dying classes" and did not draw the consequence of killing their members, or that the right to live had something to do with race and did not draw the consequence of killing "unfit races," was plainly either stupid or a coward. This stringent logicality as a guide to action permeates the whole structure of totalitarian movements and governments. It is exclusively the work of Hitler and Stalin who, although they did not add a single new thought to the ideas and propaganda slogans of their movements, for this reason alone must be considered ideologists of the greatest importance.

What distinguished these new totalitarian ideologists from their predecessors was that it was no longer primarily the "idea" of the ideology—the struggle of classes and the exploitation of the workers or the struggle of races and the care for Germanic peoples—which appealed to them, but the logical process which could be developed from it. According to Stalin, neither the idea nor the oratory but "the irresistible force of logic thoroughly overpowered [Lenin's] audience." The power, which Marx thought was born when the idea seized the masses, was discovered to reside, not in the idea itself, but in its logical process which "like a mighty tentacle seizes you on all sides as in a vise and from whose grip you are powerless to tear yourself away; you must either surrender or make up your mind to utter defeat."[3] Only when the realization of the ideological aims, the classless society or the master race, was at stake, could this force show itself. In the process of realization, the original substance upon which the ideologies based themselves as long as they had to appeal to the masses—the exploitation of the workers or the national aspirations of Germany—is gradually lost, devoured as it were by the process itself: in perfect accordance with "ice cold reasoning" and the "irresistible force of logic," the workers lost under Bolshevik rule even those rights they had been granted under Tsarist oppression and the German people suffered a kind of warfare which did not pay the slightest regard to the minimum requirements for survival of the German nation. It is in the nature of ideological politics—and is not simply a betrayal committed for the sake of self-interest or lust for power—that the real content of the ideology (the working class or the Germanic peoples), which originally had brought about the "idea" (the struggle of classes as the law of history or the struggle of races as the law of nature), is devoured by the logic with which the "idea" is carried out.

The preparation of victims and executioners which totalitarianism requires in place of Montesquieu's principle of action is not the ideology itself—racism or dialectical materialism—but its inherent logicality. The most persuasive argument in this respect, an argument of which Hitler like Stalin was very fond, is: You can't say A without saying B and C and so on, down to the end of the murderous alphabet. Here, the coercive force of logicality

[3] Stalin's speech of January 28, 1924; quoted from Lenin, *Selected Works*, Vol. I, p. 33, Moscow, 1947.—It is interesting to note that Stalin's "logic" is among the few qualities that Khrushchev praises in his devastating speech at the Twentieth Party Congress.

seems to have its source; it springs from our fear of contradicting ourselves. To the extent that the Bolshevik purge succeeds in making its victims confess to crimes they never committed, it relies chiefly on this basic fear and argues as follows: We are all agreed on the premise that history is a struggle of classes and on the role of the Party in its conduct. You know therefore that, historically speaking, the Party is always right (in the words of Trotsky: "We can only be right with and by the Party, for history has provided no other way of being in the right."). At this historical moment, that is in accordance with the law of history, certain crimes are due to be committed which the Party, knowing the law of history, must punish. For these crimes, the Party needs criminals; it may be that the Party, though knowing the crimes, does not quite know the criminals; more important than to be sure about the criminals is to punish the crimes, because without such punishment, History will not be advanced but may even be hindered in its course. You, therefore, either have committed the crimes or have been called by the Party to play the role of the criminal—in either case, you have objectively become an enemy of the Party. If you don't confess, you cease to help History through the Party, and have become a real enemy.—The coercive force of the argument is: if you refuse, you contradict yourself and, through this contradiction, render your whole life meaningless; the A which you said dominates your whole life through the consequences of B and C which it logically engenders.

Totalitarian rulers rely on the compulsion with which we can compel ourselves, for the limited mobilization of people which even they still need; this inner compulsion is the tyranny of logicality against which nothing stands but the great capacity of men to start something new. The tyranny of logicality begins with the mind's submission to logic as a never-ending process, on which man relies in order to engender his thoughts. By this submission, he surrenders his inner freedom as he surrenders his freedom of movement when he bows down to an outward tyranny. Freedom as an inner capacity of man is identical with the capacity to begin, just as freedom as a political reality is identical with a space of movement between men. Over the beginning, no logic, no cogent deduction can have any power, because its chain presupposes, in the form of a premise, the beginning. As terror is needed lest with the birth of each new human being a new beginning arise and raise its voice in the world, so the self-coercive force of logicality is mobilized lest anybody ever start thinking—which as the freest and purest of all human activities is the very opposite of the compulsory process of deduction. Totalitarian government can be safe only to the extent that it can mobilize man's own will power in order to force him into that gigantic movement of History or Nature which supposedly uses mankind as its material and knows neither birth nor death.

The compulsion of total terror on one side, which, with its iron band, presses masses of isolated men together *and* supports them in a world which has become a wilderness for them, and the self-coercive force of logical deduction on the other, which prepares each individual in his lonely isolation against all others, correspond to each other and need each other in order to set the terror-ruled movement into motion and keep it moving. Just as terror, even in its pre-total, merely tyrannical form ruins all relationships between men, so the self-compulsion of ideological thinking ruins all relationships with reality. The preparation has succeeded when people have lost contact with their fellow men as well as the reality around them; for together with these contacts, men lose the capacity of both experience and thought. The ideal subject of totalitarian rule is not the convinced Nazi or the convinced Communist, but people for whom the distinction between fact and fiction (*i.e.*, the reality of experience) and the distinction between true and false (*i.e.*, the standards of thought) no longer exist.

The question we raised at the start of these considerations and to which we now return is what kind of basic experience in the living-together of men permeates a form of government whose essence is terror and whose principle of action is the logicality of ideological thinking. That such a combination was never used before in the varied forms of political domination is obvious. Still, the basic experience on which it rests must be human and known to men, insofar as even this most "original" of all political bodies has been devised by, and is somehow answering the needs of, men.

It has frequently been observed that terror can rule absolutely only over men who are isolated against each other and that, therefore, one of the primary concerns of all tyrannical government is to bring this isolation about. Isolation may be the beginning of terror; it certainly is its most fertile ground; it always is its result. This isolation is, as it were, pretotalitarian; its hallmark is impotence insofar as power always comes from men acting together, "acting in concert" (Burke); isolated men are powerless by definition.

Isolation and impotence, that is the fundamental inability to act at all, have always been characteristic of tyrannies. Political contacts between men are severed in tyrannical government and the human capacities for action and power are frustrated. But not all contacts between men are broken and not all human capacities destroyed. The whole sphere of private life with the capacities for experience, fabrication and thought are left intact. We know that the iron band of total terror leaves no space for such private life and that the self-coercion of totalitarian logic destroys man's capacity for experience and thought just as certainly as his capacity for action.

What we call isolation in the political sphere, is called loneliness in the sphere of social intercourse. Isolation and loneliness are not the same. I can be isolated—that is in a situation in which I cannot act, because there is nobody who will act with me—without being lonely; and I can be lonely—that is in a situation in which I as a person feel myself deserted by all human companionship—without being isolated. Isolation is that impasse into which men are driven when the political sphere of their lives, where they act together in the pursuit of a common concern, is destroyed. Yet isolation, though destructive of power and the capacity for action, not only leaves intact but is required for all so-called productive activities of men.

Man insofar as he is *homo faber* tends to isolate himself with his work, that is to leave temporarily the realm of politics. Fabrication (*poiesis*, the making of things), as distinguished from action (*praxis*) on one hand and sheer labor on the other, is always performed in a certain isolation from common concerns, no matter whether the result is a piece of craftsmanship or of art. In isolation, man remains in contact with the world as the human artifice; only when the most elementary form of human creativity, which is the capacity to add something of one's own to the common world, is destroyed, isolation becomes altogether unbearable. This can happen in a world whose chief values are dictated by labor, that is where all human activities have been transformed into laboring. Under such conditions, only the sheer effort of labor which is the effort to keep alive is left and the relationship with the world as a human artifice is broken. Isolated man who lost his place in the political realm of action is deserted by the world of things as well, if he is no longer recognized as *homo faber* but treated as an *animal laborans* whose necessary "metabolism with nature" is of concern to no one. Isolation then becomes loneliness. Tyranny based on isolation generally leaves the productive capacities of man intact; a tyranny over "laborers," however, as for instance the rule over slaves in antiquity, would automatically be a rule over lonely, not only isolated, men and tend to be totalitarian.

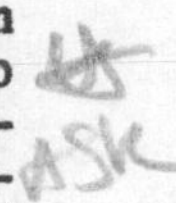

While isolation concerns only the political realm of life, loneliness concerns human life as a whole. Totalitarian government, like all tyrannies, certainly could not exist without destroying the public realm of life, that is, without destroying, by isolating men, their political capacities. But totalitarian domination as a form of government is new in that it is not content with this isolation and destroys private life as well. It bases itself on loneliness, on the experience of not belonging to the world at all, which is among the most radical and desperate experiences of man.

Loneliness, the common ground for terror, the essence of totalitarian government, and for ideology or logicality, the preparation of its executioners and victims, is closely connected with uprootedness and superfluousness which have been the curse of modern masses since the beginning of the industrial revolution and have become acute with the rise of imperialism at the end of the last century and the break-down of political institutions and social traditions in our own time. To be uprooted means to have no place in the world, recognized and guaranteed by others; to be superfluous means not to belong to the world at all. Uprootedness can be the preliminary condition for superfluousness, just as isolation can (but must not) be the preliminary condition for loneliness. Taken in itself, without consideration of its recent historical causes and its new role in politics, loneliness is at the same time contrary to the basic requirements of the human condition *and* one of the fundamental experiences of every human life. Even the experience of the materially and sensually given world depends upon my being in contact with other men, upon our *common* sense which regulates and controls all other senses and without which each of us would

be enclosed in his own particularity of sense data which in themselves are unreliable and treacherous. Only because we have common sense, that is only because not one man, but men in the plural inhabit the earth can we trust our immediate sensual experience. Yet, we have only to remind ourselves that one day we shall have to leave this common world which will go on as before and for whose continuity we are superfluous in order to realize loneliness, the experience of being abandoned by everything and everybody.

Loneliness is not solitude. Solitude requires being alone whereas loneliness shows itself most sharply in company with others. Apart from a few stray remarks—usually framed in a paradoxical mood like Cato's statement (reported by Cicero, *De Re Publica,* I, 17): *numquam minus solum esse quam cum solus esset,* "never was he less alone than when he was alone," or, rather, "never was he less lonely than when he was in solitude"—it seems that Epictetus, the emancipated slave philosopher of Greek origin, was the first to distinguish between loneliness and solitude. His discovery, in a way, was accidental, his chief interest being neither solitude nor loneliness, but being alone (*monos*) in the sense of absolute independence. As Epictetus sees it (*Dissertationes,* Book 3, ch. 13) the lonely man (*eremos*) finds himself surrounded by others with whom he cannot establish contact or to whose hostility he is exposed. The solitary man, on the contrary, is alone and therefore "can be together with himself" since men have the capacity of "talking with themselves." In solitude, in other words, I am "by myself," together with my self, and therefore two-in-one, whereas in loneliness I am actually one, deserted by all others. All thinking, strictly speaking, is done in solitude and is a dialogue between me and myself; but this dialogue of the two-in-one does not lose contact with the world of my fellow-men because they are represented in the self with whom I lead the dialogue of thought. The problem of solitude is that this two-in-one needs the others in order to become one again: one unchangeable individual whose identity can never be mistaken for that of any other. For the confirmation of my identity I depend entirely upon other people; and it is the great saving grace of companionship for solitary men that it makes them "whole" again, saves them from the dialogue of thought in which one remains always equivocal, restores the identity which makes them speak with the single voice of one unexchangeable person.

Solitude can become loneliness; this happens when all by myself I am deserted by my own self. Solitary men have always been in danger of loneliness, when they can no longer find the redeeming grace of companionship to save them from duality and equivocality and doubt. Historically, it seems as though this danger became sufficiently great to be noticed by others and recorded by history only in the nineteenth century. It showed itself clearly when philosophers, for whom alone solitude is a way of life and a condition of work, were no longer content with the fact that "philosophy is only for the few" and began to insist that nobody "understands" them. Characteristic in this respect is the anecdote reported from Hegel's deathbed which hardly could have been told of any great philosopher before him: "Nobody has understood me except one; and he also misunderstood." Conversely, there is always the chance that a lonely man finds himself and starts the thinking dialogue of solitude. This seems to have happened to Nietzsche in Sils Maria when he conceived *Zarathustra.* In two poems ("Sils Maria" and "Aus hohen Bergen") he tells of the empty expectation and the yearning waiting of the lonely until suddenly *"um Mittag war's, da wurde Eins zu Zwei . ./ Nun feiern wir, vereinten Siegs gewiss,/ das Fest der Feste;/ Freund Zarathustra kam, der Gast der Gäste!"* ("Noon was, when One became Two . . Certain of united victory we celebrate the feast of feasts; friend Zarathustra came, the guest of guests.")

What makes loneliness so unbearable is the loss of one's own self which can be realized in solitude, but confirmed in its identity only by the trusting and trustworthy company of my equals. In this situation, man loses trust in himself as the partner of his thoughts and that elementary confidence in the world which is necessary to make experiences at all. Self and world, capacity for thought and experience are lost at the same time.

The only capacity of the human mind which needs neither the self nor the other nor the world in order to function safely and which is as independent of experience as it is of thinking is the ability of logical reasoning whose premise is the self-evident. The elementary rules of cogent evidence, the truism that two and two equals four cannot be perverted even under the conditions of absolute loneliness. It is the only reliable "truth" human beings can fall back upon once they have lost the mutual guarantee, the common sense, men need in order to experience and live and know their way in a common world. But this "truth" is empty or rather no truth at all, because it does not reveal anything. (To define consistency as truth as some modern logicians do means to deny the existence of truth.) Under the conditions of loneliness, therefore, the self-evident is no longer just a means of the intellect and begins to be productive, to develop its own lines of "thought." That thought processes characterized by strict self-evident logicality, from which apparently there is no escape, have some connection with loneliness was once noticed by Luther (whose experiences in the phenomena of solitude and loneliness probably were second to no one's and who once dared to say that "there must be a God because man needs one being whom he can trust") in a little-known remark on the Bible text "it is not good that man should be alone": A lonely man, says Luther, "always deduces one thing from the other and thinks everything to the worst."[4] The famous extremism of totalitarian movements, far from having anything to do with true radicalism, consists indeed in this "thinking everything to the worst," in this deducing process which always arrives at the worst possible conclusions.

[4] *"Ein solcher (sc. einsamer) Mensch folgert immer eins aus dem andern und denkt alles zum Ärgsten."* In *Erbauliche Schriften,* "Warum die Einsamkeit zu fliehen?"

What prepares men for totalitarian domination in the non-totalitarian world is the fact that loneliness, once a borderline experience usually suffered in certain marginal social conditions like old age, has become an everyday experience of the evergrowing masses of our century. The merciless process into which totalitarianism drives and organizes the masses looks like a suicidal escape from this reality. The "ice-cold reasoning" and the "mighty tentacle" of dialectics which "seizes you as in a vise" appears like a last support in a world where nobody is reliable and nothing can be relied upon. It is the inner coercion whose only content is the strict avoidance of contradictions that seems to confirm a man's identity outside all relationships with others. It fits him into the iron band of terror even when he is alone, and totalitarian domination tries never to leave him alone except in the extreme situation of solitary confinement. By destroying all space between men and pressing men against each other, even the productive potentialities of isolation are annihilated; by teaching and glorifying the logical reasoning of loneliness where man knows that he will be utterly lost if ever he lets go of the first premise from which the whole process is being started, even the slim chances that loneliness may be transformed into solitude and logic into thought are obliterated. If this practice is compared with that of tyranny, it seems as if a way had been found to set the desert itself in motion, to let loose a sand storm that could cover all parts of the inhabited earth.

The conditions under which we exist today in the field of politics are indeed threatened by these devastating sand storms. Their danger is not that they might establish a permanent world. Totalitarian domination, like tyranny, bears the germs of its own destruction. Just as fear and the impotence from which fear springs are antipolitical principles and throw men into a situation contrary to political action, so loneliness and the logical-ideological deducing the worst that comes from it represent an antisocial situation and harbor a principle destructive for all human living-together. Nevertheless, organized loneliness is considerably more dangerous than the unorganized impotence of all those who are ruled by the tyrannical and arbitrary will of a single man. Its danger is that it threatens to ravage the world as we know it—a world which everywhere seems to have come to an end—before a new beginning rising from this end has had time to assert itself.

Apart from such considerations—which as predictions are of little avail and less consolation—there remains the fact that the crisis of our time and its central experience have brought forth an entirely new form of government which as a potentiality and an ever-present danger is only too likely to stay with us from now on, just as other forms of government which came about at different historical moments and rested on different fundamental experiences have stayed with mankind regardless of temporary defeats—monarchies, and republics, tyrannies, dictatorships and despotism.

But there remains also the truth that every end in history necessarily contains a new beginning; this beginning is the promise, the only "message"

which the end can ever produce. Begir
event, is the supreme capacity of man;
freedom. *Initium ut esset homo creat*
man was created" said Augustine.[5] Tl
new birth; it is indeed every man.

[5] *De Civitate Dei*, Book 12, chapter 20.

Bibliography

For kind permission to peruse and quote archival material, I thank the Hoover Library in Stanford, California, the Centre de Documentation Juive Contemporaine in Paris, and the Yiddish Scientific Institute in New York. Documents used in the Nuremberg Trials are quoted with their Nuremberg File Number, other documents are referred to with indication of their present location and archival number.

Abel, Theodore, *Why Hitler Came into Power; an Answer Based on the Original Life Stories of Six Hundred of His Followers,* 1938.

Adler, H. G., *Theresienstadt 1941-1945,* Tübingen, 1955.

Alquen, Gunter d', *Die SS. Geschichte, Aufgabe und Organisation der Schutzstaffeln der NSDAP* (Schriften der Hochschule für Politik), 1939.

Anweiler, Oskar, *Die Räte-Bewegung in Russland 1905-1921,* Leiden, 1958; "Lenin und der friedliche Übergang zum Sozialismus," in *Osteuropa,* 1956, vol. VI.

Armstrong, John A., *The Soviet Bureaucratic Elite: A Study of the Ukrainian Apparatus,* New York, 1959; *The Politics of Totalitarianism,* New York, 1961.

Avtorkhanov, A., "Social Differentiation and Contradictions in the Party," *Bulletin of the Institute for the Study of the USSR,* Munich, February, 1956; *Stalin and the Soviet Communist Party: A Study in the Technology of Power,* New York, 1959; (pseudonym Uvalov), *The Reign of Stalin,* London, 1953.

Bakunin, Michael, *Oeuvres,* Paris, 1907; *Gesammelte Werke,* 1921-24.

Balabanoff, Angelica, *Impressions of Lenin,* Ann Arbor, 1964.

Baldwin, Roger N., "Political Police," in *Encyclopedia of Social Sciences.*

Barruel, Abbé, *Memoire pour servir à l'histoire du Jacobinisme,* 1797.

Bataille, George, "Le Secret de Sade," *La Critique,* vol. 3, nos. 15, 16, 17, 1947; "Review of D. Rousset, *Les Jours de notre mort," La Critique,* January, 1948.

Bauer, R. A., Inkeles, A., Kluckhohn, C., *How the Soviet System Works,* Cambridge, 1956.

Bayer, Ernest, *Die SA,* Berlin, 1938.

Bayle, François, *Psychologie et Ethique du National-Socialisme. Etude Anthropologique des Dirigeants SS,* Paris, 1953.

Beck, F., and Godin, W., *Russian Purge and the Extraction of Confession,* London and New York, 1951.

Beckerath, Erwin von, "Fascism," in *Encyclopedia of Social Sciences; Wesen und Werden des faschistischen Staates,* Berlin, 1927.

Benn, Gottfried, *Der neue Staat und die Intellektuellen,* 1933.

Bennecke, H., *Hitler und die SA,* München, 1962.

Berdyaev, Nicolas, *The Origin of Russian Communism,* 1937.

Best, Werner, *Die deutsche Polizei,* 1940.

Bettelheim, Bruno, "On Dachau and Buchenwald," in *Nazi Conspiracy op. cit.*, vol. 7; "Behavior in Extreme Situations," *Journal of Abnormal and Social Psychology*, vol. 38, no. 4, 1943.
Black, C. E., editor, *Rewriting Russian History*, New York, 1956.
Blanc, R. M., *Adolf Hitler et les "Protocoles des Sages de Sion,"* 1938.
Boberach, Heinz, editor, *Meldungen aus dem Reich*, Neuwied and Berlin, 1965.
Bonhard, Otto, *Jüdische Geld- und Weltherrschraft?*, Berlin, 1926.
Borkenau Franz, *The Totalitarian Enemy*, London, 1940; *The Communist International*, London, 1938; "Die neue Komintern," *Der Monat*, no 4, 1949.
Bormann, Martin, "Relationship of National Socialism and Christianity," in *Nazi Conspiracy, op. cit.*, vol. 6; *The Bormann Letters*, ed. by H. R. Trevor-Roper, London, 1954.
Boucart, Robert, *Les Dessous de l'Intelligence Service*, 1937.
Bracher, Karl Dietrich, *Die Auflösung der Weimarer Republik*, 1955; 3rd ed., Villingen, 1960.
——, Sauer, Wolfgang, and Schulz, Gerhard, *Die nationalsozialistiche Machtergreifung*, Köln & Opladen, 1960.
Bramsted, Ernest K., *Goebbels and National Socialist Propaganda 1925-1945*, Michigan, 1965.
Brecht, Bertolt, *Stücke*, 10 vols., Frankfurt, 1953-1959; *Gedichte*, 7 vols., Frankfurt, 1960-1964.
Broszat, Martin, *Der Nationalsozialismus*, Stuttgart, 1960.
——, Jacobson, Hans-Adolf, and Krausnick, Helmut, *Konzentrationslager, Kommissarbefehl, Judenverfolgung*, Olten/Freiburg, 1965.
Brzezinski, Zbigniew, *Ideology and Power in Soviet Politics*, New York, 1962; *The Permanent Purge—Politics in Soviet Totalitarianism*, Cambridge, 1956.
Buber-Neumann, Margarete, *Under Two Dictators*, New York, 1951.
Buchheim, H., *et al.*, *Anatomie des SS-Staates*, 2 vols., Olten & Freiburg/Br., 1965.
Buchheim, Hans, "Die SS in der Verfassung des Dritten Reiches," *Vierteljahreshefte für Zeitgeschichte*, April, 1955; *Das Dritte Reich*, München, 1958; *Die SS und totalitäre Herrschaft*, München, 1962; *Die SS—das Herrschaftsinstrument—Befehl und Gehorsam*, Olten/Freiburg, 1965.
Bullock, Alan, *Hitler, a Study in Tyranny*, rev. ed., New York, 1964.

Camus, Albert, "The Human Crisis," *Twice a Year*, 1946-1947.
Carocci, Giampiero, *Storia del fascismo*, Milan, 1959.
Carr, E. H., *History of Soviet Russia*, 7 vols.. New York, 1951-1964; *Studies in Revolution*, New York, 1964.
Céline, Ferdinand, *Bagatelle pour un massacre*, 1938; *L'Ecole des cadavres*, 1940.
Chamberlin, W. H., *Blueprint for World Conquest*, 1946; *The Russian Revolution*, (1935), 1965.
Childs, H. L., and Dodd, W. E., editors, *The Nazi Primer*, New York, 1938.
Ciliga, Anton, *The Russian Enigma*, London, 1940.
Clark, Evelyn A. "Adolf Wagner. From National Economist to National Socialist," *Political Science Quarterly*, 1940, vol. 55, no. 3.
Cobban, Alfred, *National Self-determination*, London, New York, 1945; *Dictatorship; Its History and Theory*, New York, 1939.
Cohn, Norman, *Warrant for Genocide. The myth of the Jewish world-conspiracy and the "Protocols of the Elders of Zion,"* New York, 1966.
Communism in Action (United States Government House Documents, no. 754), Washington, 1946.
Crankshaw, Edward, *Gestapo, Instrument of Tyranny*, London, 1956.
Curtiss, J. S., *An Appraisal of the Protocols of Zion*, New York, 1942.

Dallin, David J., *From Purge to Coexistence*, Chicago, 1964; "Report on Russia," *The New Leader*, January 8, 1949.
—— and Nicolaevsky, Boris I., *Forced Labor in Russia*, 1947

Daniels, Robert, *The Conscience of the Revolution: Communist Opposition in Soviet Russia*, Cambridge, 1960.
The Dark Side of the Moon (preface by T. S. Eliot), New York, 1947.
Deakin, F. W., *The Brutal Friendship*, New York, 1963.
De Begnac, Yvon, *Palazzo Venezia—Storia di un regime*, Rome, 1950.
Dehillotte, Pierre, *Gestapo*, Paris, 1940.
Delarue, Jacques, *Histoire de la Gestapo*, Paris, 1962.
Deschamps, N., *Les Sociétés Secrètes et la Société*, Avignon, n.d.
Deutscher, Isaac, *Stalin: A Political Biography*, New York and London, 1949; *Prophet Armed: Trotsky, 1879-1921*, 1954; *Prophet Unarmed: Trotsky, 1921-1929*, 1959; *The Prophet Outcast: Trotsky, 1929-1940*, 1963.
"Die nationalsozialistische Revolution," *Dokumente der deutschen Politik*, vol. I.
Dobb, Maurice, "Bolshevism," in *Encyclopedia of Social Sciences*.
Dokumente der deutschen Politik und Geschichte, vol. IV.
Domarus, Max, *Hitler-Reden und Proklamationen 1932-1945*, 2 vols., 1963.
Doob, Leonard W., "Goebbels' Principles of Propaganda," in Katz, Daniel *et al.*, *Public Opinion and Propaganda*, New York, 1954.
Drucker, Peter F., *The End of Economic Man*, New York, 1939.
Deuerlein, E., "Hitlers Eintritt in die Politik und die Reichswehr," *Vierteljahreshefte für Zeitgeschichte*, München, 1959, vol. III.

Ebenstein, William, *The Nazi State*, New York, 1943.
Eckart, Dietrich, *Der Bolschewismus von Moses bis Lenin. Zwiegespräch zwischen Hitler und mir*, München, 1924.
Ehrenburg, Ilya, *Memoirs: 1921-1941*, Cleveland, 1964; *The War: 1941-1945*, Cleveland, 1965.
Engels, Friedrich, Introduction to the *Communist Manifesto*, 1890; introduction to the *Ursprung der Familie;* Funeral Speech on Marx.
Erickson, John, *The Soviet High Command 1918-1941*, New York, 1961.
Eyck, Erich, *A History of the Weimar Republic*, Cambridge, 1962.

Fainsod, Merle, *How Russia Is Ruled*, 1963; *Smolensk under Soviet Rule*, 1958.
The Fascist Era, published by the Fascist Confederation of Industrialists, Rome, 1939.
Feder, Ernest, "Essai sur la Psychologie de la terreur," *Synthèses*, Bruxelles, 1946.
Feder, Gottfried, *Das Programm der N.S.D.A.P. und seine weltanschaulichen Grundgedanken* (Nationalsozialistische Bibliothek, no. 1).
Fedotow, G. P., "Russia and Freedom," *The Review of Politics*, vol. 8, no. 1, January, 1946.
Fest, J. C., *Das Gesicht des Dritten Reiches*, München, 1963.
Finer, Herman, *Mussolini's Italy*, New York (1935), 1965.
Fischer, Louis, *The Soviets in World Affairs*, London, New York, 1930; *Life of Lenin*, New York, 1964.
Flammery, Harry W., "The Catholic Church and Fascism," *Free World*, September, 1943.
Florinsky, M. T., *Fascism and National Socialism. A Study of the Economic and Social Politics of the Totalitarian State*, New York, 1938.
Forsthoff, Ernst, *Der totale Staat*, Hamburg, 1933.
Fraenkel, Ernst, *The Dual State*, New York and London, 1941.
Frank, Hans, *Nationalsozlialistische Leitsätze für ein neues deutsches Strafrecht*, Berlin, 1935-1936; *Die Technik des Staates*, München, 1940; (editor) *Grundfragen der deutschen Polizei* (Akademie für deutsches Recht) Hamburg, 1937; *Recht und Verwaltung*, 1939; *Die Technik des Staates*, München, 1942; *Im Angesicht des Galgens*, München, 1953; editor, *Nationalsozialistisches Handbuch für Recht und Gesetzgebung*, München, 1935.
Freyer, Hans, *Pallas Athene, Ethik des politischen Volkes*, 1935.
Friedrich, C. J., editor, *Totalitarianism*, New York, 1954.
——, and Brzezinski, Z. K., *Totalitarian Dictatorship and Autocracy*, Cambridge, 1956.

Gallier-Boissière, Jean, *Mysteries of the French Secret Police*, 1938.
Gauweiler, Otto, *Rechtseinrichtungen und Rechtsaufgaben der Bewegung*, 1939.
Geigenmüller, Otto, *Die politische Schutzhaft im nationalistischen Deutschland*, 2nd ed., Würzburg, 1937.
Gerth, Hans, "The Nazi Party," *American Journal of Sociology*, vol. 45, 1940.
Gide, André, *Retour de l'URSS*, Paris, 1936.
Giles, O. C., *The Gestapo* (Oxford Pamphlets on World Affairs, no. 36), 1940.
Globke, Hans, *Kommentare zur Deutschen Rassegesetzgebung*, Munich-Berlin, 1936.
Goebbels, Joseph, *Wege ins Dritte Reich*, München, 1927; "Der Faschismus und seine praktischen Ergebnisse," *Schriften der deutschen Hochschule für Politik*, vol. I, Berlin, 1935; *Vom Kaiserhof zur Reichskanzlei*, 19. ed., München, 1937; "Rassenfrage und Weltprogramm," *Pädagogisches Magazin*, Heft 139, 1934; *The Goebbels Diaries 1942-1943*, Louis Lochner, editor, New York, 1948; *Wesen und Gestalt des Nationalsozialismus*, Berlin, 1935.
Goslar, Hans, *Jüdische Weltherrschaft. Phantasiegebilde oder Wirklichkeit*, Berlin, 1918.
Grauert, Wilhelm, "Die Entwicklung des Polizeirechts in nationalsozialistischen Staat," in *Deutsche Juristenzeitung*, 39, 1934.
Griffith, William E., editor, *Communism in Europe, Continuity, Change and the Sino-Soviet Dispute*, Cambridge, 1964.
Gross, Walter, *Der deutsche Rassengedanke und die Welt* (Schriften der Hochschule für Politik, no. 42), 1939; "Die Rassen- und Bevölkerungspolitik im Kampf um die geschichtliche Selbstbehauptung der Völker," *Nationalsozialistische Monatshefte*, no. 115, October, 1939.
Guenther, Hans, *Rassenkunde des jüdischen Volkes*, 1930; *Rassenkunde des deutschen Volkes*, 1st ed., München, 1922.
Gul, Roman, *Les Maîtres de la Tcheka*, Paris, 1938.
Gurian, Waldemar, *Bolshevism: Theory and Practice*, New York, 1932; *Bolshevism. An Introduction to Soviet Communism*, Notre Dame, 1952.

Hadamovsky, Eugen, *Propaganda und nationale Macht*, 1933.
Hafkesbrink, Hanna, *Unknown Germany*, New Haven, 1948.
Hallgarten, Georg Wolfgang F., *Hitler, Reichswehr und Industrie. Zur Geschichte der Jahre 1918-1933*, Frankfurt/M., 1955.
Hamel, Walter, "Die Polizei im neuen Reich," in *Deutsches Recht*, vol. 5, 1935.
Hammer, Hermann, "Die deutschen Ausgaben von Hitlers 'Mein Kampf,'" in *Vierteljahrshefte für Zeitgeschichte 4* (1956).
Hartshorne, Edward G., *The German Universities and National Socialism*, Cambridge, 1937.
Hayek, F. A., "The Counter-Revolution of Science," *Economics*, vol. 8, 1941.
Hayes, Carlton J. H., *Essays on Nationalism*, New York, 1926; Remarks on "The Novelty of Totalitarianism in the History of Western Civilization," *Symposion on the Totalitarian State, 1939. Proceedings of the American Philosophical Society*, vol. 82, Philadelphia, 1940; *A Generation of Materialism*, New York, 1941.
Heiden, Konrad, *Der Führer. Hitler's Rise to Power*, Boston, 1944; *A History of National Socialism*, New York, 1935; *Adolf Hitler. Das Zeitalter der Verantwortungslosigkeit. Eine Biographie*, vol. 1, Zürich, 1936; *Geschichte des Nationalsozialismus. Die Karriere einer Idee*, Berlin, 1932; *Geburt des Dritten Reiches. Die Geschichte des Nationalsozialismus bis Herbst 1933*, 2nd ed., Zürich, 1934.
Henkys, R., *Die nationalsozialistischen Gewaltverbrechen*, 1964.
Hesse, Fritz, *Das Spiel um Deutschland*, Munich, 1953.
Heydrich, Reinhard, "Die Bekämpfung der Staatsfeinde," in *Deutsches Recht*, vol. 6, 1936.
Hilberg, Raul, *The Destruction of the European Jews*, Chicago, 1961.
Himmler, Heinrich, "Männerbund auf rassischer Grundlage," *Das Schwarze Corps*, 38. Folge; *Die Schutzstaffel als antibolschewistische Kampforganisation* (Aus dem Schwarzen Korps, no. 3), 1936; "Organization and Obligation of the SS and the Police," published in *Nationalpolitischer Lehrgang der Wehrmacht vom*

15.-23. Januar 1937. Excerpts translated in *Nazi Conspiracy, op. cit.*, vol. 4; English edition: *Secret Speech by Himmler to the German Army General Staff*, published by the American Committee for Anti-Nazi Literature, 1938; *Grundfragen der deutschen Polizei*, Hamburg, 1937; "Denkschriften Himmlers über die Behandlung der Fremdvölkischen im Osten" (May 1940), *Vierteljahrshefte für Zeitgeschichte*, 5. Jg. (1957); "Die Schutzstaffel," *Grundlagen, Aufbau und Wirtschaftsordnung des nationalsozialistischen Staates*, Nr. 7b.

Hitler, Adolf, *Mein Kampf*, 1925-1927. Unexpurgated English edition, New York, 1939; *Reden*, ed. by Ernst Boepple, München, 1933; *Hitler's Speeches, 1922-1939*, ed. by N. H. Baynes, London, 1942; *Ausgewählte Reden des Führers*, 1939; *Die Reden des Führers nach der Machtübernahme*, 1940; *Der grossdeutsche Freiheitskampf*, Reden Hitlers vom 1.9.1939-10.3.1940; *Hitler's Table Talks*, New York, 1953; *Hitler's Secret Book*, New York, 1962; *Der grossdeutsche Freiheitskampf—Reden Adolf Hitlers*, vols. I and II, 3rd ed., München, 1943.

Hocke, Werner, ed., *Die Gesetzgebung des Kabinetts Hitler*, vol. 1, Berlin, 1933.

Hoehn, Reinhard, *Rechtsgemeinschaft und Volksgemeinschaft*, Hamburg, 1935.

Hoettl, Wilhelm, *The Secret Front: The Story of Nazi Political Espionage*, New York, 1954.

Holldack, Heinz, *Was wirklich geschah*, 1949.

Horneffer, Reinhold, "Das Problem der Rechtsgeltung und der Restbestand der Weimarer Verfassung," in *Zeitschrift für die gesamte Staatswissenschaft 99*, 1938.

Höss, Rudolf, *Commandant of Auschwitz*, New York, 1960.

Hossbach, Friedrich, *Zwischen Wehrmacht und Hitler 1934-1938*, Wolfenbüttel-Hannover, 1949.

Huber, Ernst R., "Die deutsche Polizei," *Zeitschrift für die gesamte Staatswissenschaft*, vol. 101, 1940/1.

Hudal, Bischof Alois, *Die Grundlagen des Nationalsozialismus*, 1937.

Inkeles, A., and Bauer, R. A., *The Soviet Citizen: Daily Life in a Totalitarian Society*, Cambridge, 1959.

Jäger, Herbert, *Verbrechen unter totalitärer Herrschaft*, Olten & Freiburg/Br., 1967.

Jetzinger, Franz, *Hitlers Jugend*, Wien, 1956.

Jünger, Ernst, *The Storm of Steel*, London, 1929.

Keiser, Guenther, "Der jüngste Konzentrationsprozess," *Die Wirtschaftskurve*, vol. 18, no. 148, 1938.

Kennan, George F., *Russia and the West under Lenin and Stalin*, Boston, 1961.

Khrushchev, N., "The Crimes of the Stalin Era," edited and annotated by Boris Nicolaevsky, New York, *The New Leader*, 1956.

Klein, Fritz, "Zur Vorbereitung der faschistischen Diktatur durch die deutsche Grossbourgeoisie 1929-1932," *Zeitschrift für Geschichtswissenschaft*, 1.Jg, 1953.

Kluke, Paul, "Nationalsozialistische Europaideologie," *Vierteljahrshefte für Zeitgeschichte*, 8. Jg. (1960).

Koch, Erich, "Sind wir Faschisten?," in *Arbeitertum* 1, H. 9 (1.Juli 1931).

Koellenreuter, Otto, *Volk und Staat in der Weltanschauung des Nationalsozialismus*, 1935; *Der deutsche Führerstaat*, Tübingen, 1934.

Koettgen, Arnold, "Die Gesetzmässigkeit der Verwaltung im Führerstaat," *Reichsverwaltungsblatt*, 1936.

Kogon, Eugen, *The Theory and Practice of Hell*, 1956.

Kohn-Bramstedt, Ernst, *Dictatorship and Political Police; the Technique of Control by Fear*, London, 1945.

Koyré, Alexandre, "The Political Function of the Modern Lie," *Contemporary Jewish Record*, June, 1945.

Kravchenko, Victor, *I Chose Freedom. The Personal and Political Life of a Soviet Official*, New York, 1946.

Krivitsky, W., *In Stalin's Secret Services*, New York, 1939.

Kuhn, Karl G., "Die Judenfrage als weltgeschichtliches Problem," in *Forschugen zur Judenfrage*, 1939.

Laporte, Maurice, *Histoire de l'Okhrana*, Paris, 1935.
Latour, Contamine de, "Le Maréchal Pétain," *Revue de Paris*, vol. 1.
Lebon, Gustave, *La Psychologie des foules*, 1895.
Lederer, Zdenek, *Ghetto Theresienstadt*, London, 1953.
Lenin, V. I., *What Is to Be Done?*, 1902; *State and Revolution*, 1917.
Leutwein, Paul, editor, *Kämpfe um Afrika; sechs Lebensbilder*, Luebeck, 1936.
Lewy, Guenter, *The Catholic Church and Nazi Germany*, New York and Toronto, 1964.
Ley, Robert, *Der Weg zur Ordensburg*, no date.
Lösener, Bernhard, *Die Nürnberger Gesetze*, Berlin, 1936.
Lowenthal, Richard, *World Communism. The Disintegration of a Secular Faith*, New York, 1964.
Luedecke, Winfred, *Behind the Scenes of Espionage. Tales of the Secret Service*, 1929.
Luxemburg, Rosa, *The Russian Revolution*, Ann Arbor, 1961.

Martin, Alfred von, "Zur Soziologie der Gegenwart," *Zeitschrift für Kulturgeschichte*, vol. 27.
Massing, Paul W., *Rehearsal for Destruction*, New York, 1949.
Mathias, Erich, and Morsey, Rudolph, editors, *Das Ende der Parteien 1933*, Düsseldorf, 1960.
Maunz, Theodor, *Gestalt und Recht der Polizei*, Hamburg, 1943.
McKenzie, Kermit E., *Comintern and World Revolution 1928-1934*, New York, 1964.
Micaud, Charles A., *The French Right and Nazi Germany. 1933-1939*, 1943.
Moeller van den Bruck, Arthur, *Das Dritte Reich*, 1923; English edition *Germany's Third Empire*, New York, 1934.
Monas, Sidney, *The Third Section: Police and Society in Russia under Nicholas I*, Cambridge, 1961.
Moore, Barrington, *Terror and Progress USSR; Some Sources of Change and Stability in the Soviet Dictatorship*, Cambridge, 1954.
Morstein Marx, Fritz, "Totalitarian Politics," *Symposion on the Totalitarian State, 1939. Proceedings of the American Philosophical Society*, vol. 82, Philadelphia, 1940.
Mosse, George J., *The Crisis of German Ideology: Intellectual Origins of the Third Reich*, New York, 1964.
Muller, H. S., "The Soviet Master Race Theory," *The New Leader*, July 30, 1949.
Müller, Josef, *Die Entwicklung des Rassenantisemitismus in den letzten Jahrzehnten des 19. Jahrhundert* (*Historische Studien*, H. 372), Berlin, 1940.
Mussolini, Benito, "Relativismo et Fascismo," *Diuturna*, Milano, 1924; *Four Speeches on the Corporate State*, Rome, 1935; *Opera Omnia di Benito Mussolini*, vol. IV, Florence, 1951.

Nansen, Odd, *Day after Day*, London, 1949.
Naumann, Bernd, *Auschwitz*, New York, 1966.
Nazi Conspiracy and Aggression, Office of the United States Chief of Counsel for the Prosecution of Axis Criminality, U. S. Government, Washington, 1946.
Nazi-Soviet Relations, 1939-1941. Documents from the Archives of the German Foreign Office, edited by Raymond James Sontag and James Stuart Beddie, Washington, 1948.
Neesse, Gottfried, *Partei und Staat*, 1936; "Die verfassungsrechtliche Gestaltung der Ein-Partei," *Zeitschrift für die gesamte Staatswissenschaft*, vol. 98, 1938.
Neumann, Franz, *Behemoth*, 1942.
Neusüss-Hunkel, Ermenhild, *Die SS*, Hannover-Frankfurt a.M., 1956.
Newman, Bernard, *Secret Servant*, New York, 1936.
Nicolaevsky, Boris I., *Bolsheviks and Bureaucrats*, New York, 1965; *Power and the Soviet Elite*, New York, 1965; (——), *Letter of an Old Bolshevik*, New York, 1937.

Nicolai, Helmut, *Die rassengesetzliche Rechtslehre. Grundzüge einer nationalsozialistischen Rechtsphilosophie* (Nationalsozialistische Bibliothek, H. 39), 3rd ed., München, 1934.

Nomad, Max, *Apostles of Revolution*, Boston, 1939.

Olgin, Moissaye J., *The Soul of the Russian Revolution*, New York, 1917.

Organisationsbuch der NSDAP, many editions.

Orlov, A., *The Secret History of Stalin's Crimes*, New York, 1953.

Ortega y Gasset, José, *The Revolt of the Masses*, New York, 1932.

Paetel, Karl O., "Die SS," *Vierteljahreshefte für Zeitgeschichte*, January, 1954; "Der schwarze Orden. Zur Literatur über die 'SS,'" in *Neue Politische Literatur 3*, 1958.

Parsons, Talcott, "Some Sociological Aspects of the Fascist Movement," *Essays in Sociological Theory*, Glencoe, 1954.

Pascal, Pierre, *Avvakum et les débuts du raskol* (Institut Français de Leningrad, Bibliothèque, vol. 18), Paris, 1938.

Paulhan, Jean, "Introduction" to Marquis de Sade, *Les Infortunes de la Vertu*, Paris, 1946.

Payne, Stanley G., *A History of Spanish Fascism*, Stanford, 1961.

Pencherlo, Alberto, "Antisemitism," in *Encyclopedia Italiana*.

Petegroski, D. W., "Antisemitism, the Strategy of Hatred," *Antioch Review*, vol. 1, no. 3, 1941.

Pfenning, Andreas, "Gemeinschaft und Staatswissenschaft," *Zeitschrift für die gesamte Staatswissenschaft*, vol. 96.

Poliakov, Léon, *Bréviaire de la Haine*, Paris, 1951; "The Weapon of Antisemitism," *The Third Reich*, London, 1955, UNESCO.

——, and Wulf, Josef, *Das Dritte Reich und die Juden*, Berlin, 1955.

Poncins, Léon de, *Les Forces secrètes de la Révolution; F.·. M.·.-Judaïsme*, revised ed., 1929 (translated into German, English, Spanish, Portuguese); *Les Juifs Maîtres du Monde*, 1932; *La Dictature des puissances occultes; La F.·. M.·.*, 1932; *La mystérieuse Internationale juive*, 1936; *La Guerre occulte*, 1936.

Rauschning, Hermann, *Hitler Speaks*, 1939; *The Revolt of Nihilism*, 1939.

Reck-Malleczewen, Friedrich Percyval, *Tagebuch eines Verzweifelten*, Stuttgart, 1947.

Reitlinger, Gerald, *The Final Solution*, 1953; *The SS—Alibi of a Nation*, London, 1956.

Reveille, Thomas, *The Spoil of Europe*, 1941.

Reventlow, Graf Ernst zu, *Deutschlands auswärtige Politik. 1888-1914*, 1916; *Judas Kampf und Niederlage in Deutschland*, 1937.

Riesman, David, "The Politics of Persecution," *Public Opinion Quarterly*, vol. 6, 1942; "Democracy and Defamation," *Columbia Law Review*, 1942.

Riess, Curt, *Joseph Goebbels: A Biography*, New York, 1948.

Ripka, Hubert, *Munich: Before and After*, London, 1939.

Ritter, Gerhard, *Carl Goerdeler's Struggle against Tyranny*, New York, 1958.

Roberts, Stephen H., *The House that Hitler Built*, London, 1939.

Robinson, Jacob, and Friedman, Philip, *Guide to Jewish History under Nazi Impact*, a bibliography published jointly by YIVO Institute for Jewish Research and Yad Washem, New York and Jerusalem, 1960.

Rocco, Alfredo, *Scritti e discorsi politici*, 3 vols., Milan, 1938.

Roehm, Ernst, *Die Geschichte eines Hochverräters*, Volksausgabe, 1933; *Die Memoiren des Stabschefs Roehm*, Saarbrücken, 1934; *Warum SA?*, Berlin, 1933; "SA und deutsche Revolution," in *Nationalsozialistische Monatshefte*, Nr. 31, 1933.

Rollin, Henri, *L'Apocalypse de notre temps*, Paris, 1939.

Rosenberg, Alfred, *Die Protokolle der Weisen von Zion und die jüdische Weltpolitik*, München, 1923; *Der Mythos des zwanzigsten Jahrhunderts*, 1930.

Rosenberg, Arthur, *A History of Bolshevism*, London, 1934; *Geschichte der deutschen Republik*, 1936.

Rousset, David, *Les Jours de notre mort*, Paris, 1947; *The Other Kingdom*, 1947.

Rush, Myron, *Political Succession in the USSR*, New York, 1965; *The Rise of Khrushchev*, Washington, 1958.

SA-Geist im Betrieb. Vom Ringen um die Durchsetzung des deutschen Sozialismus, edited by Oberste SA-Führung, München, 1938.

Salisbury, Harrison E., *Moscow Journal: The End of Stalin*, Chicago, 1961; *American in Russia*, New York, 1955.

Salvemini, Gaetano, *La terreur fasciste 1922-1926*, Paris, 1938; *The Fascist Dictatorship in Italy* (1927), New York, 1966.

Schäfer, Wolfgang, *NSDAP, Entwicklung und Struktur der Staatspartei des Dritten Reiches*, Hannover-Frankfurt a.M., 1956.

Schapiro, L., *The Communist Party of the Soviet Union*, 1960; *The Government and Politics of the Soviet Union*, New York, 1965.

Schellenberg, Walter, *The Schellenberg Memoirs*, London, 1956.

Schemann, Ludwig, *Die Rasse in den Geisteswissenschaften. Studie zur Geschichte des Rassengedankens*, 3 vols., München, Berlin, 1928.

Scheuner, Ulrich, "Die nationale Revolution. Eine staatsrechtliche Untersuchung," in *Archiv des öffentlichen Rechts* (1933/34).

Schmitt, Carl, *Politische Romantik*, Munich, 1925; *Staat, Bewegung, Volk*, 1934; "Totaler Feind, totaler Krieg, totaler Staat," *Völkerbund und Völkerrecht*, vol. 4, 1937; *Verfassungsrechtliche Aufsätze aus den Jahren 1924-1954. Materialien zu einer Verfassungslehre*, Berlin, 1958.

Schnabel, Raimund, *Macht ohne Moral. Eine Dokumentation über die SS*, Frankfurt/M., 1957.

Schumann, Fr. L., *The Nazi Dictatorship*, 1939.

Schwartz, Dieter, *Angriffe auf die nationalsozialistische Weltanschauung* (Aus dem Schwarzen Korps, no. 2), 1936.

Schwartz-Bostunitsch, Gregor, *Jüdischer Imperialismus*, 5th edition, 1939.

Seraphim, Hans-Günther, *Das politische Tagebuch Alfred Rosenbergs aus den Jahren 1934/5 und 1939/40*, Göttingen-Berlin-Frankfurt/M., 1956; "SS-Verfügungstruppe und Wehrmacht," in *Wehrwissenschaftliche Rundschau 5*, 1955.

Seraphim, P. H., *Das Judentum im osteuropäischen Raum*, Essen, 1938; "Der Antisemitismus in Osteuropa," *Osteuropa*, vol. 14, no. 5, February, 1939.

Seton-Watson, Hugh, *From Lenin to Khrushchev*, New York, 1960.

Simmel, Georg, "Sociology of Secrecy and of Secret Societies," *The American Journal of Sociology*, vol. 11, no. 4, 1906; *The Sociology of Georg Simmel*, translated by K. H. Wolff, 1950.

Six, F. A., *Die politische Propaganda der NSDAP im Kampf um die Macht*, 1936.

Smith, Bruce, "Police," in *Encyclopedia of Social Sciences*.

Souvarine, Boris, *Stalin. A Critical Survey of Bolshevism*, New York, 1939; translated from the French *Staline, Aperçu historique du Bolshévisme*, Paris, 1935.

Spengler, Oswald, *The Decline of the West*, 1928-1929.

SS-Hauptamt-Schulungsamt, *Wesen und Aufgabe der SS und der Polizei; Der Weg der SS; SS-Mann und Blutsfrage. Die biologischen Grundlagen und ihre sinngemässe Anwendung für die Erhaltung und Mehrung des nordischen Blutes.*

Stalin, J. V., *Leninism*, London, 1933; *Mastering Bolshevism*, New York, 1946; *History of the Communist Party of the Soviet Union (Bolsheviks): Short Course*, New York, 1939.

Starlinger, Wilhelm, *Grenzen der Sowjetmacht*, Würzburg, 1955.

Starr, Joshua, "Italy's Antisemites," *Jewish Social Studies*, 1939.

Stein, Alexander, *Adolf Hitler, Schüler der "Weisen von Zion,"* Karlsbad, 1936.

Stein, George H., *The Waffen SS: Hitler's Elite Guard at War, 1939-45*, Ithaca, 1966.

Stuckart, Wilhelm, and Globke, Hans, *Reichsbürgergesetz, Blutschutzgesetz und Ehegesundheitsgesetz (Kommentare zur deutschen Rassengesetzgebung)*, vol. 1, München, Berlin, 1936.

Tasca, Angelo (pseudonym Angelo Rossi), *The Rise of Italian Fascism, 1918-1922* (1938), New York, 1966.

Thyssen, Fritz, *I Paid Hitler*, London, 1941.
Tobias, Fritz, *The Reichstag Fire*, New York, 1964.
Trevor-Roper, H. R., *The Last Days of Hitler*, 1947.
The Trial of the Major War Criminals, 42 vols., Nürnberg, 1947-1948.
Trials of War Criminals before the Nuremberg Military Tribunals, 15 vols., Washington, 1949-1953.
Trotsky, Leon, *The History of the Russian Revolution*, New York, 1932.
Tucker, Robert C., *The Soviet Political Mind*, New York, 1963; "The Deradicalization of Marxist Movements," *The American Political Science Review*, vol. LXI, no. 2, June, 1967.
——, and Cohen, Stephen F., editors, *The Great Purge Trial*, New York, 1965.

Ulam, Adam B., *The Bolsheviks: The Intellectual and Political History of the Triumph of Communism in Russia*, New York, 1965; *The New Face of Soviet Totalitarianism*, Cambridge, 1963.
Ullmann, A., *La Police, quatrième Pouvoir*, Paris, 1935.

Vardys, V. Stanley, "How the Baltic Republics Fare in the Soviet Union," *Foreign Affairs*, April, 1966.
Vassilyev, A. T., *The Ochrana*, 1930.
Venturi, Franco, *Roots of Revolution. A History of the Populist and Socialist Movements in Nineteenth Century Russia*, (1952), New York, 1966.
Verfassung, Die, des Sozialistischen Staates der Arbeiter und Bauern, Strasbourg, 1937.
Volkmann, Erich, Elster, Alexander, and Küchenhoff, Günther, editors, *Die Rechtsentwicklung der Jahre 1933 bis 1935/6*, Handwörterbuch der Rechtswissenschaft, vol. VIII, Berlin, Leipzig, 1937.

Warmbrunn, Werner, *The Dutch under German Occupation, 1940-1945*, Stanford, 1963.
Weinreich, Max, *Hitler's Professors*, New York, 1946.
Weissberg, Alexander, *The Accused*, New York, 1951.
Weizmann, Chaim, *Trial and Error*, New York, 1949.
Wighton, Charles, *Heydrich: Hitler's Most Evil Henchman*, Philadelphia, 1962.
Wirsing, Giselher, *Zwischeneuropa und die deutsche Zukunft*, Jena, 1932.
Wolfe, Bertram D., *Three Men Who Made a Revolution: Lenin—Trotsky—Stalin*, New York, 1948.
Wolin, Simon, and Slusser, Robert M., editors, *The Soviet Secret Police*, New York, 1957.

Zielinski, T., "L'Empereur Claude et l'idée de la domination mondiale des Juifs," *Revue Universelle*, Bruxelles, 1926-1927.

Index

Authors are listed only in case of special discussion or reference. Subjects of footnotes are listed. Chapter headings and subheadings and bibliographical references are not included.

BOOKS BY HANNAH ARENDT
AVAILABLE FROM HARCOURT, INC.
IN HARVEST PAPERBACK EDITIONS

Crises of the Republic

The Life of the Mind *(one-volume edition)*

Men in Dark Times

On Violence

The Origins of Totalitarianism *(three volumes)*
PART I: ANTISEMITISM
PART II: IMPERIALISM
PART III: TOTALITARIANISM

The Origins of Totalitarianism *(one-volume edition)*

Rahel Varnhagen:
THE LIFE OF A JEWISH WOMAN

HANNAH ARENDT AND KARL JASPERS

Correspondence 1926–1969

HANNAH ARENDT AND MARY MCCARTHY

Between Friends: The Correspondence of Hannah Arendt and Mary McCarthy, 1949–1975

CPSIA information can be obtained
at www.ICGtesting.com
Printed in the USA
LVHW101950160322
713506LV00015B/1516

9 780156 906500